EVOLUTIONARY GAME DYNAMICS
Agent Based Methods

EVOLUTIONARY GAME DYNAMICS
Agent Based Methods

BY

JACK WILLIAMS
BASTIAAN GRAHAM

KNOWLEDGE

KNOWLEDGE BAKERS

ISBN: 9789390013296 (HB)

Published by : **Knowledge Bakers**
Pune, India
Email: knowledgebakers2019@gmail.com

Digitally Printed at : **Replika Press Pvt. Ltd.**

PREFACE

Evolutionary game theory describes systems where individual success is based on the interaction with others. We consider a system in which players unconditionally imitate more successful strategies but sometimes also explore the available strategies at random. Most research has focused on how strategies spread via genetic reproduction or cultural imitation, but random exploration of the available set of strategies has received less attention so far. In genetic settings, the latter corresponds to mutations in the DNA, whereas in cultural evolution, it describes individuals experimenting with new behaviors. Genetic mutations typically occur with very small probabilities, but random exploration of available strategies in behavioral experiments is common. We term this phenomenon "exploration dynamics" to contrast it with the traditional focus on imitation. As an illustrative example of the emerging evolutionary dynamics, we consider a public goods game with cooperators and defectors and add punishers and the option to abstain from the enterprise in further scenarios. For small mutation rates, cooperation (and punishment) is possible only if interactions are voluntary, whereas moderate mutation rates can lead to high levels of cooperation even in compulsory public goods games.

Evolutionary game theory originated as an application of the mathematical theory of games to biological contexts, arising from the realization that frequency dependent fitness introduces a strategic aspect to evolution. Recently, however, evolutionary game theory has become of increased interest to economists, sociologists, and anthropologists--and social scientists in general--as well as philosophers. The interest among social scientists in a theory with explicit biological roots derives from three facts. First, the 'evolution' treated by evolutionary game theory need not be biological evolution. 'Evolution' may, in this context, often be understood as *cultural* evolution, where this refers to changes in beliefs and norms over time. Second, the rationality assumptions underlying evolutionary game theory are, in many cases, more appropriate for the modelling of social systems than those assumptions underlying the traditional theory of games. Third, evolutionary game theory, as an explicitly dynamic theory, provides an important element missing from the traditional theory.

The present book provides an overview of the book and introduces the concept of agent-based modeling in the context of evolutionary game dynamics and introduces the reader to the basics of agent-based modeling and evolutionary game dynamics. Explores the behaviour of agents when they are connected in a network rather than a grid. This chapter examines the impact of different revision protocols and payoff functions on the behavior of agents. Focuses on the formation of networks as an endogenous process that arises from the interactions among agents and also deals with games involving more than two populations. Introduces a technique for solving the mean dynamics of a system at runtime also provides a summary of the models presented in the book, including their key features and results. It is primarily aimed at researchers, students, and professionals interested in the fields of game theory, evolutionary dynamics, and agent-based modeling. It is also relevant to those working in related areas such as computational social science, artificial intelligence, and complexity science.

We are grateful to all those persons as well as various books, manuals, periodicals, magazines, journals etc. that helped in the preparation of this book. In spite of the best efforts, it is possible that some errors may have occurred into the compilation and editing of the book. Further queries, constructive suggestions and criticisms for the improvement of the book are always welcomed and shall be thankfully acknowledged.

Jack Williams
Bastiaan Graham

CONTENTS

0. INTRODUCTION

0.1. Introduction to evolutionary game theory

Evolutionary Game Theory (EGT) is a branch of a more general discipline called game theory. Therefore, to understand what EGT is about, we believe it is useful to get familiar with the basic ideas underlying game theory first.

1. What is game theory?

Game theory is a discipline devoted to studying social interactions where individuals' decisions are interdependent, i.e. situations where the outcome of the interaction for any individual generally depends not only on her own choices, but also on the choices made by every other individual. Thus, several scholars have pointed out that game theory could well be defined as 'interactive decision theory' (Myerson, 1997, p. 1). Some examples of interactive decisions for which game theory is useful are:

1. Choosing the side of the road on which to drive.
2. Choosing WhatsApp or Facebook messenger as your default text messaging app.
3. Choosing which restaurant to go in the following situation:

> Imagine that over breakfast your partner and you decided to have lunch together, but you did not specify where. Right before lunch time you discover that you left your cellphone at home, and there is no other way to contact your partner quickly. Fortunately, you are not completely lost: there are only two restaurants that you both love in town. Which one should you go to?

Interactive social interactions like the ones outlined above are modeled in game theory as *games*. A game is an abstract representation of a social interaction which is meant to capture its most basic properties. In particular, a game typically comprises:

- the set of individuals who interact (called *players*),
- the different choices available to each of the individuals when they are called upon to act (named actions or *pure strategies*),
- the *information* individuals have at the time of making their decisions,
- and a *payoff* function that assigns a value to each individual for each possible combination of choices made by every individual (Fig. 1). In most cases, payoffs represent the preferences of each individual over each possible outcome of the social interaction,[1] though there are some

1. A common misconception about game theory relates to the roots of players' preferences. There is no assumption in game theory that dictates that players' preferences are formed in complete disregard of each other's interests. On the contrary, preferences in game theory are assumed to account for anything, i.e. they may include altruistic

evolutionary models where payoffs represent Darwinian fitness.

		Player 2	
		Player 2 chooses **A**	Player 2 chooses **B**
Player 1	Player 1 chooses **A**	1 , 1	0 , 0
	Player 1 chooses **B**	0 , 0	2 , 2

Figure 1. Payoff matrix of a 2-player 2-strategy game. For each possible combination of pure strategies there is a corresponding pair of numbers (x , y) in the matrix whose first element x represents the payoff for player 1, and whose second element y represents the payoff for player 2.

Note that the payoff matrix shown in Fig. 1 could well be used for the three examples outlined above, assuming that there is one side of the road, one text messaging app, and one restaurant in town that is preferred, if only slightly. To be sure, let us model the example about choosing a restaurant as a game, identifying each of its elements:

- The players would be you and your partner.
- Each of you may choose restaurant A or restaurant B.
- Neither of you have any information about the other's choice at the time of making your decision.
- Both of you prefer eating together rather than being alone, no matter where, and you both prefer restaurant B over restaurant A. Thus, the best possible outcome for both would be to meet at restaurant B; second best would be meeting at restaurant A; and any lack of coordination would be equally awful.[2]

The three examples above are very different in many aspects, but they all could be modeled using the same game. This is so because games are abstractions that are meant to capture the bare essentials of the original social interaction and, at least to some extent, the three examples above share the same strategic backbone.

Having seen this, it may not come as a surprise that the sort of issues for which game theory can be useful is impressively broad and diverse, including applications in international relations, resource management, network routing (of vehicles or information packages), voting systems, linguistics, law, distributed control, evolutionary biology, design of incentive systems, and business and environmental regulations.

---

motivations, moral principles, and social constraints (see e.g. Colman (1995, p. 301), Vega-Redondo (2003, p. 7), Binmore and Shaked (2010, p. 88), Binmore (2011, p. 8) or Gintis (2014, p. 7)).

2. Note that there is no inconsistency in being indifferent about outcomes {A, B} and {B, A}, even if you prefer restaurant B. It is sufficient to assume that you care about your partner as much as about yourself.

2. Traditional game theory

Game theory has nowadays various branches. Historically, the first branch to be developed was Traditional Game Theory (TGT) (von Neumann and Morgenstern (1944), Nash (1950), Selten (1965, 1975), Harsanyi (1967, 1968a, 1968b)). TGT is also the branch where most of the work has been focused, and the one with the largest representation in most game theory textbooks and academic courses.[3]

In TGT, payoffs reflect preferences and players are assumed to be rational, meaning that they act as if they have consistent preferences and unlimited computational capacity to achieve their well-defined objectives. The aim of the discipline is to study how these instrumentally rational players would behave in order to obtain the maximum possible payoff in the formal game.

A key problem in TGT is that, in general, assuming rational behavior for any one player rules out very few actions -and consequently very few outcomes- in the absence of strong assumptions about what players know about others' rationality, knowledge and actions. Hence, in order to derive specific predictions about how rational players would behave, it is often necessary to make very stringent assumptions about everyone's beliefs and their reciprocal consistency. If one assumes common knowledge of rationality and consistency of beliefs, then the outcome of the game is a *Nash equilibrium*, which is a set of strategies, one for each player, such that no player, knowing the other players' strategies in that set, could improve her expected payoff by unilaterally changing her own strategy (see Samuelson (1997, pp. 10-12) and Holt and Roth (2004) for several interpretations). An equivalent definition is the following: A Nash equilibrium is a strategy profile (i.e. one strategy for each player in the game) where every player is best responding to the strategies of the others.

Oftentimes, games have several Nash equilibria. As an example, the game depicted in Fig. 1 has three different Nash equilibria: the two strategy profiles where both players choose the same action (i.e. {A, A} and {B, B}), and a third equilibrium in *mixed* strategies, which means that players choose each action with a certain probability. In this third Nash equilibrium, both players choose action A with probability ⅔ (and action B with probability ⅓), a strategy that we denote (⅔, ⅓).

The equilibrium in mixed strategies is unsatisfactory for a number of reasons. First, since both actions can be chosen with strictly positive probability by each player, any observation of the actions actually taken by the two players would be consistent with this Nash equilibrium. Therefore, this equilibrium cannot be falsified by observing the outcome of the game. Another disappointing property of the Nash equilibrium in mixed strategies is the low payoff that players are expected to receive when they play it. In that equilibrium, outcome {B, B} would occur with probability ⅓ × ⅓, outcome {A, A} would occur with probability ⅔ × ⅔, and players would not coordinate with probability 2 × ⅓ × ⅔ , yielding a total expected payoff of ⅔ for each of them. Thus, this equilibrium is worse than any of the other

3. TGT can be divided further into cooperative and non-cooperative game theory. In *cooperative* game theory, it is assumed that players may negotiate binding agreements that can be externally enforced (by e.g. contract law). In *non-cooperative* game theory, such agreements cannot be enforced externally, so they are relevant only to the extent that abiding by them is in each individual's interest.

two Nash equilibria for *both* players. Finally, the mixed-strategy equilibrium does not seem to be very robust. Imagine that one of the players deviates from this equilibrium only slightly, by choosing action B with a probability marginally greater than ⅓. Then the other player's best response would be to choose action B with probability 1, and the deviator's best response to that reaction would be to play B with probability 1, too. Thus, this mixed-strategy equilibrium does not seem to be very stable.[4]

One could think that this diversity of equilibria, and the existence of the mixed-strategy equilibrium, may be partly an artifact of the fact that the game is played just once. It seems intuitive to think that if the game was played repeatedly, rational individuals would manage to coordinate in the (unique) *Pareto optimal*[5] outcome {B, B}, and the other suboptimal outcomes would not be observed in any Nash equilibrium. However, that natural intuition turns out to be wrong. To understand this, let us briefly review how repeated games are modeled in TGT.

In a *repeated game*, a certain basic game (called *stage game*) is played a number of rounds; the payoff obtained by each player in the repeated game is the sum of the (potentially discounted) payoffs obtained in each of the rounds. At any round, all the actions chosen by each of the players in previous rounds are known by everyone. A strategy in this repeated game is a complete plan of action for every possible contingency that may occur. For instance, in our coordination game, a possible strategy for the 3-round repeated game would be:

- At initial round $t = 1$, play B.
- At round $t > 1$, play B if the other player chose B at time $t - 1$. Otherwise play A.

Importantly, note that, even though the game is played repeatedly, the interaction only occurs once, since the strategies of the individuals dictate what to do in every possible history of the long game. Players could send their strategies by mail, and robots could implement them.

So, does repetition lead to sharper predictions about how rational players may interact? Not at all, rather the opposite. It turns out that when a game is repeated, the number of Nash equilibria generally multiplies, and there is a wide range of possible outcomes that can be supported by them. As an example, in our coordination game, any sequence formed by combining the three Nash equilibria of the stage game is a Nash equilibrium of the repeated game, and there are many more.[6]

The approach followed to model repeated interactions in Evolutionary Game Theory is rather different, as we explain below.

---

4. The same logic applies if one assumes that the deviation consists in choosing action B with a probability marginally *less* than ⅓. In this case, the other player's best response would be to choose action A with probability 1.
5. An outcome is Pareto optimal if it is impossible to make one player better off without making at least one other player worse off
6. In general, any strategy profile which at every round prescribes the play of a Nash equilibrium of the stage game regardless of history is a (subgame perfect) Nash equilibrium of the repeated game. This can be easily proved using the one-shot deviation principle.

3. Evolutionary Game Theory

3.1. The beginnings

Some time after the emergence of traditional game theory, biologists realized the potential of game theory to formally study adaptation and coevolution of biological populations, particularly in contexts where the fitness of a phenotype depends on the composition of the population (Hamilton, 1967). The initial development of the evolutionary approach to game theory came with important changes on how the main elements of a game (i.e. players, strategies, information and payoffs) were interpreted and used:

- Players (who most often represented non-human animals) were assumed to be pre-programmed to play one given strategy, i.e. players were seen as mere carriers of a particular fixed strategy that had been genetically endowed to them and could not be changed during the course of the player's lifetime. As for the number of players, the main interest in early EGT was to study *large populations* of animals, where the actions of one single individual could not significantly affect the overall success of any strategy in the population.
- Strategies, therefore, were not assumed to be selected by players, but rather hardwired in the animals' genetic make-up. Strategies were, basically, phenotypes.

> The concept is couched in terms of a 'strategy' because it arose in the context of animal behaviour. The idea, however, can be applied equally well to any kind of phenotypic variation, and the word strategy could be replaced by the word phenotype; for example, a strategy could be the growth form of a plant, or the age at first reproduction, or the relative numbers of sons and daughters produced by a parent. Maynard Smith (1982, p. 10)

- Since strategies are not consciously chosen by players, but they are simply hardwired, information at the time of making the decision plays no significant role.
- Payoffs did not represent any order of preference, but Darwinian fitness, i.e. the expected reproductive contribution to future generations.

The main assumption underlying evolutionary thinking was that strategies with greater payoffs at a particular time would tend to spread more and thus have better chances of being present in the future. The first models in EGT, which were developed for biological contexts, assumed that this selection biased towards individuals with greater payoffs occurred at the population level, through a process of natural selection. As a matter of fact, early EGT models embraced a fairly direct interpretation of the essence of Wallace and Darwin's idea of evolution by natural selection.

> As many **more individuals of each species are born than can possibly survive**; and as,

> consequently, there is a frequently recurring struggle for existence, it follows that any being, if it **vary** however slightly in any manner profitable to itself, under the complex and sometimes varying conditions of life, will have a **better chance of surviving**, and thus be *naturally selected*. From the strong **principle of inheritance**, any **selected variety will tend to propagate its new and modified form.** Darwin (1859, p. 5)

The essence of this simple and groundbreaking idea could be algorithmically summarized as follows:

> **IF**:
>
> - More offspring are produced than can survive and reproduce, and
> - variation within populations:
>   - affects the fitness (i.e. the expected reproductive contribution to future generations) of individuals, and
>   - is heritable,
>
> **THEN**:
>
> - evolution by natural selection occurs.

The key insight that game theory contributed to evolutionary biology is that, once the strategy distribution changes as a result of the evolutionary process, the relative fitness of the remaining strategies may also change, so previously unsuccessful strategies may turn out to be successful in the new environment, and thus increase their prevalence. In other words, the fitness landscape is not static, but it also evolves as the distribution of strategies changes.

An important concept developed in this research programme was the notion of *Evolutionarily Stable Strategy* (ESS), put forward by Maynard Smith and Price (1973) for 2-player symmetric games played by individuals belonging to the same population. Informally, a strategy **I** (for **I**ncumbent) is an ESS if and only if, when adopted by all members of a population, it enjoys a uniform invasion barrier in the sense that any other strategy **M** (for **M**utant) that could enter the population (in sufficiently low proportion) would obtain a strictly lower expected payoff in the postentry population than the incumbent strategy **I**. The ESS concept is a refinement of (symmetric) Nash equilibrium.

As an example, in the coordination game depicted in Fig. 1 both pure strategies are ESSs, but the mixed strategy (⅔ , ⅓), corresponding to the symmetric Nash equilibrium in mixed strategies, is not an ESS. The intuition for this is clear: a population where every agent is playing strategy **I** = (⅔ , ⅓) would be invadable by e.g. a small fraction of mutants playing action B (i.e. strategy (0,1)). This is so because the mutants would obtain the same payoff against the incumbents as the incumbents among themselves (i.e. ⅔ on average), but a strictly greater payoff whenever they met other mutants (i.e. 2 for certain). Thus, natural selection would gradually favor the mutants over the incumbents.[7]

The basic ideas behind EGT –i.e. that strategies with greater payoffs tend to spread more, and that fitness is frequency-dependent– soon transcended the borders of biology and started to permeate many other disciplines. In economic contexts, it was understood that natural selection would derive from competition among entities for scarce resources or market shares. In other social contexts, evolution was often understood as *cultural* evolution, and it referred to dynamic changes in behavior or ideas over time (Nelson and Winter (1982), Boyd and Richerson (1985)).

3.2. An interpretation of evolutionary game theory where strategies are *explicitly selected* by individuals

Evolutionary ideas proved very useful to understand several phenomena in many disciplines, but –at the same time– it became increasingly clear that a *direct* application of the principles of *Darwinian* natural selection was not always appropriate for the study of (non-Darwinian) social evolution.[8] In many contexts, it seems more natural to assume that players are capable of adapting their behavior within their lifetime, occasionally revising their strategy in a way that tends to favor strategies leading to higher payoffs over strategies leading to lower payoffs. The key distinction is that, in this latter interpretation, strategies are selected at the individual level (rather than at the population level). Also, in this view of selection taking place at the individual level, payoffs do not have to represent Darwinian fitness anymore, but can perfectly well represent a preference ordering, and interpersonal comparisons of payoffs may not be needed. Following this interpretation, the algorithmic view of the process by which strategies with greater payoffs gradually displace strategies with lower payoffs would look as follows:

IF:

- Players using different strategies obtain different payoffs, and
- they occasionally revise their strategies (by e.g. imitation or direct reasoning over gathered information), preferentially switching to strategies that provide greater payoffs,

THEN:

- the frequency of strategies with greater payoffs will tend to increase (and this change in strategy

7. Note that mutants playing action A (i.e. strategy (1,0)) would also be able to invade the incumbent population.
8. As an example, note that payoffs interpreted as Darwinian fitness are added across different players to determine the relative frequency of different types of players (i.e. strategies) in succeeding generations. These interpersonal comparisons are inherent to the notion of biological evolution by natural selection, and pose no problems if payoffs reflect Darwinian fitness. However, if evolution is interpreted in cultural terms, presuming the ability to conduct interpersonal comparisons of payoffs across players may be controversial. In this link, you can watch a video that shows how unconvinced John Maynard Smith was by direct applications of the principles of *Darwinian* natural selection in Economics.

frequencies may alter the future relative success of strategies).

In this interpretation, the canonical evolutionary model typically comprises the following elements:

- A population of agents,
- a game that is recurrently played by the agents,
- a procedure by which revision opportunities are assigned to agents, and
- a revision protocol, which dictates how individual agents choose their strategy when they are given the opportunity to revise.

Note that this approach to EGT can *formally* encompass the biological interpretation, since one can always interpret the revision of a strategy as a death and birth event, rather than as a conscious decision. Having said that, it is clear that different interpretations may seem more natural in different contexts. The important point is that the framework behind the two interpretations is the same.

To conclude this section, let us revisit our coordination example (with payoff matrix shown in Fig. 1) in a population context. We will analyze two revision protocols that lead to different results: imitative pairwise-difference protocol and best experienced payoff protocol.

- Under the *imitative pairwise-difference protocol* (Helbing (1992), Hofbauer (1995), Schlag (1998)), a revising agent looks at another individual at random and imitates her strategy only if that strategy yields a higher expected payoff than his current strategy; in this case he switches with probability proportional to the payoff difference. It can be proved that the dynamics of this protocol in large populations will tend to approach the state where every agent plays action B if the initial proportion of B-players is greater than ⅓, and will tend to approach the state where every agent plays action A if the initial proportion of B-players is less than ⅓ (Fig. 2).[9]

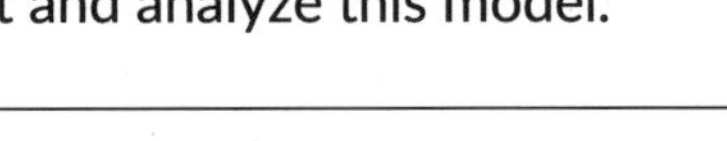

Figure 2. Mean dynamic of the imitative pairwise-difference protocol in a coordination game.

The following video shows some NetLogo simulations that illustrate these dynamics. In this book, we will learn to implement and analyze this model.[10]

A video element has been excluded from this version of the text. You can watch it online here: https://wisc.pb.unizin.org/agent-based-evolutionary-game-dynamics/?p=94

---

9. To prove this statement, note that the mean dynamic of this revision protocol is the well-known replicator dynamic (Taylor and Jonker, 1978)
10. See exercise 5 in section 1.0 and exercise 3 in section 1.4

Simulation runs of the imitative pairwise-difference protocol in coordination game [[1 0][0 2]]

- Under the *best experienced payoff protocol* (Osborne and Rubinstein (1998), Sethi (2000, 2019), Sandholm et al. (2019, 2020)), a revising agent tests each of the two strategies against a random agent, with each play of each strategy being against a newly drawn opponent. The revising agent then selects the strategy that obtained the greater payoff in the test, with ties resolved at random. It can be proved that the dynamics of this protocol in large populations will tend to approach the state where every agent plays action B from any initial condition (other than the state where everyone plays A; see Fig. 3).[11]

Figure 3. Mean dynamic of the best experienced protocol in a coordination game.

The following video shows some NetLogo simulations that illustrate these dynamics. In this book, we will learn to implement and analyze this model.[12]

> *A video element has been excluded from this version of the text. You can watch it online here: https://wisc.pb.unizin.org/agent-based-evolutionary-game-dynamics/?p=94*

Simulation runs of the best experienced payoff protocol in coordination game [[1 0][0 2]]

The example above shows that different protocols can lead to very different dynamics in non-trivial ways. Both protocols above tend to favor best-performing strategies, and in both the mixed-strategy Nash equilibrium is unstable. However, given an initial state where 80% of the population is playing strategy A, one of the protocols will almost certainly lead the population to the state where everyone plays A, while the other protocol will lead the population to the state where everyone plays B. In this book, we will learn a range of different concepts and techniques that will help us understand these differences.

Evolutionary Game Theory and Engineering

Many engineering infrastructures are becoming increasingly complex to manage due to their large-scale distributed nature and the nonlinear interdependences between their components (Quijano et al., 2017). Examples include communication networks, transportation systems, sensor and data networks, wind farms, power grids, teams of autonomous vehicles, and urban drainage systems. Controlling such large-scale distributed systems requires the implementation of decision rules for the interconnected components that guarantee the accomplishment of a collective objective in an environment that is often dynamic and uncertain. To achieve this goal, traditional control

11. This statement is a direct application of Proposition 5.11 in Sandholm et al. (2020)
12. See exercise 6 in section 1.0 and exercise 4 in section 1.4

theory is often of little use, since distributed architectures generally lack a central entity with access or authority over all components (Marden and Shamma, 2015).

The concepts developed in EGT can be very useful in such situations. The analogy between distributed systems in engineering and the social interactions analyzed in EGT has been formally established in various engineering contexts (Marden and Shamma, 2015). In EGT terms, the goal is to identify revision protocols that will lead to desirable outcomes using limited local information only. As an example, at least in the coordination game discussed above, the best experienced payoff protocol is more likely to lead to the most efficient outcome than the imitative pairwise-difference protocol.

3.3. Take-home message

EGT is devoted to the study of the evolution of strategies in a population context where individuals repeatedly interact to play a game. Strategies are subjected to evolutionary pressures in the sense that the relative frequency of strategies which obtain higher payoffs in the population will tend to increase at the expense of those which obtain relatively lower payoffs. The aim is to identify which strategies are most likely to thrive in this "evolving ecosystem of strategies" and which will be wiped out, under different evolutionary dynamics. In this sense, note that EGT is an inherently dynamic theory.

There are two ways of interpreting the process by which strategies are selected. In biological systems, players are typically assumed to be pre-programmed to play one given strategy throughout their whole lifetime, and strategy composition changes by natural selection. By contrast, in socio-economic models, players are usually assumed capable of adapting their behavior within their lifetime, revising their strategy in a way that tends to favor strategies that provide greater payoffs at the time of revision.

Whether strategies are selected by natural selection or by individual players is rather irrelevant for the formal analysis of the system, since in both cases the interest lies in studying the evolution of strategies. In this book, we will follow the approach which assumes that strategies are selected by individuals using a revision protocol.

3.4. Relation with other branches

The differences between TGT and EGT are quite clear and rather obvious. TGT players are rational and forward-looking, while EGT players adapt in a fairly gradual and myopic fashion. TGT is a theory stated in terms of a one-time interaction: even if the interaction is a repeated game, this long game is played just once. In stark contrast, dynamics are at the core of EGT: the outcomes of the game shape the distribution of strategies in the population, and this change in distribution modifies the relative success of different strategies when the game is played again. Finally, TGT is mainly focused on the study of end-states and possible equilibria, paying hardly any attention to how such equilibria might be reached. By contrast, EGT is concerned with the evolution of the strategy composition in a population, which in some cases may never settle down on an equilibrium.

The branch of game theory that is closest to EGT is the Theory of Learning in Games (TLG). Like EGT, TLG abandons the demanding assumptions of TGT on players' rationality and beliefs, and assumes instead that players learn over time about the game and about the behavior of others (e.g. through reinforcement, imitation, or belief updating).

The process of learning in TLG can take many different forms, depending on the available information and feedback, and the way these are used to modify behavior. The assumptions made in these regards give rise to different models of learning. In most models of TLG, players use the history of the game to decide what action to take. In the simplest forms of learning (e.g. reinforcement or imitation) this link between acquired information and action is direct (e.g. in a stimulus-response fashion); in more sophisticated learning, players use the history of the game to form expectations or beliefs about the other players' behavior, and they then react optimally to these inferred expectations.[13]

The interpretation of EGT which assumes that players can revise their strategy is very similar to TLG. The main differences between these two branches are:

- EGT tends to study *large* populations of *small* agents, who interact *anonymously*. This implies that players' payoffs only depend on the distribution of strategies in the population, and also that any one player's actions have little or no effect on the aggregate success of any strategy at the population level. In contrast, TLG is mainly concerned with the analysis of small groups of players who repeatedly play a game among them, each of them in her particular role.
- The revision protocols analyzed in EGT tend to be fairly simple and use information about the current state of the population only. By contrast, the sort of algorithms analyzed in TLG tend to be more sophisticated, and make use of the history of the game to decide what action to take.

4. How can I learn game theory?

To learn more about game theory, we recommend the following material:

- Overviews:
  - Introductory: Colman (1995).
  - Advanced: Vega-Redondo (2003).
- Traditional game theory:
  - Introductory: Dixit and Nalebuff (2008).
  - Intermediate: Osborne (2004).
  - Advanced: Fudenberg and Tirole (1991), Myerson (1997), Binmore (2007).
- Evolutionary game theory:

13. Izquierdo et al. (2012) provide a succinct overview of some of the learning models that have been studied in TLG. For a more detailed account, see chapters 11 and 12 in Vega-Redondo (2003).

    - Introductory: Maynard Smith (1982), Gintis (2009), Sandholm (2009).
    - Advanced: Hofbauer and Sigmund (1988), Weibull (1995), Samuelson (1997), Sandholm (2010).
    - Recent literature review: Newton (2018).
- The theory of learning in games:
    - Introductory: Vega-Redondo (2003, chapters 11 and 12).
    - Advanced: Fudenberg and Levine (1998), Young (2004).

0.2. Introduction to agent-based modeling

1. What is agent-based modeling?

Agent-based modeling (ABM) is a methodology used to build formal models of real-world systems that are made up by *individual* units (such as e.g. atoms, cells, animals, people or institutions) which *repeatedly interact* among themselves and/or with their environment.

The essence of agent-based modeling

The defining feature of the agent-based modeling approach is that it establishes a direct and explicit correspondence

- between the individual units in the target system to be modeled and the parts of the model that represent these units (i.e. the agents), and also
- between the interactions of the individual units in the target system and the interactions of the corresponding agents in the model (figure 1).

This approach contrasts with e.g. equation-based modeling, where entities of the target system may be represented via average properties or via single representative agents.

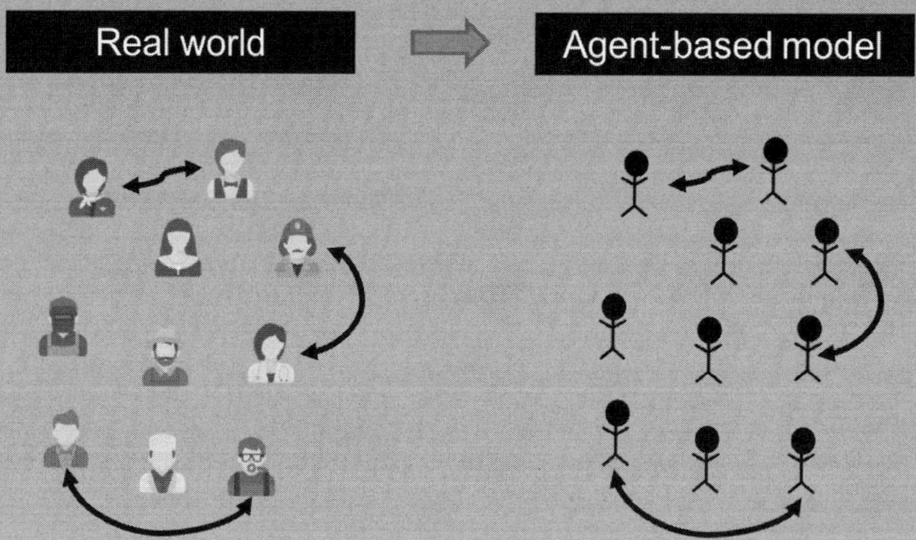

Figure 1. In an agent-based model, the individual units of the real-world system to be modeled and their interactions are explicitly and individually represented in the model.

Thus, in an agent-based model, the individual units of the system and their repeated interactions are *explicitly* and *individually* represented in the model (Edmonds, 2001).[1] Beyond this, no further assumptions are made in agent-based modeling.

1. These three videos by Bruce Edmonds and Michael Price and Uri Wilensky nicely describe what ABM is about.

At this point, you may be wondering whether game theory is part of ABM, since in game theory players are indeed explicitly and individually represented in the models.[2] The key to answer that question is the last sentence in the box above, i.e. "*Beyond this, no further assumptions are made in agent-based modeling*". There are certainly many disciplines (e.g. game theory and cellular automata theory) that analyze models where individuals and their interactions are represented explicitly. The key distinction is that these disciplines make further assumptions, i.e. impose additional structure on their models. These additional assumptions constrain the type of models that are analyzed and, by doing so, they often allow for more accurate predictions and/or greater understanding within their (somewhat more limited) scope. Thus, when one encounters a model that fits perfectly into the framework of a particular discipline (e.g. game theory), it seems more appropriate to use the more specific name of the particular discipline, and leave the term "agent-based" for those models which satisfy the defining feature of ABM mentioned above and they do not currently fit in any more specific area of study.

The last sentence in the box also uncovers a key feature of ABM: its *flexibility*. In principle, you can make your agent-based model as complex as you wish. This has pros and cons. Adding complexity to your model allows you to study any phenomenon you may be interested in, but it also makes analyzing and understanding the model harder (or even sometimes practically impossible) using the most advanced mathematical techniques. Because of this, agent-based models are generally implemented in a programming language and explored using computer simulation. This is so common that the terms agent-based modeling and agent-based simulation are often used interchangeably. The following is a list of some features that traditionally have been difficult to analyze mathematically, and for which agent-based modeling can be useful (Epstein and Axtell, 1996):

- Agents' heterogeneity. Since agents are explicitly represented in the model, they can be as heterogeneous as the modeler deems appropriate.
- Interdependencies between processes (e.g. demographic, economic, biological, geographical, technological) that have been traditionally studied in different disciplines, and are not often analyzed together. There is no restriction on the type of rules that can be implemented in an agent-based model, so models can include rules that link disparate aspects of the world that are often studied in different disciplines.
- Out-of-equilibrium dynamics. Dynamics are inherent to ABM. Running a simulation consists in applying the rules that define the model over and over, so agent-based models almost invariably include some notion of time within them. Equilibria are never imposed a priori: they may emerge as an outcome of the simulation, or they may not.
- The micro-macro link. ABM is particularly well suited to study how global phenomena emerge from the interactions among individuals, and also how these emergent global phenomena may constrain and shape back individuals' actions.
- Local interactions and the role of physical space. The fact that agents and their environment

2. The extent to which *repeated* interactions are *explicitly* represented in traditional game theoretical models is not so clear.

are represented explicitly in ABM makes it particularly straightforward and natural to model local interactions (e.g. via networks).

As you can imagine, introducing any of the aspects outlined above in an agent-based model often means that the model becomes mathematically intractable, at least to some extent. However, in this book we will learn that, in many cases, there are various aspects of agent-based models that can be analytically solved, or described using formal approximation results. Our view is that the most useful agent-based models lie at the boundaries of theoretical understanding, and help us push these boundaries. They are advances sufficiently small so that simplified versions of them (or certain aspects of their behaviour) can be fully understood in mathematical terms –thus retaining its analytical rigour–, but they are steps large enough to significantly extend our understanding beyond what is achievable using the most advanced mathematical techniques available.

> In my personal (albeit biased) view, the best simulations are those which just peek over the rim of theoretical understanding, displaying mechanisms about which one can still obtain causal intuitions. Probst (1999)

2. What is an agent?

In this book we will use the term *agent* to refer to a distinct part of our (computational) model that is meant to represent a decision-maker. Agents could represent human beings, non-human animals, institutions, firms, etc. The agents in our models will always play a game, so in this book we will use the term agent and the term player interchangeably.

Agents have *individually-owned variables*, which describe their internal state (e.g. a strategy), and are able to conduct certain computations or tasks, i.e. they are able to run *instructions* (e.g. to update their strategy). These instructions are sometimes called decision rules, or rules of behavior, and most often imply some kind of interaction with other agents or with the environment.

The following are some of the individually-owned variables that the agents we are going to implement in this book may have:

- strategy (a number)
- payoff (a number)
- my-coplayers (the set of agents with whom this agent plays the game)
- color (the color of this agent)

And the following are examples of instructions that the agents in most of our models will be able to run:

- to play (play a certain game with my-coplayers and set the payoff appropriately)
- to update-strategy (revise strategy according to a certain revision protocol)

- to update-color (set color according to strategy)

3. A paradigmatic example

In this section we present a model that captures the spirit of ABM. The model implements the main features of a family of models proposed by Sakoda (1949, 1971) and –independently– by Schelling (1969, 1971, 1978).[3][4] Specifically, here we present a computer implementation put forward by Edmonds and Hales (2005).[5]

In this model there are 133 blue agents and 133 orange agents who live in a 2-dimensional grid made up of 20×20 cells (figure 2). Agents are initially located at random on the grid. The neighborhood of a cell is defined by the eight neighboring cells (i.e. the eight cells which surround it).[6]

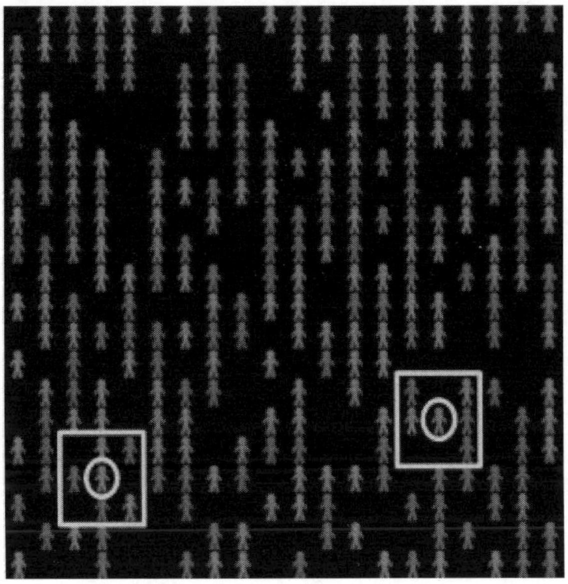

Figure 2. Grid of Schelling-Sakoda model (20×20), with 133 blue agents, 133 orange agents. The agents in yellow circles have 2 out of 5 neighbors of the same color.

Agents may be happy or unhappy. An agent is happy if the proportion of other agents of its same colour in its neighbourhood is greater or equal than a certain threshold (*%-similar-wanted*), which is a parameter of the model; otherwise the agent is said to be unhappy. Agents with no neighbors are assumed to be happy regardless of the value of *%-similar-wanted*. In each iteration of the model one unhappy agent is randomly selected to move to a random empty cell in the lattice.

---

3. Hegselmann (2017) provides a detailed and fascinating account of the history of this family of models.
4. Our implementation is not a precise instance of neither Sakoda's nor Schelling's family of models, because unhappy agents in our model move to a *random* location. We chose this migration regime to make the code simpler. For details, see Hegselmann (2017, footnote 124).
5. Izquierdo et al. (2009, appendix B) analyze this model as a Markov chain.
6. Cells on a side have five neighbors and cells at a corner have three neighbors.

As an example, the two agents surrounded by a circle in figure 2 have 2 out of 5 neighbors of the same color as them, i.e. 40%. This means that in simulation runs where *%-similar-wanted* ≤ 40% these agents would be happy, and would not move. On the other hand, in simulations where *%-similar-wanted* > 40% these two agents would move to a random location.

Individually-owned variables and instructions

In this model, agent's individually-owned variables are:

- color, which can be either blue or orange,
- (xcor, ycor), which determine the agent's location on the grid, and
- happy?, which indicates whether the agent is happy or not.

Agents are able to run the following instructions:

- to move, to change the agent's location to a random empty cell, and
- to update-happiness, to update the agent's individually-owned variable happy?.

Now imagine that we simulate a society where agents require at least 60% of their neighbors to be of the same color as them in order to be happy (i.e. *%-similar-wanted* = 60%). These are pretty strong segregationist preferences, so one would expect a fairly clear pattern of spatial segregation at the end. The following video shows a representative run. You may wish to run the simulations yourself downloading this model's code.

A video element has been excluded from this version of the text. You can watch it online here: https://wisc.pb.unizin.org/agent-based-evolutionary-game-dynamics/?p=40

Simulation run of Schelling-Sakoda model with %-similar-wanted = 60.

As expected, the final outcome of the simulation shows clearly distinctive ghettos. To measure the level of segregation of a certain spatial pattern we define a global variable named *avg-%similar*, which is the average proportion (across agents) of an agent's neighbors that are the same color as the agent. Extensive Monte Carlo simulation shows that a good estimate of the expected *avg-%similar* is about 95.7% when *%-similar-wanted* is 60%.

What is really surprising is that even with only mild segregationist preferences, such as *%-similar-wanted* = 40%, we still obtain fairly segregated spatial patterns (expected *avg-%similar* ≈ 82.7%). The following video shows a representative run.

A video element has been excluded from this version of the text. You can watch it online here: https://wisc.pb.unizin.org/agent-based-evolutionary-game-dynamics/?p=40

Simulation run of Schelling-Sakoda model with %-similar-wanted = 40.

And even with segregationist preferences as weak as *%-similar-wanted* = 30% (i.e. you are happy unless strictly less than 30% of your neighbors are of the same color as you), the emergent spatial patterns show significant segregation (expected *avg-%similar* ≈ 74.7%). The following video shows a representative run.

> *A video element has been excluded from this version of the text. You can watch it online here:* https://wisc.pb.unizin.org/agent-based-evolutionary-game-dynamics/?p=40

Simulation run of Schelling-Sakoda model with %-similar-wanted = 30.

So this agent-based model illustrates how strong spatial segregation can result from only weakly segregationist preferences (e.g. trying to avoid an acute minority status). This model has been enriched in a number of directions (e.g. to include heterogeneity between and within groups),[7] but the implementation discussed here is sufficient to illustrate a non-trivial phenomenon that emerges from agents' individual choices and their interactions.

4. Agent-based modeling and evolutionary game theory

Given that models in Evolutionary Game Theory (EGT) comprise many *individuals* who repeatedly *interact* among them and occasionally revise their *individually-owned* strategy, it seems clear that agent-based modelling is certainly an appropriate methodology to build EGT models. Therefore, the question is whether other approaches may be more appropriate or convenient. This is an important issue, since nowadays most models in EGT are equation-based, and therefore –in general– more amenable to mathematical analysis than agent-based models. This is a clear advantage for equation-based models. Why bother with agent-based modeling then?

The reason is that mathematical tractability often comes at a price: equation-based models tend to incorporate several assumptions that are made solely for the purpose of guaranteeing mathematical tractability. Examples include assuming that the population is infinite, or assuming that revising agents are able to evaluate strategies' expected payoffs. These assumptions are clearly made for mathematical convenience, since there are no infinite populations in the real world, and –in general– it seems more natural to assume that agents' choices are based on information obtained from experiences with various strategies, or from observations of others' experiences. Are assumptions made for mathematical convenience harmless? We cannot know unless we study models where such assumptions are not made. And this is where agent-based modelling can play an important role.

Agent-based modeling gives us the potential to build models closer to the real-world systems that we want to study, because in an agent-based model we are free to choose the sort of assumptions

7. See Aydinonat (2007).

that we deem appropriate in purely scientific terms. We may not be able to fully analyze all aspects of the resulting agent-based model mathematically, but we will certainly be able to explore it using computer simulation, and this exploration can help us assess the impact of assumptions that are made only for mathematical tractability. In this way, we will be able to shed light on questions such as: how large must a population be for the mathematical model to be a good description of the dynamics of the finite-population model? and, how much do dynamics change if agents cannot evaluate strategies' expected payoffs with infinite precision?

5. How can I learn about agent-based modeling?

A wonderful classic book to learn the fundamental concepts and appreciate the kind of models you can build using ABM is Epstein and Axtell (1996). In this short book, the authors show how to build an artificial society where agents, using extremely simple rules, are able to engage in a wide range of activities such as sex, cultural exchange, trade, combat, disease transmission, etc. Epstein and Axtell (1996)'s interdisciplinary book shows how complex patterns can emerge from very simple rules of interaction.

Epstein and Axtell (1996)'s seminal book focuses on the fundamental concepts without discussing any code whatsoever. The following books are also excellent introductions to scientific agent-based modeling, and all of them make use of NetLogo: Gilbert (2007), Railsback and Grimm (2019), Wilensky and Rand (2015) and Janssen (2020)[8]. Hamill and Gilbert (2016) discuss the implementation of several NetLogo models in the context of Economics. Most of these models are significantly more sophisticated than the ones we implement and analyze in this book.

8. Free online book

0.3. Introduction to NetLogo

1. What is NetLogo?

> NetLogo is a well-written, easy-to-install, easy-to-use, easy-to-extend, and easy-to-publish-online environment. The entry level is simple enough and the tutorials provided in the package are straightforward and clear enough that anyone who can read and is comfortable using a keyboard and mouse could create their own models in a short time, with little or no additional instruction. Sklar (2007, p. 7)

NetLogo (Wilensky, 1999) is a modeling environment designed for coding and running agent-based simulations.[1] Nowadays, there are many languages and software platforms that can be employed to create agent-based models,[2] and at the time of writing NetLogo is the most widely used. We recommend NetLogo and will use it throughout this book for the many reasons we outline below.

Easy to learn

> NetLogo stands out as the quickest to learn and the easiest to use. Gilbert (2007, p. 49)

The language used to code models within NetLogo –which is also called NetLogo– has been designed following a "Low Threshold, No Ceiling" philosophy (Wilensky and Rand, 2015). All reviews of the software highlight how easy it is to learn. To be concrete, we would estimate that an average scholar without previous coding experience can learn the basics of the language and be in a position to write a simple agent-based model after 2-4 days of work. Someone with programming experience could reduce the estimated time to 1-2 days.

---

1. NetLogo was created by Uri Wilensky and is under continuous development at the Northwestern's Center for Connected Learning and Computer-Based Modeling. It is also important to acknowledge Seth Tisue, who "*worked meticulously to guarantee the quality of the NetLogo software*" (Wilensky and Rand, 2015, p. xxii) as lead developer for over a decade.
2. To our knowledge, the most up-to-date and comprehensive review of agent-based simulation software has been conducted by Abar et al. (2017), who compare 85 tools using a convenient tabular and chart format, and deem NetLogo both *easy to use* and also *appropriate to execute medium/large-scale simulations*. Another recent review that assesses and compares NetLogo with other platforms has been published by Kravari and Bassiliades (2015). There is also a wikipedia page set up by Nikolai and Madey (2009) which provides an up-to-date comparison of agent-based software toolkits. Finally, it is also possible to code agent-based models using general-purpose programming languages directly. In the context of evolutionary game theory, Isaac (2008) convincingly demonstrates how this can be easily done with Python.

One characteristic that makes the NetLogo language easy to learn is that it is remarkably close to natural language. As a matter of fact, NetLogo language could perfectly be used as pseudo-code to communicate algorithms implemented in other languages.

> Since NetLogo was designed to be easily readable, we believe that NetLogo code is about as easy to read as any pseudo-code we would have used. NetLogo also has the big advantage over pseudo-code of being executable, so the user can run and test the examples. (Wilensky and Rand, 2015, p. xiv)

NetLogo language is definitely simpler to use than e.g. Java or Objective-C, and can often reduce programming efforts significantly when compared with other languages.

Powerful

> NetLogo has become a standard platform for agent-based simulation, yet there appears to be widespread belief that it is not suitable for large and complex models due to slow execution. Our experience does not support that belief. Railsback et al. (2017, abstract)

NetLogo is powerful in that it can accommodate reasonably large and complex simulations, and its execution speed is more than acceptable for most purposes. NetLogo can easily run simulations with several tens of thousands of agents.

Excellent documentation

> NetLogo is by far the most professional platform in its appearance and documentation. Railsback et al. (2006, p. 613)

One of the reasons why NetLogo is so easy to learn is that it is very well documented. The user manual includes three tutorials to help beginners get started, an excellent programming guide, and a comprehensive dictionary with the definitions of all NetLogo primitives, including examples of how to use them. NetLogo also comes with an extensive library of models from different disciplines (e.g. art, biology, chemistry, computer science, mathematics, networks, philosophy, physics, psychology, and other social sciences) and several code examples which succinctly illustrate particular features and coding techniques.

Possibility to interact with the model at runtime

NetLogo is designed to allow the user to interact with the model during runtime in a variety of ways:

- By modifying parameter values at runtime, with immediate effect on the simulation. This feature is very convenient to assess the impact of different assumptions in the model and conduct exploratory work.
- By running commands in the middle of a run to e.g. create new agents, remove others, or make a subset of them take some action.
- By probing agents to see –and potentially set– the value of any of their individually-owned variables at any time.

Automatic exploration of parameter space

NetLogo includes a software tool named BehaviorSpace (Wilensky and Shargel, 2002) which greatly facilitates running a model many times, systematically varying the desired parameter values, and keeping a record of the results of each run. Besides, computational experiments set up with BehaviorSpace can be run from the command line, i.e. without having to open NetLogo's graphical user interface. This feature is particularly useful for launching large-scale experiments in computer clusters.

Open-source and free

NetLogo can be downloaded for free at http://ccl.northwestern.edu/netlogo/. Its source code is publicly hosted on GitHub at https://github.com/NetLogo/NetLogo, where users can open issues to request the implementation of new features or to report bugs.

Multiplatform and online execution of models

NetLogo can run on Windows, Mac or Linux. Most modern computers will run NetLogo without any trouble. It can also be used online through NetLogo Web. NetLogo Web can also be used to create stand-alone versions of NetLogo models in HTML format. These self-contained versions can be run in any browser without having to install any software.[3]

Great support and active user community

NetLogo developers are always happy to receive feedback and enhancement requests (at feedback@ccl.northwestern.edu), and bug reports (at bugs@ccl.northwestern.edu). There is also

3. This can be done by uploading any NetLogo model to NetLogo Web and exporting it as HTML.

an active community of NetLogo users who post their questions and help each other at the NetLogo-Users Google group and on StackOverflow.

Abundance of quality resources

At https://ccl.northwestern.edu/netlogo/resources.shtml you can find plenty of quality resources to learn NetLogo. These include references to textbooks, papers that make use of NetLogo, courses given at middle schools, high schools and Universities all around the world, competitions and tutorials. There are also many video tutorials on YouTube.

> This reviewer, who has used NetLogo for both research and teaching at several levels, highly recommends it for instructors from elementary school to graduate school and for researchers from a wide range of fields. Sklar (2007, p. 8)

Extensions to fulfill specialised needs

Extensions are add-ons that extend the NetLogo language with new primitives created to fulfill specialised needs. Some of these extensions come bundled with NetLogo, some have been created by NetLogo developers but must be downloaded separately, and others have been created by third parties. Four representative examples of useful extensions that come with NetLogo are:

- The rnd extension, which provides efficient primitives to make random weighted selections, with or without replacement.
- The nw extension, which adds many primitives to generate networks, compute several network-related metrics, and import and export network data.
- The matrix extension, which adds a matrix data structure to NetLogo and several primitives to operate with it.
- The GIS (Geographic Information Systems) extension.

Useful to conduct experiments with real people and for participatory modeling

The NetLogo release includes HubNet (Wilensky and Stroup, 1999), a technology that enables users to communicate and interact with each other through NetLogo. Thus, Hubnet can be very useful to run participatory simulations and experiments, in which human users can be part of the simulation and interact among themselves and with artificial agents.

Happy to link with other software

> NetLogo is now a powerful tool widely used in science and we recommend it strongly, especially for those new to modeling and programming but also for serious scientists with software experience. Lytinen and Railsback (2012)

NetLogo can be linked with advanced software tools like R (R Core Team, 2019), Python (Python Software Foundation, 2019), Mathematica (Wolfram Research, Inc., 2019) or Matlab (The MathWorks, Inc., 2019). Specifically, using an R package called RNetLogo (Thiele (2014); Thiele et al. (2012a, 2012b, 2014)), it is possible to run and control NetLogo models from R, execute NetLogo commands, and obtain any information from a NetLogo model. The connector PyNetLogo (Jaxa-Rozen and Kwakkel, 2018) provides the same functionalty for Python, and the so-called Mathematica link (Bakshy and Wilensky, 2007) for Mathematica. The Mathematica link comes bundled as part of the latest NetLogo releases.

Conversely, one can also call R, Python and Matlab commands from within NetLogo using the R-Extension (Thiele and Grimm, 2010), the NetLogo Python extension (Head, 2018) and MatNet (Biggs and Papin, 2013) respectively.

2. How to learn NetLogo

To make the most of this book, we recommend you get familiar with the NetLogo environment and with NetLogo programming before moving to the next chapter. This will normally take from a few hours to a couple of days, depending on your programming skills, and can be accomplished doing the following tasks:

- Download and install NetLogo following the instructions at https://ccl.northwestern.edu/netlogo/. In this book we will be using NetLogo version 6.1.1.[4]
- Go through the three tutorials in the NetLogo user manual, i.e.
    - Tutorial #1: Models
    - Tutorial #2: Commands
    - Tutorial #3: Procedures

After having gone through the previous material, you will have obtained the required NetLogo background to follow this text without any problems. In the next section we review the main concepts of NetLogo and give an overview of the structure of most NetLogo models, using the Schelling-Sakoda model as an illustration.

---

4. Please, make sure you download version 6.1.1 or greater. NetLogo syntax changed significantly in version 6.0, and a little bit in 6.1.

0.4. The fundamentals of NetLogo

This section provides a succinct overview of the fundamentals of NetLogo. It is strongly based on the excellent NetLogo user manual, version 6.1.1 (Wilensky, 2019). By no means do we claim originality on the content of this section; all credit should go to Uri Wilensky and his team. The following table provides links to the different aspects of NetLogo programming that we cover here.

Very basics	More advanced	Final polishing
The three tabs	Ask	Consistency within procedures
Types of agents	Lists	Breeds
Instructions	Agentsets	Ticks and Plotting
Variables	Synchronization	Skeleton of many NetLogo models
		The code for Schelling-Sakoda model

Feel free to skip this section if you are already familiar with NetLogo. For future reference, you may wish to download our NetLogo quick guide, which is a 6-page pdf file containing the main concepts outlined here.

1. The three tabs

The main window of NetLogo contains three tabs, i.e. the interface tab, the info tab and the code tab (see figure 1).

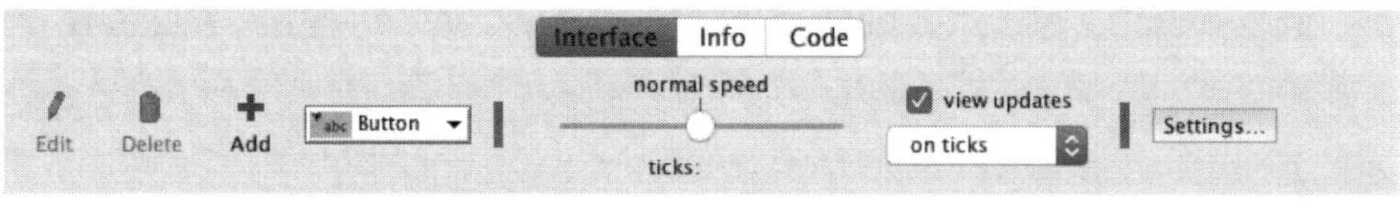

Figure 1. Top bar of the NetLogo Interface tab, where you can select the tab you want to see.

The interface tab is used to run the model. It often contains buttons, sliders, switches, plots... Most models include a button labeled setup, which is used to initialize the model, and another button labeled go, which is used to run the model.

The Info tab can be used to include the documentation of the model.

Finally, **the code tab** contains most of the code of the model. We say *most* because in some models part of the code is included within the plots in the interface tab.

2. Types of agents

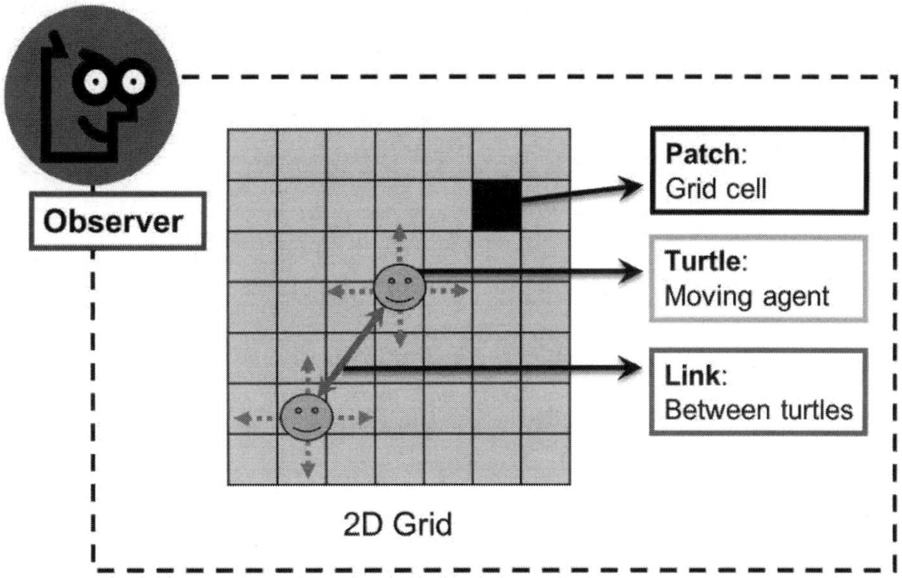

Figure 2. The NetLogo world is made up of turtles, patches, links and the observer.

The NetLogo world is made up by four types of agents (see figure 2), i.e.:

- **Turtles**. Turtles are agents that can move.
- **Patches**: The NetLogo world is two-dimensional and is divided up into a grid of patches. Each patch is a square piece of "ground" over which turtles can move.
- **Links**: Links are agents that connect two turtles. Links can be directed (from one turtle to another turtle) or undirected (one turtle with another turtle).
- **The observer**: There is only one observer and it does not have a location. You can think of the observer as the conductor of the whole NetLogo orchestra.

Note that in many descriptions of agent-based models, the word *agent* is used only to refer to the turtles (i.e. the *mobile* agents in NetLogo), while patches and links are not considered *agents* (and the observer is not even mentioned). However, when reading NetLogo documentation, it is important to remember that these four types of entities are all agents in NetLogo.

3. Instructions

Instructions tell agents what to do. Three characteristics are useful to remember about instructions:

- Whether the instruction is **implemented by the user** (*procedures*), **or** whether it is **built into NetLogo** (*primitives*). Once you define a procedure, you can use it elsewhere in your program. The NetLogo Dictionary has a complete list of built-in instructions (i.e. primitives). The following code is an example of the implementation of procedure to setup:

```
to setup                ;; comments are written after semicolon(s)
  clear-all             ;; clear everything
  create-turtles 10     ;; make 10 new turtles
end                     ; (one semicolon is enough, but I like two)
```

The instruction to setup is a procedure (since it is implemented by us), whereas `clear-all` and `create-turtles` are both primitives (they are built into NetLogo).

Note that primitives are nicely colored, and you can click on them and press F1 to see their syntax, functionality, and examples. You may want to copy and paste the code above to see all this for yourself.

- Whether the instruction produces an **output** (*reporters*) **or not** (*commands*).
    - A reporter computes a result and **reports** it. Most reporters are nouns or noun phrases (e.g. "average-wealth", "most-popular-girl"). These names are preceded by the keyword `to-report`. The keyword `end` marks the end of the instructions in the procedure.

```
to-report average-wealth              ;; this reporter returns the
  report mean [wealth] of turtles ;; average wealth in the
end                                   ;; population of turtles
```

    - A command is an action for an agent to carry out. Most commands begin with verbs (e.g. "create", "die", "jump", "inspect", "clear"). These verbs are preceded by the keyword `to` (instead of `to-report`). The keyword `end` marks the end of the procedure.

```
to go
  ask turtles [
    forward 1         ;; all turtles move forward one step
    right random 360 ;; and turn a random amount
  ]
end
```

Note that primitive commands are colored in `blue` while primitive reporters are colored in `purple`. Keywords are colored in `green`.

- Whether the instruction takes an **input** (or several inputs) **or not**. Inputs are values that the instruction uses in carrying out its actions.

```
to-report absolute-value [number]      ;; number is the input
  ifelse number >= 0              ;; if number is already non-negative
    [ report number ]             ;; return number (a non-negative value).
    [ report (- number) ]         ;; Otherwise, return the opposite, which
end                               ;; is then necessarily positive.
```

4. Variables

Variables are places to store values (such as numbers). A variable can be a *global* variable, a *turtle* variable, a *patch* variable, a *link* variable, or a *local* variable (local to a procedure). To change the value of a variable you can use the `set` command. If you don't set the variable to any value, it starts out storing a value of zero.

- **Global variables**: If a variable is a global variable, there is only one value for the variable, and every agent can access it. You can declare a new global variable either *in the Interface tab* -by adding a switch, a slider, a chooser or an input box- *or in the Code tab* -by using the `globals` keyword at the beginning of your code, like this:

```
globals [ n-of-strategies ]
```

- **Turtle, patch, and link variables**: Each turtle has its own value for every turtle variable, each patch has its own value for every patch variable, and each link has its own value for every link variable. Turtle, patch, and link variables can be *built-in* or *defined by the user*.
  - **Built-in** variables: For example, all turtles and all links have a `color` variable, and all patches have a `pcolor` variable. If you set this variable, the corresponding turtle, link or patch changes color. Other built-in turtle variables are `xcor`, `ycor`, and `heading`. Other built-in patch variables include `pxcor` and `pycor`. Other built-in link variables are `end1`, `end2`, and `thickness`. You can find the complete list in the NetLogo Dictionary.
  - **User-defined** turtle, patch and link variables: You can also define new turtle, patch or link variables using the `turtles-own`, `patches-own`, and `links-own` keywords respectively, like this:

```
turtles-own [ energy ]     ;; each turtle has its own energy
patches-own [ roughness ] ;; each patch has its own roughness
links-own   [ weight ]     ;; each link has its own weight
```

- **Local variables**: A local variable is defined and used only in the context of a particular procedure or part of a procedure. To create a local variable, use the `let` command. You can use this command anywhere. If you use it at the top of a procedure, the variable will exist throughout the procedure. If you use it inside a set of square brackets, for example inside an `ask`, then it will exist only inside those brackets.

```
to swap-colors [turtle1 turtle2]  ;; turtle1 and turtle2 are inputs
  let temp ([color] of turtle1)   ;; store the color of turtle1 in temp
  ask turtle1 [ set color ([color] of turtle2) ]
        ;; set turtle1's color to turtle2's color
  ask turtle2 [ set color temp ]
        ;; now set turtle2's color to turtle1's (original) color
end     ;; (which was conveniently stored in local variable "temp").
```

Setting and reading the value of variables

Global variables can be read and set at any time by any agent. Every agent has direct access to her own variables, both for reading and setting. Sometimes you will want an agent to read or set a different agent's variable; to do that, you can use ask (which is explained in further detail later):

```
ask turtle 5 [ show color ]       ;; turtle 5 shows its color
ask turtle 5 [ set color blue ]   ;; turtle 5 becomes blue
```

You can also use of to make one agent read another agent's variable. of is written in between the variable name and the relevant agent (i.e. [*reporter*] of *agent*). Example:

```
show [color] of turtle 5 ;; observer shows turtle 5's color
```

Finally, a turtle can read and set the variables of the patch it is standing on directly, e.g.

```
ask turtles [ set pcolor red ]
```

The code above causes every turtle to make the patch it is standing on red. (Because patch variables are shared by turtles in this way, you cannot have a turtle variable and a patch variable with the same name –e.g. that is why we have color for turtles and pcolor for patches).

5. Ask

NetLogo uses the ask command to specify instructions that are to be run by turtles, patches or links. Usually, the observer uses ask to ask all turtles or all patches to run commands. Here's an example of the use of ask syntax in a NetLogo procedure:

```
to setup
  clear-all                ;; clear everything
  create-turtles 100       ;; create 100 new turtles with random heading
  ask turtles [            ;; ask them
    set color red          ;; to turn red and
    forward 50             ;; to move 50 steps forward
  ]
  ask patches [            ;; ask patches
    if (pxcor > 0) [       ;; with pxcor greater than 0
      set pcolor green ;; to turn green
    ]
  ]
end
```

You can also use ask to have an individual turtle, patch or link run commands. The reporters turtle, patch, link, and patch-at are useful for this technique. For example:

```
to setup
  clear-all                   ;; clear the world
  create-turtles 3            ;; make 3 turtles
  ask turtle 0 [ fd 10 ]      ;; tell the first one to go forward 10 steps
  ask turtle 1 [              ;; ask the second turtle (with who number 1)
    set color green           ;; ... to become green
  ]
  ask patch 2 -2 [            ;; ask the patch at (2,-2)...
    set pcolor blue           ;; ... to become blue
  ]
  ask turtle 0 [                ;; ask the first turtle (with who number 0)
    create-link-to turtle 2 ;; to link to turtle with who number 2
  ]
  ask link 0 2 [              ;; ask the link between turtle 0 and 2...
    set color blue            ;; ... to become blue
  ]
  ask turtle 0 [              ;; ask the turtle with who number 0
    ask patch-at 1 0 [        ;; ... to ask the patch to her east
      set pcolor red          ;; ... to become red
    ]
  ]
end
```

6. Lists

In the simplest models, each variable holds only one piece of information, usually a number or a string. Lists let you store multiple pieces of information in a single variable by collecting those pieces of information in a list. Each value in the list can be any type of value: a number, a string, an agent, an agentset, or even another list.

Constant lists

You can make a list by simply putting the values you want in the list between brackets, e.g.:

```
set my-list [2 4 6 8]
```

Building lists on the fly

If you want to make a list in which the values are determined by reporters, as opposed to being a series of constants, use the `list` reporter. The `list` reporter accepts two other reporters, runs them, and reports the results as a list.

```
set my-random-list list (random 10) (random 20)
```

To make shorter or longer lists, you can use the `list` reporter with fewer or more than two inputs, but in order to do so, you must enclose the entire call in parentheses, e.g.:

```
show (list random 10)
show (list (random 10) (turtle 3) "a" 30)  ;; inner () are not necessary
```

The `of` primitive lets you construct a list from an agentset (i.e. a set of agents). It reports a list containing each agent's value for the given reporter (syntax: *[reporter]* `of` *agentset*).

```
set fitness-list ([fitness] of turtles)
      ;; list containing the fitness of each turtle (in random order)
show [pxcor * pycor] of patches
```

See also: `n-values`, `range`, `sentence` and `sublist`.

Reading and changing list items

List items can be accessed using `first`, `last` and `item`. The first element of a list is item 0. Technically, lists cannot be modified, but you can construct new lists based on old lists. If you want the new list to replace the old list, use `set`. For example:

```
set my-list [2 7 5 "Bob" [3 0 -2]]       ;; my-list is now [2 7 5 "Bob" [3 0 -2]]
set my-list replace-item 2 my-list 10   ;; my-list is now [2 7 10 "Bob" [3 0 -2]]
```

See also: `but-first`, `but-last`, `fput`, `lput`, `length`, `shuffle`, `position` and `remove-item`.

Iterating over lists

To apply a function (procedure) on each item in a list, you can use `foreach` or `map`. The function to be applied is usually defined using anonymous procedures, with the following syntax:

```
[ [input-1 input-2 ...] -> code of the procedure ]
  ;; this syntax was different in versions before NetLogo 6.0
```

The names assigned to the inputs of the procedure (i.e. *input-1* and *input-2* above) may be used within the code of the procedure just like you would use any other variable within scope. You can use any name you like for these local variables (complying with the usual restrictions). An example of an anonymous procedure that implements the absolute value is:

```
[ [x] -> abs x ]  ;; you can use any symbol instead of x
[  x  -> abs x ]  ;; if there is just one input
                  ;; you do not need the square brackets
```

`foreach` is used to run a command on each item in a list. It takes as inputs the list and the command to be run on each element of the list, e.g.:

```
foreach [1.2 4.6 6.1] [ n -> show (word n " rounded is " round n) ]
  ;; output: "1.2 rounded is 1" "4.6 rounded is 5" "6.1 rounded is 6"
```

`map` is similar to `foreach`, but it is a reporter (it returns a list). It takes as inputs a list and a reporter; and returns an output list containing the results of applying the reporter to each item in the input list. As in `foreach`, procedures can be anonymous.

```
map [ element -> round element ] [1.2 2.2 2.7]          ;; returns [1 2 3]
```

Simple uses of foreach, map, n-values, and related primitives can be written more concise.

```
map round [1.2 2.2 2.7]
  ;; (see Anonymous procedures in Programming Guide)
```

Both foreach and map can take multiple lists as input; in that case, the procedure is run once for the first items of all input lists, once for the second items, and so on.

```
(map [[el1 el2] -> el1 + el2] [1 2 3] [10 20 30])  ;; returns [11 22 33]
(map + [1 2 3] [10 20 30])                          ;; a shorter way of writing the same
```

See also: reduce, filter, sort-by, sort-on, and -> (anonymous procedure).

7. Agentsets

An agentset is a set of agents; all agents in an agentset must be of the same type (i.e. turtles, patches, or links). An agentset is not in any particular order. In fact, it's always in a random order.[1] What's powerful about the agentset concept is that you can construct agentsets that contain only some agents. For example, all the *red* turtles, or the patches with positive pxcor, or all the links departing from a certain agent. These agentsets can then be used by ask or by various reporters that take agentsets as inputs, such as one-of, n-of, with, with-min, max-one-of, etc. The primitive with and its siblings are very useful to build agentsets. Here are some examples:

```
turtles with [color = red]          ;; all red turtles
patches with [pxcor > 0]            ;; patches with positive pxcor
[my-out-links] of turtle 0          ;; all links outgoing from turtle 0
turtles in-radius 3                 ;; all turtles three or fewer patches away
other turtles-here with-min [size] ;; other turtles with min size on my patch
(patch-set self neighbors4)         ;; von Neumann neighborhood of a patch
```

Once you have created an agentset, here are some simple things you can do:

- Use ask to make the agents in the agentset do something.
- Use any? to see if the agentset is empty.
- Use all? to see if every agent in an agentset satisfies a condition.
- Use count to find out exactly how many agents are in the set.

1. If you want agents to do something in a fixed order, you can make a list of the agents instead.

Here are some more complex things you can do:

```
ask one-of turtles [ set color green ]
        ;; one-of reports a random agent from an agentset

ask (max-one-of turtles [wealth]) [ donate ]
        ;; max-one-of agentset [reporter] reports an agent in the
        ;; agentset that has the highest value for the given reporter

show mean ([wealth] of turtles with [gender = male])
        ;; Use of to make a list of values, one for each agent in the agentset.

show (turtle-set turtle 0 turtle 2 turtle 9 turtles-here)
        ;; Use turtle-set, patch-set and link-set reporters to make new
        ;; agentsets by gathering together agents from a variety of sources

show (turtles with [gender = male]) = (turtles with [wealth > 10])
        ;; Check whether two agentsets are equal using = or !=

show member? (turtle 0) turtles with-min [wealth]
        ;; Use member? to see if an agent is a member of an agentset.

if all? turtles [color = red]      ;; use all? to see if every agent in the
  [ show "every turtle is red!" ] ;; agentset satisfies a certain condition

ask turtles [
  create-links-to other turtles-here ;; on same patch as me, not me,
    with [color = [color] of myself] ;; and with same color as me.
]

show [([color] of end1) - ([color] of end2)] of links   ;; check everything's OK
```

8. Synchronization

When you ask a set of agents to run more than one command, each agent must finish all the commands in the block before the next agent starts. One agent runs all the commands, then the next agent runs all of them, and so on. As mentioned before, the order in which agents are chosen to run the commands is random. To be clear, consider the following code:

```
ask turtles [
  forward random 10 ;; move forward a random number of steps (0–9)
  wait 0.5          ;; wait half a second
  set color blue    ;; set your color to blue
]
```

The first (randomly chosen) turtle will move forward some steps, she will then wait half a second, and she will finally set her color to blue. Then, and only then, another turtle will start doing the same; and so on until all turtles have run the commands inside ask without being interrupted by any other turtle. The order in which turtles are selected to run the commands is random. If you want all turtles to move, and then all wait, and then all become blue, you can write it this way:

```
ask turtles [ forward random 10 ]
ask turtles [ wait 0.5 ]         ;; note that you will have to wait
ask turtles [ set color blue ]   ;; (0.5 * number-of-turtles) seconds
```

Finally, you can make agents execute a set of commands in a certain order by converting the agentset into a list. There are three primitives that help you do this: `sort`, `sort-by` and `sort-on`.

```
set my-list-of-agents sort-by [[t1 t2] -> [size] of t1 < [size] of t2] turtles
 ;; This sets my-list-of-agents to a list of turtles sorted in
 ;; ascending order by their turtle variable size. For simple orderings
 ;; like this, you can use sort-on, e.g.: sort-on [size] turtles

foreach my-list-of-agents [ ag ->
    ask ag [              ;; each agent undertakes the list of commands
    forward random 10     ;; (forward, wait, and set) without being
    wait 0.5              ;; interrupted, i.e. the next agent does not
    set color blue        ;; start until the previous one has finished.
  ]
]
```

9. Consistency within procedures

Some primitives in NetLogo can only be run by a certain type of agent. For instance, `forward` can only be run by turtles, since turtles are the only type of agent that can move. An easy way of knowing which type of agent can run a certain primitive is to find the primitive in the NetLogo Dictionary and look at the icon beneath the name of the primitive. If you click on `forward`, you will see the icon, which denotes turtles. The icons for the other types of agent are: for the observer, for patches, and for links. There are primitives that can be run by more than one type of agent. For instance, reporter `turtles-here` can be run by turtles and by patches.

The question that naturally comes to mind now is: How do we tell NetLogo what type of agent should run a certain procedure (which *we* implement)? The answer is simple: we don't. NetLogo infers that from the code of the procedure; we just have to be consistent. An example of inconsistency would be to code a procedure containing two primitives that can be run *only* by two different types of agents, as in the following example:

```
to setup
  create-turtles 10
  forward 1
end
```

If we implement this code, we obtain the following error message: "You can't use FORWARD in an observer context, because FORWARD is turtle-only" (see figure 3).

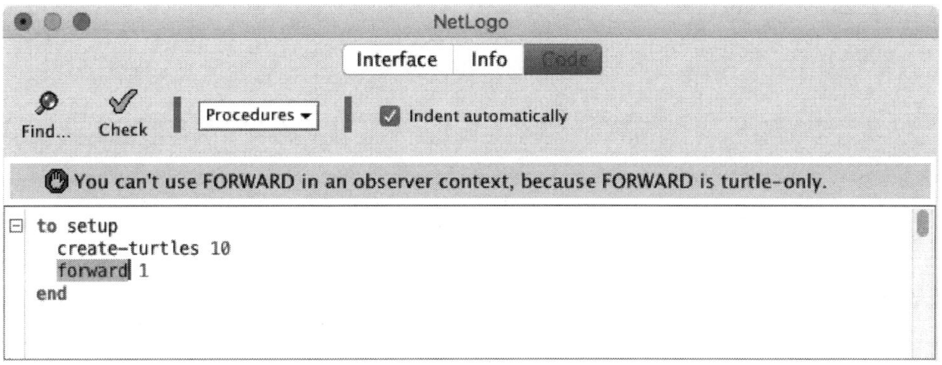

Figure 3. Inconsistency error.

The reason is that NetLogo reads the primitive `create-turtles` and, since it can only be run by the observer, NetLogo infers that the procedure to setup will be run only by the observer, i.e. everything inside is in an observer context. Then, NetLogo reads the primitive `forward`, which can only be run by turtles, and throws the error.

We would obtain similar inconsistency errors if we tried to access individually-owned variables within procedures that can only be run by a type of agent that cannot access those variables, as in the following examples.

```
to setup
  create-turtles 10
  show xcor
end
;; Here we would obtain the error:
;; "You can't use XCOR in an observer context, because XCOR is turtle-only"
```

```
to setup
  create-turtles 10
  show pxcor
end
;; Here we would obtain the error:
;; "You can't use PXCOR in an observer context, because PXCOR is turtle/patch-
only"
```

Note that in the example above, NetLogo says that `pxcor` is "turtle/patch-only". This is because all patch variables can be directly accessed by any turtle standing on the patch (see section Variables above).

```
to setup
  create-turtles 10
  show end1
end
;; Here we would obtain the error:
;; "You can't use END1 in an observer context, because END1 is link-only"
```

10. Breeds

NetLogo allows you to have different types of turtles and different types of links. There are called breeds. Here we discuss breeds of turtles only, since breeds of links follow the same logic. Breeds are defined with the syntax:

```
breed [plural-name singular-name]
```

For instance, to define a breed of sellers and a breed of buyers, we would type the following at the top of our code:

```
breed [sellers seller]
breed [buyers buyer]
```

From then onwards, we could assign different individually-owned variables to each of the breeds, using the keywords `sellers-own` and `buyers-own`. Also, there are a number of primitives that are automatically added to the NetLogo language once you have defined a breed, such as `create-sellers`, `hatch-sellers`, `sprout-sellers`, `sellers-here`, `sellers-at`, `sellers-on`, and `is-seller?`.

11. Ticks and Plotting

In most NetLogo models, time passes in discrete steps called "ticks". NetLogo includes a built-in tick counter so you can keep track of how many ticks have passed. The current value of the tick counter is shown above the view. Note that –since NetLogo 5.0– ticks and plots are closely related.

You can write code inside the plots. Every plot and each of its pens have *setup* and *update* **code fields** where you can write commands. All these fields must be edited directly in each plot –i.e. in the interface, not in the code tab. To execute the commands written inside the plots, you can use `setup-plots` and `update-plots`, which run the corresponding fields in every plot and in every pen. However, in models that use the tick counter, these two primitives are not normally used because they are automatically triggered by tick-related commands, as explained below.

To use the tick counter, first you must `reset-ticks`; this command resets the tick counter to zero, sets up all plots (i.e. triggers `setup-plots`), and then updates all plots (i.e. triggers `update-plots`); thus, the initial state of the world is plotted. Then, you can use the `tick` command, which advances the tick counter by one and updates all plots.

See also: `plot`, `plotxy`, and `ticks`.

12. Skeleton of many NetLogo models

In most NetLogo models there are two basic procedures that are run by the observer: to setup and to go.

Procedure to setup is run just once at the beginning of the simulation, most often by clicking a button in the interface tab. In this procedure:

- we initialize the model from scratch using the primitive `clear-all`,
- we set up all initial conditions (this often implies creating several agents), and
- we finish with the primitive `reset-ticks`.

Procedure to go contains all the actions that will be executed repeatedly in the model. Some of these actions will be executed directly by the observer, while others will be run by the turtles, the patches or the links. In any case, procedure to go is run by the observer, so it is the observer who must ask the other agents to run the appropriate instructions, using the primitive `ask`. Most often, procedure to go contains the primitive tick, which advances the (discrete) NetLogo clock in one unit.

```
globals [ … ]      ;; global variables (also defined with sliders, …)
turtles-own [ … ]  ;; user-defined turtle variables (also <breeds>-own)
patches-own [ … ]  ;; user-defined patch variables
links-own [ … ]    ;; user-defined link variables (also <link-breeds>-own)
…

to setup
  clear-all
  …
  setup-patches  ;; procedure where patches are initialized
  …
  setup-turtles  ;; procedure where turtles are created
  …
  reset-ticks
end
…

to go
  conduct-observer-procedure
  …
  ask turtles [conduct-turtle-procedure]
  …
  ask patches [conduct-patch-procedure]
  …
  tick ;; this will update every plot and every pen in every plot
end
…

to-report a-particular-statistic
  …
  report the-result-of-some-formula
end
```

13. The code for Schelling-Sakoda model

To conclude this section, we present some simple code that implements the Schelling-Sakoda model described in section 0.2 "Introduction to agent-based modeling". The code we show here is simpler than the one used for the videos in section 0.2, which is more efficient but less readable.[2] In the interface, we have used two sliders to define parameters *number-of-agents* and *%-similar-wanted* (see figure 4).

2. Both implementations lead to exactly the same dynamics.

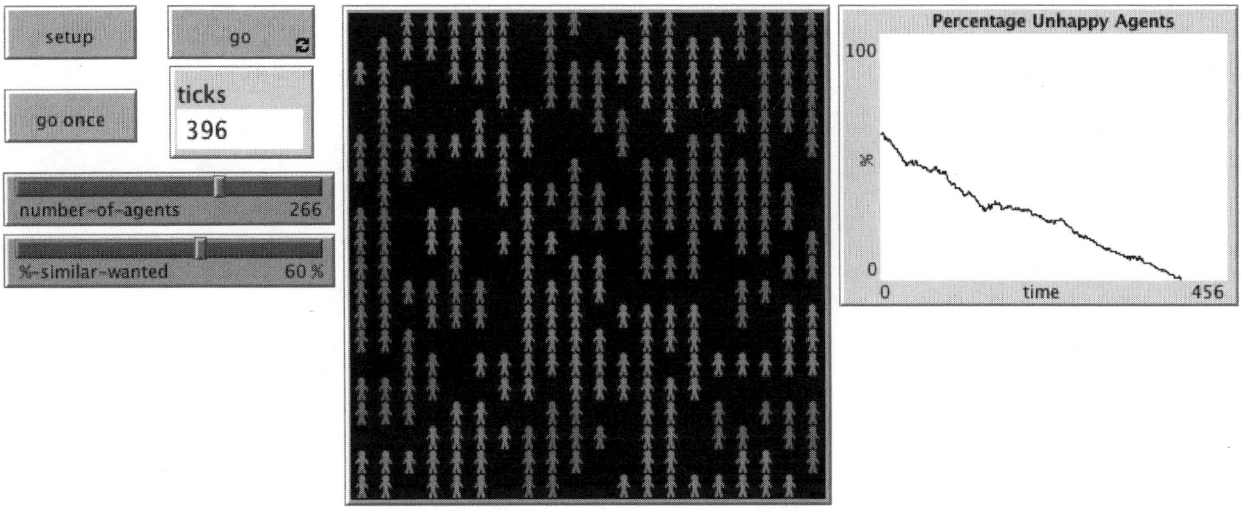

Figure 4. Interface of a simple version of Schelling-Sakoda model.

The code that goes in the code tab is shown below. You can download the whole model here and take this code as a test to check whether you are ready to proceed to the next chapter. If you can understand most of it, you are definitely prepared!

To work your way through the code, you will most likely have to use the NetLogo Dictionary intensively, and run small pieces of code in the Command Center (especially because the model includes several NetLogo primitives that we have not seen yet). You can also inspect individual turtles and make them run (turtle) instructions such as:

```
ask turtles-on neighbors [set label
"Hi!"]
```

You will have to type these instructions on the bottom line of the window that pops up when you inspect a turtle (see figure 5). To inspect a turtle, right-click on it, select the name of the turtle (e.g. turtle 21), and click on "inspect". Alternatively, you can just type the following instruction in the command center:

```
inspect turtle 21
```

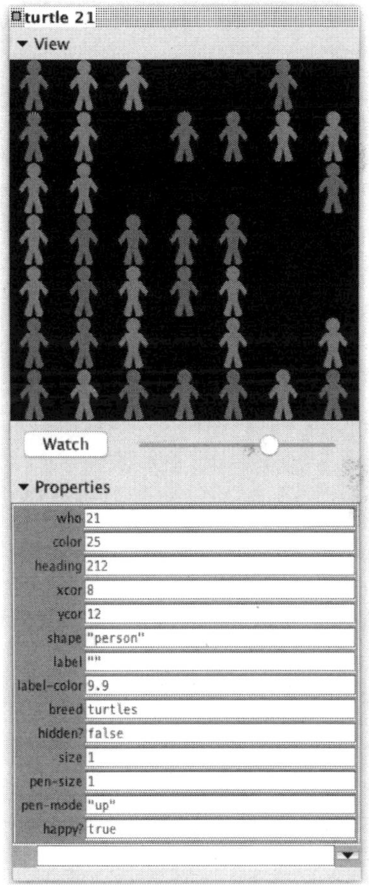

Figure 5. Window that pops up when you inspect a turtle. You can ask the turtle to execute instructions by typing them on the bottom line.

Developing these skills will be useful, since programming in NetLogo most often involves looking up the dictionary very often and testing short snippets of code. Once you have understood most of the code below we can start building our first agent-based evolutionary model in the next chapter!

```
;;;;;;;;;;;;;;;;;
;;; VARIABLES ;;;
;;;;;;;;;;;;;;;;;

turtles-own [
  happy?
]

;;;;;;;;;;;;;;;;;;;;;;;;
;;; SETUP PROCEDURES ;;;
;;;;;;;;;;;;;;;;;;;;;;;;

to setup
  clear-all
  setup-agents
  reset-ticks
end

to setup-agents
  set-default-shape turtles "person"
  ask n-of number-of-agents patches
    [ sprout 1 [set color cyan] ]
  ask n-of (number-of-agents / 2) turtles
    [ set color orange ]
  ask turtles [update-happiness]
end

;;;;;;;;;;;;;;;;;;;;;;
;;; MAIN PROCEDURE ;;;
;;;;;;;;;;;;;;;;;;;;;;

to go
  if all? turtles [happy?] [stop]
  ask one-of turtles with [not happy?] [move]
  ask turtles [update-happiness]
  tick
end

;;;;;;;;;;;;;;;;;;;;;;;;;;;
;;; TURTLES' PROCEDURES ;;;
;;;;;;;;;;;;;;;;;;;;;;;;;;;

to move
  move-to one-of patches with [not any? turtles-here]
end

to update-happiness
  let my-nbrs (turtles-on neighbors)
  let n-of-my-nbrs (count my-nbrs)
  let similar-nbrs (count my-nbrs with [color = [color] of myself])
  set happy? similar-nbrs >= (%-similar-wanted * n-of-my-nbrs / 100)
end
```

1. OUR FIRST AGENT-BASED EVOLUTIONARY MODEL

1.0. Our very first model

1. Goal

The goal of this section is to create our first agent-based evolutionary model in NetLogo. Being our first model, we will keep it simple; nonetheless, the model will already contain the four building blocks that define most models in agent-based evolutionary game theory, namely:

- a population of agents,
- a game that is recurrently played by the agents,
- an assignment rule, which determines how revision opportunities are assigned to agents, and
- a revision protocol, which specifies how individual agents update their (pure) strategies when they are given the opportunity to revise.

In particular, in our model the number of (individually-represented) agents in the population will be chosen by the user. These agents will repeatedly play a symmetric 2-player 2-strategy game, each time with a randomly chosen counterpart. The payoffs of the game will be determined by the user. Agents will revise their strategy with a certain probability, also to be chosen by the user. The revision protocol these agents will use is called "imitate-the-better-realization", which dictates that a revising agent imitates the strategy of a randomly chosen player, if this player obtained a payoff greater than the revising agent's.

This fairly general model will allow us to explore a variety of specific questions, like the one we outline next.

2. Motivation. Cooperation in social dilemmas

There are many situations in life where we have the option to make a personal effort that will benefit others beyond the personal cost incurred. This type of behavior is often termed "to cooperate", and can take a myriad forms: from paying your taxes, to inviting your friends over for a home-made dinner. All these situations, where cooperating involves a personal cost but creates net social value, exhibit the somewhat paradoxical feature that individuals would prefer not to pay the cost of cooperation, but everyone prefers the situation where everybody cooperates to the situation where no one does. Such counterintuitive characteristic is the defining feature of social dilemmas, and life is full of them (Dawes, 1980).

The essence of many social dilemmas can be captured by a simple 2-person game called the Prisoner's Dilemma. In this game, the payoffs for the players are: if both cooperate, R (Reward); if both defect, P (Punishment); if one cooperates and the other defects, the cooperator obtains S (Sucker) and the defector obtains T (Temptation). The payoffs satisfy the condition T > R > P > S. Thus, in a Prisoner's Dilemma, both players prefer mutual cooperation to mutual defection (R > P), but two motivations may drive players to behave uncooperatively: the temptation to exploit (T > R), and the fear to be exploited (P > S).

Let us see a concrete example of a Prisoner's Dilemma. Imagine that you have $1000, which you may keep for yourself, or transfer to another person's account. This other person faces the same decision: she can transfer her $1000 money to you, or else keep it. Crucially, whenever money is transferred, the money doubles, i.e. the recipient gets $2000.

Try to formalize this situation as a game, assuming you and the other person only care about money.

The game can be summarized using the payoff matrix in Fig. 1. To see that this game is indeed a Prisoner's Dilemma, note that transferring the money would be what is often called "to cooperate", and keeping the money would be "to defect".

		Player 2	
		Keep	Transfer
Player 1	Keep	**1000 , 1000**	**3000 , 0**
	Transfer	**0 , 3000**	**2000 , 2000**

Figure 1. Payoff matrix of a Prisoner's Dilemma game.

To explore whether cooperation may be sustained in a simple evolutionary context, we can model a population of agents who are repeatedly matched to play the Prisoner's Dilemma. Agents are either cooperators or defectors, but they can occasionally revise their strategy. A revising agent looks at another agent in the population and, if the observed agent's payoff is greater than the revising agent's payoff, the revising agent copies the observed agent's strategy. Do you think that cooperation will be sustained in this setting? Here we are going to build a model that will allow us to investigate this question... and many others!

3. Description of the model

In this model, there is a population of *n-of-players* agents who repeatedly play a symmetric 2-player 2-strategy game. The two possible strategies are labeled 0 and 1. The *payoffs* of the game are determined by the user in the form of a matrix [[A_{00} A_{01}] [A_{10} A_{11}]], where A_{ij} is the payoff that an agent playing strategy *i* obtains when meeting an agent playing strategy *j* ($i, j \in \{0, 1\}$).

Initially, the number of agents playing strategy 1 is a (uniformly distributed) random number between

0 and the number of players in the population. From then onwards, the following sequence of events –which defines a tick– is repeatedly executed:

1. Every agent obtains a payoff by selecting another agent at random and playing the game.
2. With probability *prob-revision*, individual agents are given the opportunity to revise their strategies. The revision rule –called "**imitate the better realization**"– reads as follows:[1]

> Look at another (randomly selected) agent and adopt her strategy if and only if her payoff was greater than yours.

The model shows the evolution of the number of agents choosing each of the two possible strategies at the end of every tick.

CODE 4. Interface design

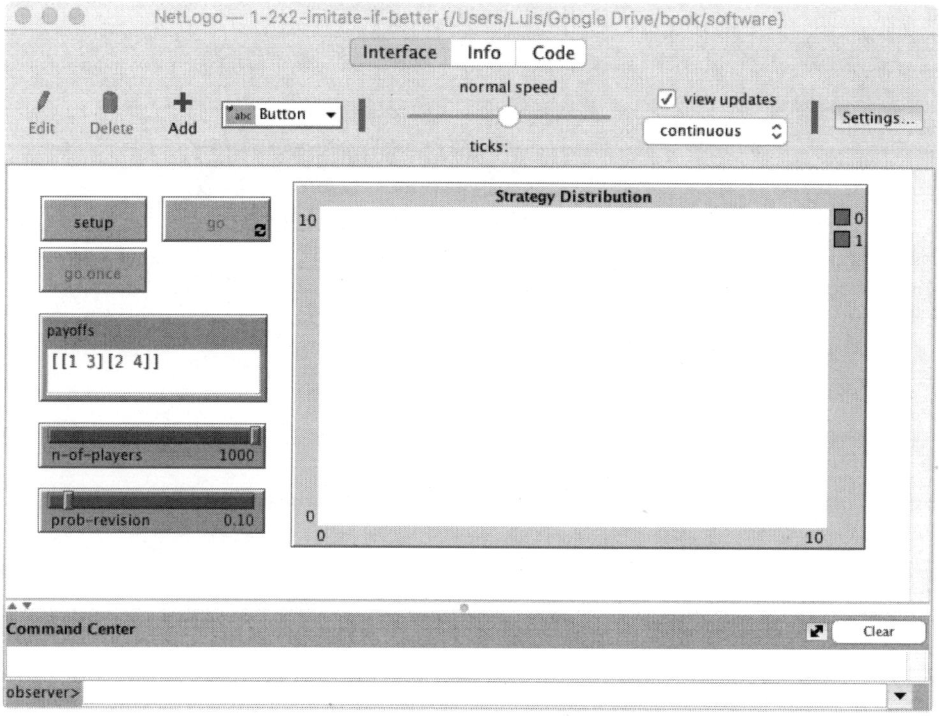

Figure 2. Interface design.

The interface (see figure 2) includes:

- Three buttons:
    1. One button named setup, which runs the procedure to setup.
    2. One button named go once, which runs the procedure to go.
    3. One button named go, which runs the procedure to go indefinitely.

1. This protocol has been studied by Izquierdo and Izquierdo (2013) and Loginov (2019).

In the Code tab, write the procedures to setup and to go, without including any code inside for now.

```
to setup
  ;; empty for now
end

to go
  ;; empty for now
end
```

In the Interface tab, create a button and write setup in the "commands" box. This will make the procedure to setup run whenever the button is pressed.

Create another button for the procedure to go (i.e., write go in the commands box) with display name go once to emphasize that pressing the button will run the procedure to go just once.

Finally, create another button for the procedure to go, but this time tick the "forever" option. When pressed, this button will make the procedure to go run repeatedly until the button is pressed again.

- A slider to let the user select the number of players.

Create a slider for global variable *n-of-players*. You can choose limit values 2 (as the minimum) and 1000 (as the maximum), and an increment of 1.

- An input box where the user can write a string of the form [[A_{00} A_{01}] [A_{10} A_{11}]] containing the payoffs A_{ij} that an agent playing strategy *i* obtains when meeting an agent playing strategy *j* ($i, j \in \{0, 1\}$).

Create an input box with associated global variable *payoffs*. Set the input box type to "String (reporter)". Note that the content of *payoffs* will be a string (i.e. a sequence of characters) from which we will need to extract the payoff numeric values.

- A slider to let the user select the probability of revision.

Create a slider with associated global variable *prob-revision*. Choose limit values 0 and 1, and an increment of 0.01.

- A plot that will show the evolution of the number of agents playing each strategy.

Create a plot and name it Strategy Distribution. Since we are not going to use the 2D view (i.e. the large black square in the interface) in this model, you may want to overlay it with the newly created plot.

CODE 5. Code

5.1. Skeleton of the code

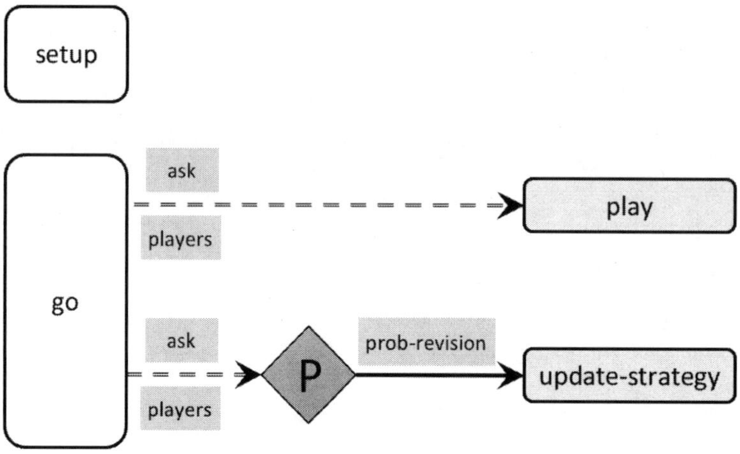

Figure 3. Skeleton of the code

5.2. Global variables and individually-owned variables

First we declare the global variables that we are going to use and we have not already declared in the interface. We will be using a global variable named payoff-matrix to store the payoff values on a list, so the first line of code in the Code tab will be:

```
globals [payoff-matrix]
```

Next we declare a breed of agents called "players". If we did not do this, we would have to use the default name "turtles", which may be confusing to newcomers.

```
breed [players player]
```

Individual players have their own strategy (which can be different from the other agents' strategy) and their own payoff, so we need to declare these *individually-owned variables* as follows:

```
players-own [
  strategy
  payoff
]
```

5.3. Setup procedures

In the setup procedure we want:

- To clear everything up. We initialize the model afresh using the primitive clear-all:

```
clear-all
```

- To transform the string of characters the user has written in the *payoffs* input box (e.g. "[[1 2][3 4]]") into a list (of 2 lists) that we can use in the code (e.g. [[1 2][3 4]]). This list of lists will be stored in the global variable named payoff-matrix. To do this transformation (from string to list, in this case), we can use the primitive read-from-string as follows:

```
set payoff-matrix read-from-string payoffs
```

- To create *n-of-players* players and set their individually-owned variables to an appropriate initial value. At first, we set the value of payoff and strategy to 0:[2]

```
create-players n-of-players [
  set payoff 0
  set strategy 0
]
```

Note that the primitive `create-players` does not appear in the NetLogo dictionary; it has been automatically created after defining the breed "players". Had we not defined the breed "players", we would have had to use the primitive create-turtles instead.

Now we will ask a random number of players (between 0 and *n-of-players*) to set their strategy to 1, using one of the most important primitives in NetLogo, namely ask. The instruction will be of the form:

```
ask AGENTSET [set strategy 1]
```

where `AGENTSET` should be a random subset o players.

To randomly select a certain number of agents from an agentset (such as players), we can use the primitive n-of (which reports another -usually smaller- agentset):

```
ask (n-of SIZE players) [set strategy 1]
```

where `SIZE` is the number of players we would like to select.

2. By default, user-defined variables in NetLogo are initialized with the value 0, so there is no actual need to explicitly set the initial value of individually-owned variables to 0, but it does no harm either.

Finally, to generate a random integer between 0 and *n-of-players* we can use the primitive random:

```
random (n-of-players + 1)
```

The resulting instruction will be:

```
ask n-of (random (n-of-players + 1)) players [set strategy 1]
```

- To initialize the tick counter. At the end of the setup procedure, we should include the primitive reset-ticks, which resets the tick counter to zero (and also runs the "plot setup commands", the "plot update commands" and the "pen update commands" in every plot, so the initial state of the model is plotted):

```
reset-ticks
```

Thus, the code up to this point should be as follows:

```
globals [
  payoff-matrix
]

breed [players player]

players-own [
  strategy
  payoff
]

to setup
  clear-all
  set payoff-matrix read-from-string payoffs
  create-players n-of-players [
    set payoff 0
    set strategy 0
  ]
  ask n-of random (n-of-players + 1) players [set strategy 1]
  reset-ticks
end

to go

end
```

5.4. Go procedure

The procedure to go contains all the instructions that will be executed in every tick. In this particular model, these instructions include *a)* asking all players to interact with another (randomly selected) player to obtain a payoff and *b)* asking all players to revise their strategy with probability *prob-revision*.

To keep things nice and modular, we will create two separate procedures *to be run by players* named to play and to update-strategy. Writing short procedures with meaningful names will make our code elegant, easy to understand, easy to debug, and easy to extend... so we should definitely aim for that. Following this modular design, the procedure to go is particularly easy to code and understand:

```
ask players [play]
ask players [
  if (random-float 1 < prob-revision) [update-strategy]
]
```

Note that condition

```
(random-float 1 < prob-revision)
```

will be true with probability *prob-revision*.

Having the agents go once through the code above will mark an evolution step (or generation), so, to keep track of these cycles and have the plots in the interface automatically updated at the end of each cycle, we include the primitive tick at the end of to go.

```
tick
```

5.5 Other procedures

to play

Importantly, note that the procedure to play *will be run by a particular player*. Thus, within the code of this procedure, we can access and set the value of player-owned variables strategy and payoff.

Here we want the player running this procedure (let us call her the running player) to play with some other player and get the corresponding payoff. First, we will (randomly) select a counterpart and store it in a local variable named mate:

```
let mate one-of other players
```

Now we need to compute the payoff that the running player will obtain when she plays the game with her mate. This payoff is an element of the payoff-matrix list, which is made up of two sublists (e.g., [[1 2][3 4]]).

Note that the first sublist (i.e., `item` 0 payoff-matrix) corresponds to the case in which the running player plays strategy 0. We want to consider the sublist corresponding to the player's strategy, so we type:

```
item strategy payoff-matrix
```

In a similar fashion, the payoff to extract from this sublist is determined by the strategy of the running player's mate (i.e., [strategy] `of` mate). Thus, the payoff obtained by the running agent is:

```
item ([strategy] of mate) (item strategy payoff-matrix)
```

Finally, to make the running agent store her payoff, we can write:

```
set payoff item ([strategy] of mate) (item strategy payoff-matrix)
```

This line of code concludes the definition of the procedure to play.

to update-strategy

In this procedure, which is also *to be run by individual players*, we want the running player to look at some other random player (which we will call the observed-agent) and, if the payoff of the observed-agent is greater than her own payoff, adopt the observed-agent's strategy.

To select a random player and store it in the local variable observed-agent, we can write:

```
let observed-agent one-of other players
```

To compare the payoffs and, if appropriate, adopt the observed-agent's strategy, we can write:

```
if ([payoff] of observed-agent) > payoff [
  set strategy ([strategy] of observed-agent)
]
```

This concludes the definition of the procedure to update-strategy and, actually, of all the code in the Code tab, which by now should look as shown below.

5.6. Complete code in the Code tab

```
globals [
  payoff-matrix
]

breed [players player]

players-own [
  strategy
  payoff
]

to setup
  clear-all
  set payoff-matrix read-from-string payoffs
  create-players n-of-players [
    set payoff 0
    set strategy 0
  ]
  ask n-of random (n-of-players + 1) players [set strategy 1]
  reset-ticks
end

to go
  ask players [play]
  ask players [
    if (random-float 1 < prob-revision) [update-strategy]
  ]
  tick
end

to play
  let mate one-of other players
  set payoff item ([strategy] of mate) (item strategy payoff-matrix)
end

to update-strategy
  let observed-agent one-of other players
  if ([payoff] of observed-agent) > payoff [
    set strategy ([strategy] of observed-agent)
  ]
end
```

5.7. Code in the plots

Finally, let us set up the plot to show the number of agents playing each strategy. This is something that can be done directly on the plot, in the Interface tab.

Edit the plot by right-clicking on it, choose a color and a name for the pen showing the number of agents with strategy 0, and in the "pen update commands" area write:

```
plot count players with [strategy = 0]
```

Add a second pen to show the number of players with strategy 1.

6. Sample runs

Now that we have the model, we can investigate the question we posed at the motivation above. Let strategy 0 be "Defect" and let strategy 1 be "Cooperate". We can use *payoffs* [[1 3][0 2]]. Note that we could choose any other numbers (as long as they satisfy the conditions that define a Prisoner's Dilemma), since our revision protocol only depends on ordinal properties of payoffs. Let us set *n-of-players* = 100 and *prob-revision* = 0.1, but feel free to change these values.

If you run the model with these settings, you will see that in nearly all runs all agents end up defecting in very little time.[3] The video below shows some representative runs.

A video element has been excluded from this version of the text. You can watch it online here: https://wisc.pb.unizin.org/agent-based-evolutionary-game-dynamics/?p=18

Note that at any population state, defectors will tend to obtain a greater payoff than cooperators, so they will be preferentially imitated. Sadly, this drives the dynamics of the process towards overall defection.

7. Exercises

You can use the following link to download the complete NetLogo model: 2×2-imitate-if-better.

3. All simulations will necessarily end up in one of the two absorbing states where all agents are using the same strategy. The absorbing state where everyone defects (henceforth D-state) can be reached from any state other than the absorbing state where everyone cooperates (henceforth C-state). The C-state can be reached from any state with at least two cooperators, so –in principle– any simulation with at least two agents using each strategy could end up in either absorbing state. However, it is overwhelmingly more likely that the final state will be the D-state. As a matter of fact, one single defector is extremely likely to be able to invade a whole population of cooperators, regardless of the size of the population.

Exercise 1. Consider a coordination game with payoffs [[3 0][0 2]] such that both players are better off if they coordinate in one of the actions (0 or 1) than if they play different actions. Run several simulations with 1000 players and probability of revision 0.1. (You can easily do that by leaving the button go pressed down and clicking the setup button every time you want to start again from random initial conditions.)

Picture by Caleb Whiting

Do simulations end up with all players choosing the same action? Does the strategy with a greater initial presence tend to displace the other strategy? How does changing the payoff matrix to [[30 0][0 2]] make a difference on whether agents coordinate on 0 or strategy 1?

P.S. You can explore this model's (deterministic) mean dynamic approximation with this program.

Exercise 2. Consider a Stag hunt game with payoffs [[3 0][2 1]] where strategy 0 is "Stag" and strategy 1 is "Hare". Does the strategy with greater initial presence tend to displace the other strategy?

P.S. You can explore this model's (deterministic) mean dynamic approximation with this program.

Picture by Ming Jun Tan

Exercise 3. Consider a Hawk-Dove game with payoffs [[0 3][1 2]] where strategy 0 is "Hawk" and strategy 1 is "Dove". Do all players tend to choose the same strategy? Reduce the number of players to 100 and observe the difference in behavior (press the setup button after changing the number of players). Reduce the number of players to 10 and observe the difference.

P.S. You can explore this model's (deterministic) mean dynamic approximation with this program.

Exercise 4. Create a stand-alone version of the model we have implemented in this section. To do this, you will have to upload the model to NetLogo Web and then export it in HTML format.

CODE Exercise 5. Reimplement the procedure to update-strategy so the revising agent uses the imitative pairwise-difference protocol that we saw in section 0.1.

CODE Exercise 6. Reimplement the procedure to update-strategy so the revising agent uses the best experienced payoff protocol that we saw in section 0.1.

1.1. Extension to any number of strategies

1. Goal

Our goal here is to extend the model we have created in the previous section –which accepted games with 2 strategies only– to model (2-player symmetric) games with any number of strategies.

2. Motivation. Rock, paper, scissors

The model we will develop in this section will allow us to explore games such as Rock-Paper-Scissors. Can you guess what will happen in our model if agents are matched to play Rock-Paper-Scissors and they keep on using the "imitate-the-better-realization" rule whenever they revise?

3. Description of the model

In this model, there is a population of *n-of-players* agents who repeatedly play a symmetric 2-player game with any number of strategies. The *payoffs* of the game are determined by the user in the form of a matrix [[A_{00} A_{01} ... A_{0n}] [A_{10} A_{11} ... A_{1n}] ... [A_{n0} A_{n1} ... A_{nn}]] containing the payoffs A_{ij} that an agent playing strategy *i* obtains when meeting an agent playing strategy *j* ($i, j \in \{0, 1, ..., n\}$). The number of strategies is inferred from the number of rows in the payoff matrix.

Initially, players choose one of the available strategies at random (uniformly). From then onwards, the following sequence of events –which defines a tick– is repeatedly executed:

1. Every agent obtains a payoff by selecting another agent at random and playing the game.
2. With probability *prob-revision*, individual agents are given the opportunity to revise their strategies. The revision rule –called **"imitate the better realization"**– reads as follows:

   > Look at another (randomly selected) agent and adopt her strategy if and only if her payoff was greater than yours.

The model shows the evolution of the number of agents choosing each of the possible strategies at the end of every tick.

CODE 4. Interface design

We depart from the model we developed in the previous section (so if you want to preserve it, now is a good time to duplicate it).

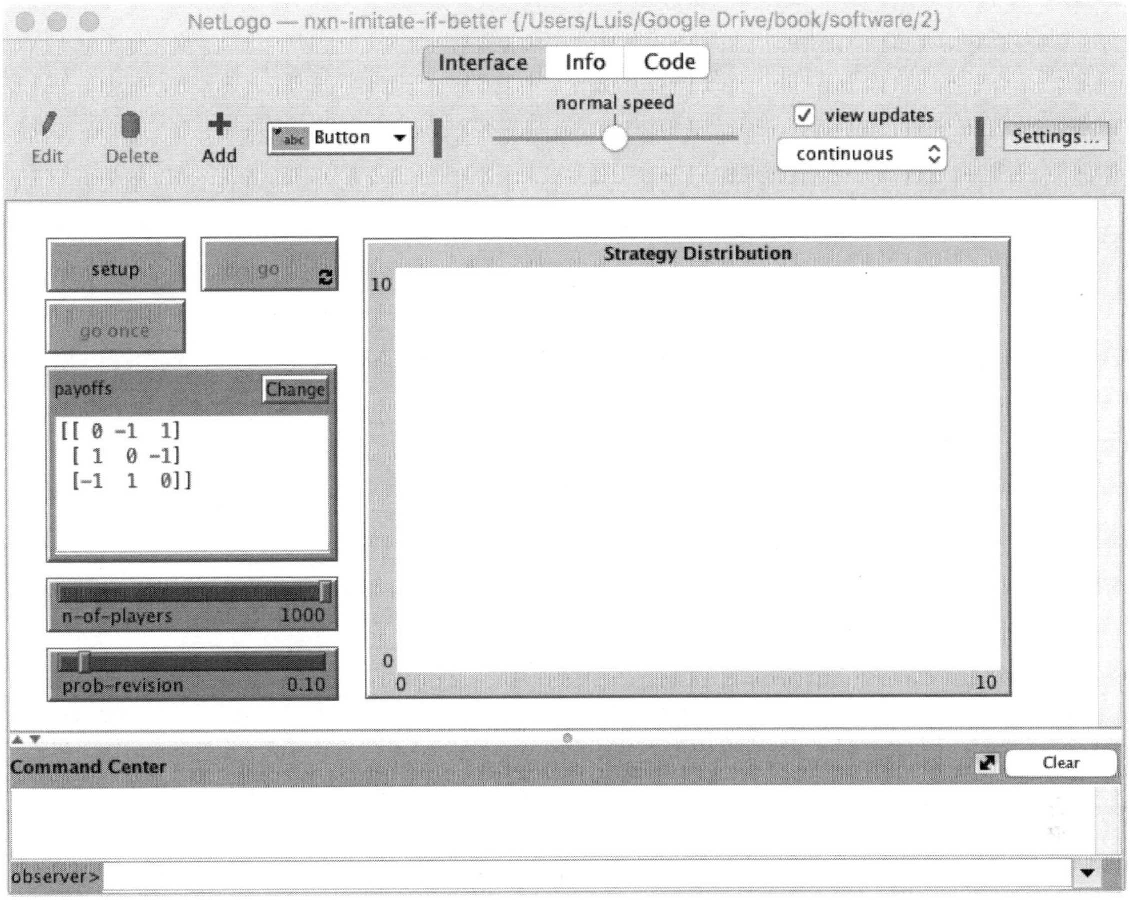

Figure 1. Interface design

The new interface (see figure 1 above) requires just two simple modifications:

- Make the *payoffs* input box bigger and let its input contain several lines.

> In the Interface tab, select the input box (by right-clicking on it) and make it bigger. Then edit it (by right-clicking on it) and tick the "Multi-Line" box.

- Remove the "pens" in the Strategy Distribution plot. Since the number of strategies is unknown until the payoff matrix is read, we will need to create the required number of "pens" via code.

> In the Interface tab, edit the Strategy Distribution plot and delete both pens.

CODE 5. Code

5.1. Skeleton of the code

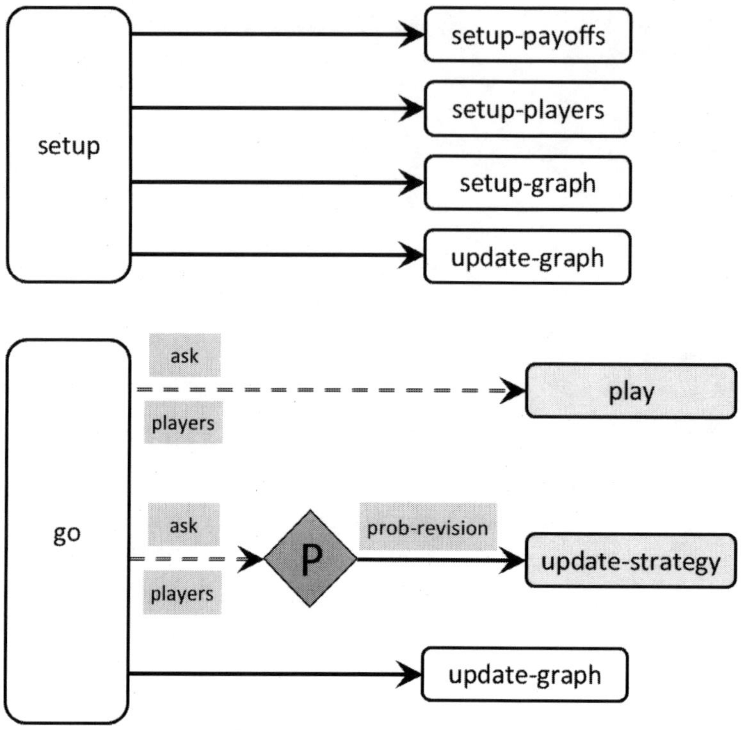

Figure 2. Skeleton of the code

5.2. Global variables and individually-owned variables

It will be handy to have a variable store the number of strategies. Since this information will likely be used in various procedures, it makes sense to define the new variable as global. A natural name for this new variable is n-of-strategies. The modified code will look as follows, then:

```
globals [
  payoff-matrix
  n-of-strategies
]
```

5.3. Setup procedures

The current setup procedure is the following:

```
to setup
  clear-all
  set payoff-matrix read-from-string payoffs
  create-players n-of-players [
    set payoff 0
    set strategy 0
  ]
  ask n-of random (n-of-players + 1) players [set strategy 1]
  reset-ticks
end
```

Note that the code in the current setup procedure performs several unrelated tasks –namely clear everything, set up the payoffs, set up the players, and set up the tick counter–, and now we will need to set up the graph as well (since we have to create as many pens as strategies). Let us take this opportunity to modularize our code and improve its readability by creating new procedures with descriptive names for groups of related instructions, as follows:

```
to setup
  clear-all
  setup-payoffs
  setup-players
  setup-graph
  reset-ticks
  update-graph
end
```

to setup-payoffs

The procedure to setup-payoffs will include the instructions to read the payoff matrix, and will also set the value of the global variable n-of-strategies. We will use the primitive `length` to obtain the number of rows in the payoff matrix.

```
to setup-payoffs
  set payoff-matrix read-from-string payoffs
  set n-of-strategies length payoff-matrix
end
```

to setup-players

The procedure to setup-players will create the players and set the initial values for their individually-owned variables. The initial payoff will be 0 and the initial strategy will be a random integer between 0 and (n-of-strategies – 1).

```
to setup-players
 create-players n-of-players [
   set payoff 0
   set strategy (random n-of-strategies)
 ]
end
```

to setup-graph

The procedure to setup-graph will create the required number of pens –one for each strategy– in the Strategy Distribution plot. To this end, we must first specify that we wish to work on the Strategy Distribution plot, using the primitive `set-current-plot`.

```
set-current-plot "Strategy Distribution"
```

Then, for each strategy $i \in \{0, 1, ..., (\text{n-of-strategies} - 1)\}$, we do the following tasks:

1. Create a pen with the name of the strategy. For this, we use the primitive `create-temporary-plot-pen` to create the pen, and the primitive `word` to turn the strategy number into a string.

   ```
   create-temporary-plot-pen (word i)
   ```

2. Set the pen mode to 1 (bar mode) using `set-plot-pen-mode`. We do this because we plan to create a stacked bar chart for the distribution of strategies.

   ```
   set-plot-pen-mode 1
   ```

3. Choose a color for each pen. See how colors work in NetLogo.

   ```
   set-plot-pen-color 25 + 40 * i
   ```

Now we have to actually loop through the number of each strategy, making *i* take the values 0, 1, ..., (n-of-strategies – 1). There are several ways we can do this. Here, we do it by creating a list [0 1 2 ... (n-of-strategies – 1)] containing the strategy numbers and going through each of its elements. To create the list, we use the primitive `range`.

```
range n-of-strategies
```

The final code for the procedure to setup-graph is then:

```
to setup-graph
  set-current-plot "Strategy Distribution"
  foreach (range n-of-strategies) [ i ->
    create-temporary-plot-pen (word i)
    set-plot-pen-mode 1
    set-plot-pen-color 25 + 40 * i
  ]
```

```
end
```

to update-graph

Procedure to update-graph will draw the strategy distribution using a stacked bar chart, like the one shown in figure 3 below. This procedure is called at the end of setup to plot the initial distribution of strategies, and then also at the end of procedure to go, to plot the strategy distribution at the end of every tick.

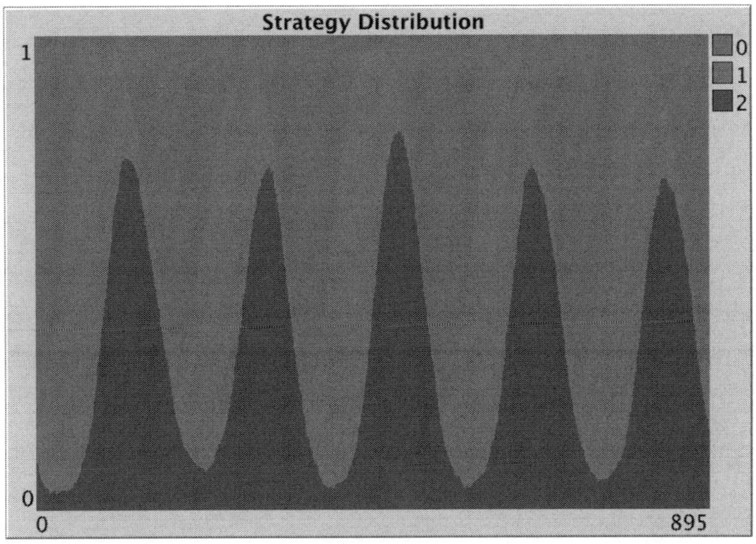

Figure 3. Example of stacked bar chart showing the strategy distribution as ticks go by

We start by creating a list containing the strategy numbers [0 1 2 ... (n-of-strategies – 1)], which we store in local variable strategy-numbers.

```
let strategy-numbers (range n-of-strategies)
```

To compute the (relative) strategy frequencies, we apply to each element of the list strategy-numbers, i.e. to each strategy number, the operation that calculates the fraction of players using that strategy. To do this, we use primitive map. Remember that map requires as inputs a) the function to be applied to each element of the list and b) the list containing the elements on which you wish to apply the function. In this case, the function we wish to apply to each strategy number (implemented as an anonymous procedure) is:

```
[n -> ( count (players with [strategy = n]) ) / n-of-players]
```

In the code above, we first identify the subset of players that have a certain strategy (using with), then we count the number of players in that subset (using count), and finally we divide by the total number of players n-of-players. Thus, we can use the following code to obtain the strategy frequencies, as a list:

```
map [n -> count players with [strategy = n] / n-of-players] strategy-numbers
```

Finally, to build the stacked bar chart, we begin by plotting a bar of height 1, corresponding to the first strategy. Then we repeatedly draw bars on top of the previously drawn bars (one bar for each of the remaining strategies), with the height diminished each time by the relative frequency of the corresponding strategy. The final code of procedure to update-graph will look as follows:

```
to update-graph
  let strategy-numbers (range n-of-strategies)
  let strategy-frequencies map [ n ->
        count players with [strategy = n] / n-of-players
      ] strategy-numbers

  set-current-plot "Strategy Distribution"
  let bar 1
  foreach strategy-numbers [ n ->
    set-current-plot-pen (word n)
    plotxy ticks bar
    set bar (bar - (item n strategy-frequencies))
  ]
  set-plot-y-range 0 1
end
```

5.4. Go procedure

The only change needed in the go procedure is the call to procedure to update-graph, which will draw the fraction of agents using each strategy at the end of every tick:

```
to go
  ask players [play]
  ask players [
    if (random-float 1 < prob-revision) [update-strategy]
  ]
  tick
  update-graph
end
```

5.5. Other procedures

Note that there is no need to modify the code of to play or to update-strategy.

5.6. Complete code in the Code tab

The Code tab is ready!

```
globals [
  payoff-matrix
  n-of-strategies
]

breed [players player]

players-own [
  strategy
  payoff
]

to setup
  clear-all
  setup-payoffs
  setup-players
  setup-graph
  reset-ticks
  update-graph
end

to setup-payoffs
  set payoff-matrix read-from-string payoffs
  set n-of-strategies length payoff-matrix
end

to setup-players
  create-players n-of-players [
    set payoff 0
    set strategy (random n-of-strategies)
  ]
end

to setup-graph
  set-current-plot "Strategy Distribution"
  foreach (range n-of-strategies) [ i ->
    create-temporary-plot-pen (word i)
    set-plot-pen-mode 1
    set-plot-pen-color 25 + 40 * i
  ]
end

to go
  ask players [play]
  ask players [
    if (random-float 1 < prob-revision) [update-strategy]
  ]
  tick
  update-graph
end
```

```
to play
  let mate one-of other players
  set payoff item ([strategy] of mate) (item strategy payoff-matrix)
end

to update-strategy
  let observed-player one-of other players
  if ([payoff] of observed-player) > payoff [
    set strategy ([strategy] of observed-player)
  ]
end

to update-graph
  let strategy-numbers (range n-of-strategies)
  let strategy-frequencies map [n -> count players with [strategy = n] / n-of-
players] strategy-numbers

  set-current-plot "Strategy Distribution"
  let bar 1
  foreach strategy-numbers [ n ->
    set-current-plot-pen (word n)
    plotxy ticks bar
    set bar (bar - (item n strategy-frequencies))
  ]
  set-plot-y-range 0 1
end
```

5.7. Code inside the plots

Note that we take care of all plotting in the update-graph procedure. Thus there is no need to write any code inside the plot. We could instead have written the code of procedure to update-graph inside the plot, but given that it is somewhat lengthy, we find it more convenient to group it with the rest of the code in the Code tab.

6. Sample run

Now that we have implemented the model, we can explore the behavior of a population who are repeatedly matched to play a Rock-Paper-Scissors game. To do that, let us use payoff matrix [[0 -1 1][1 0 -1][-1 1 0]], a population of 500 agents and a 0.1 probability of revision. The following video shows a representative run with these settings.

A video element has been excluded from this version of the text. You can watch it online here: https://wisc.pb.unizin.org/agent-based-evolutionary-game-dynamics/?p=98

Note that soon in the simulation run, one of the strategies will get a greater share by chance (due to the inherent randomness of the model). Then, the next strategy (modulo 3) will enjoy a payoff advantage, and thus will tend to be imitated. For example, if "Paper" is the most popular strategy, then agents playing "Scissors" will tend to get higher payoffs, and thus be imitated. As the fraction of agents playing "Scissors" grows, strategy "Rock" becomes more attractive... and so on and so forth. These cycles get amplified until one of the strategies disappears. At that point, one of the two remaining strategies is superior and finally prevails. The three strategies have an equal change of being the "winner" in the end, since the whole model setting is symmetric.

7. Exercises

You can use the following link to download the complete NetLogo model: nxn-imitate-if-better.

Exercise 1. Consider a Rock-Paper-Scissors game with payoff matrix [[0 -1 1][1 0 -1][-1 1 0]]. Here we ask you to explore how the dynamics are affected by the number of players *n-of-players* and by the probability of revision *prob-revision*. Explore simulations with a small population (e.g. *n-of-players* = 50) and with a large population (e.g. *n-of-players* = 1000). Also, for each case, try both a small probability of revision (e.g. *prob-revision* = 0.01) and a large probability of revision (e.g. *prob-revision* = 0.5).

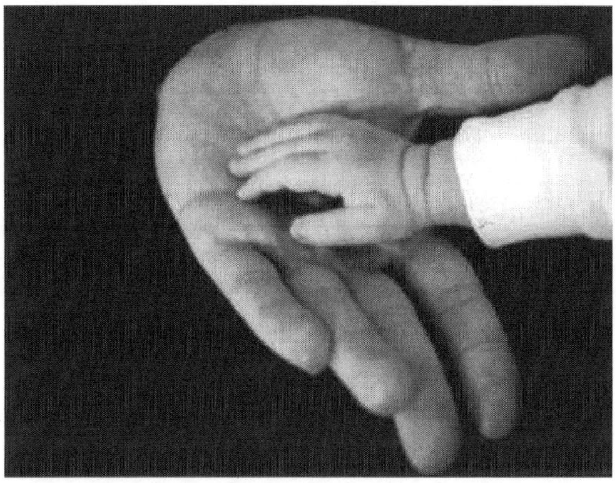

Picture by Liane Metzler

How do your insights change if you use payoff matrix [[0 -1 10][10 0 -1][-1 10 0]]?

Exercise 2. Consider a game with payoff matrix [[1 1 0][1 1 1][0 1 1]]. Set the probability of revision to 0.1. Press the setup button and run the model for a while (then press the setup button again to change the initial conditions). Can you explain what happens?

CODE Exercise 3. How would you create the list [0 1 2 ... (n-of-strategies - 1)] using `n-values` instead of `range`?

CODE Exercise 4. Implement the procedure to setup-graph:

1. using the primitive `repeat` instead of `foreach`.
2. using the primitive `while` instead of `foreach`.
3. using the primitive `loop` instead of `foreach`.

CODE Exercise 5. Reimplement the procedure to update-strategy so the revising agent looks at five (randomly selected) other agents and copies the strategy of the agent with the highest payoff (among these five observed agents). Resolve ties as you wish.

CODE Exercise 6. Reimplement the procedure to update-strategy so the revising agent selects the strategy that is the best response to (i.e. obtains the greatest payoff against) the strategy of another (randomly) observed agent. This is an instance of the so-called *sample best response revision protocol* (Sandholm (2001), Kosfeld et al. (2002), Oyama et al. (2015)). Resolve ties as you wish.

1.2. Noise and initial conditions

1. Goal

Our goal is to extend the model we have created in the previous section by adding two features that will prove very useful:

- The possibility of setting initial conditions explicitly. This is an important feature because initial conditions can be very relevant for the evolution of a system.
- The possibility that revising agents select a strategy at random with a small probability. This type of noise in the revision process may account for experimentation or errors in economic settings, or for mutations in biological contexts. The inclusion of noise in a model can sometimes change its dynamical behavior dramatically, even creating new attractors. This is important because dynamic characteristics of a model –such as attractors, cycles, repellors, and other patterns– that are not robust to the inclusion of small noise may not correspond to relevant properties of the real-world system that we aim to understand. Besides, as a positive side-effect, adding small amounts of noise to a model often makes the analysis of its dynamics easier to undertake.

2. Motivation. Rock, paper, scissors

In the previous section we saw that simulations of the Rock-Paper-Scissors game under the "imitate-the-better-realization" revision protocol end up in a state where everyone is choosing the same strategy. Can you guess what will happen in this model if we add a little bit of noise?

3. Description of the model

In this model, there is a population of *n-of-players* agents who repeatedly play a symmetric 2-player game with any number of strategies. The *payoffs* of the game are determined by the user in the form of a matrix [[A_{00} A_{01} ... A_{0n}] [A_{10} A_{11} ... A_{1n}] ... [A_{n0} A_{n1} ... A_{nn}]] containing the payoffs A_{ij} that an agent playing strategy i obtains when meeting an agent playing strategy j ($i, j \in \{0, 1, ..., n\}$). The number of strategies is inferred from the number of rows in the payoff matrix.

Initial conditions are set with parameter *n-of-players-for-each-strategy*, using a list of the form [a_0 a_1 ... a_n], where item a_i is the initial number of agents with strategy i. Thus, the total number of agents is the sum of all elements in this list. From then onwards, the following sequence of events –which defines a tick– is repeatedly executed:

1. Every agent obtains a payoff by selecting another agent at random and playing the game.
2. With probability *prob-revision*, individual agents are given the opportunity to revise their

strategies. In that case, with probability *noise*, the revising agent will adopt a random strategy; and with probability (1 – *noise*), the revising agent will choose her strategy following the **"imitate the better realization"** protocol:

> Look at another (randomly selected) agent and adopt her strategy if and only if her payoff was greater than yours.

The model shows the evolution of the number of agents choosing each of the possible strategies at the end of every tick.

CODE 4. Interface design

We depart from the model we developed in the previous section (so if you want to preserve it, now is a good time to duplicate it).

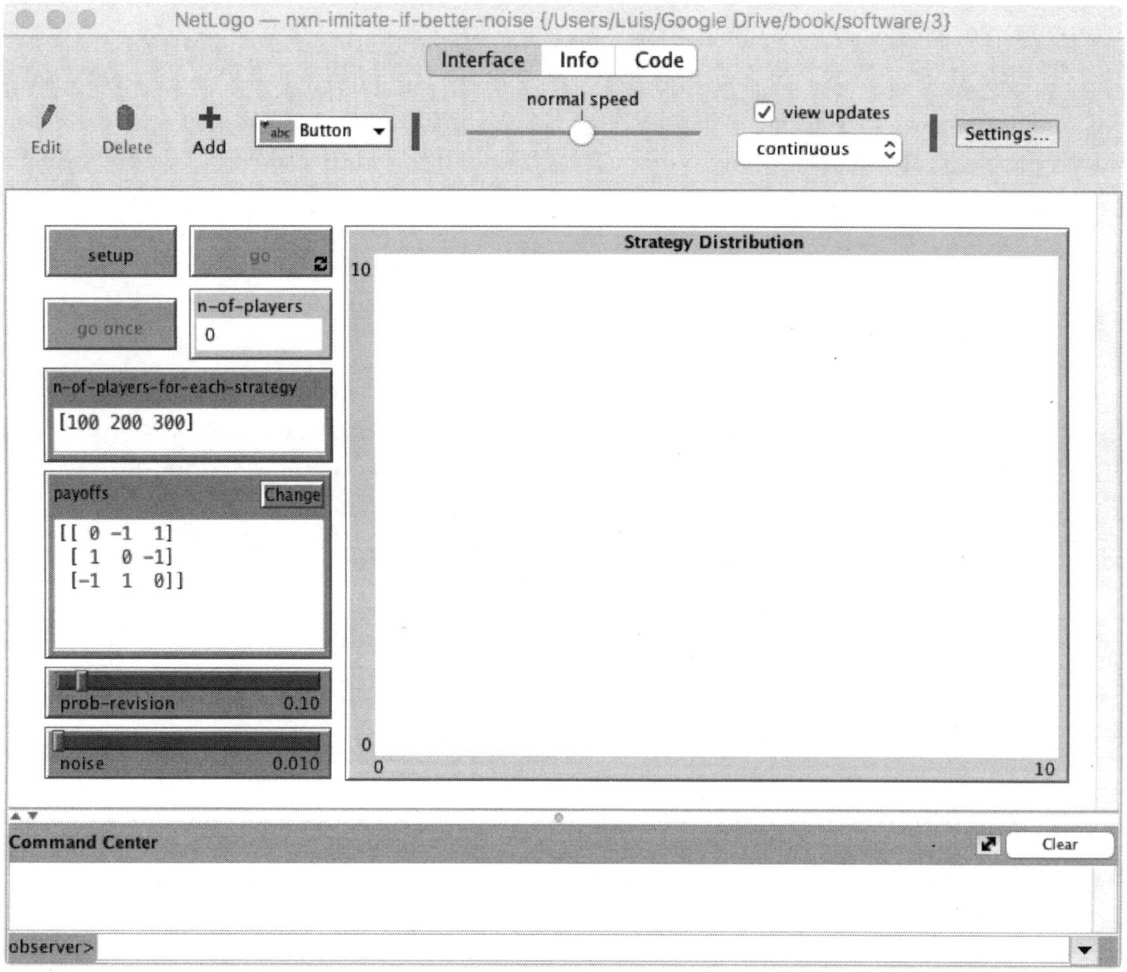

Figure 1. Interface design

The new interface (see figure 1 above) requires a few simple modifications:

- Create an input box to let the user set the initial number of players using each strategy.

In the Interface tab, add an input box with associated global variable *n-of-players-for-each-strategy*. Set the input box type to "String (reporter)".

- Note that the total number of players (which was previously set using a slider with associated global variable *n-of-players*) will now be computed totaling the items of the list *n-of-players-for-each-strategy*. Thus, we should remove the slider, and include the global variable n-of-players in the Code tab.

```
globals [
  payoff-matrix
  n-of-strategies
  n-of-players
]
```

- Add a monitor to show the total number of players. This number will be stored in the global variable n-of-players, so the monitor must show the value of this variable.

In the Interface tab, create a monitor. In the "Reporter" box write the name of the global variable n-of-players.

- Create a slider to choose the value of parameter *noise*.

In the Interface tab, create a slider with associated global variable *noise*. Choose limit values 0 and 1, and an increment of 0.001.

CODE 5. Code

5.1. Skeleton of the code

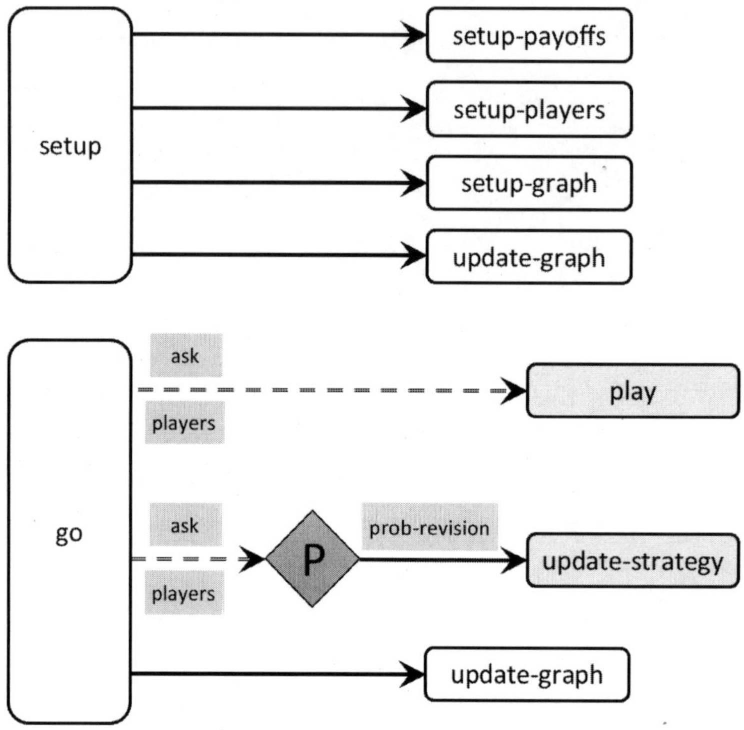

Figure 2. Skeleton of the code

5.2. Global variables and individually-owned variables

The only change required regarding user-defined variables is the inclusion of global variable n-of-players in the Code tab, as explained in the previous section.

5.3. Setup procedures

To read the initial conditions specified with parameter *n-of-players-for-each-strategy* and set up the players accordingly, it is clear that we only have to modify the code in procedure to setup-players. Note that making our code modular, implementing short procedures with specific tasks and meaningful names, makes our life easy when we extend the model.

to setup-players

Since the content of parameter *n-of-players-for-each-strategy* is a string, the first we should do is to turn it into a list that we can use in our code. To this end, we use the primitive `read-from-string` and store its output in a new local variable named initial-distribution, as follows:

```
let initial-distribution read-from-string n-of-players-for-each-strategy
```

Next, we can check that the number of elements in the list initial-distribution matches the number of possible strategies (i.e. the number of rows in the payoff matrix stored in payoff-matrix), and issue a warning message otherwise, using primitive `user-message`. Naturally, this is by no means compulsory, but it is a thoughtful touch that will make our program more user-friendly. To this end, we can use the code below.

```
if length initial-distribution != length payoff-matrix [
  user-message (word "The number of items in\n"
      ;; "\n" is used to jump to the next line
    "n-of-players-for-each-strategy (i.e. "
    length initial-distribution "):\n"
    n-of-players-for-each-strategy
    "\nshould be equal to the number of rows\n"
    "in the payoff matrix (i.e. "
    length payoff-matrix "):\n"
    payoffs
  )
]

;; It is not necessary to show the user
;; the value of n-of-players-for-each-strategy
;; and payoffs again,
;; but when creating an error message,
;; it is good practice to give the user
;; as much information as possible,
;; so the error can be easily corrected.
```

Now, let us create as many players using each strategy as indicated by the values in the list initial-distribution. For instance, if initial-distribution is [5 10 15], we should create 5 players with strategy 0, 10 players with strategy 1, and 15 players with strategy 2. Since we want to perform a task for each element of the list, primitive `foreach` will be handy.

Besides going through each element on the list using `foreach`, we would also like to keep track of the position being read on the list, which is the corresponding strategy number. For this, we create a counter i which we start at 0:

```
let i 0
foreach initial-distribution [ j ->
  create-players j [
    set payoff 0
    set strategy i
  ]
  set i (i + 1)
```

```
]
```

Finally, let us set the value of the global variable n-of-players:

```
set n-of-players count players
```

The line above concludes the definition of procedure to setup-players, and the implementation of the user-chosen initial conditions.

5.4. Go and other main procedures

To implement the choice of a random strategy with probability *noise* by revising agents, we have to modify the code of procedure to update-strategy. At present, the code of this procedure looks as follows:

```
to update-strategy
  let observed-player one-of other players
  if ([payoff] of observed-player) > payoff [
    set strategy ([strategy] of observed-player)
  ]
end
```

We can implement the noise feature using primitive `ifelse`, whose structure is

```
ifelse CONDITION
   [ COMMANDS EXECUTED IF CONDITION IS TRUE ]
   [ COMMANDS EXECUTED IF CONDITION IS FALSE ]
```

In our case, the `CONDITION` should be true with probability *noise*. Bearing all this in mind, the final code for procedure to update-strategy could be as follows:

```
to update-strategy
  ifelse random-float 1 < noise
  ;; the condition is true with probability noise
    [ ;; code to be executed if there is noise
      set strategy (random n-of-strategies)
    ]
    [ ;; code to be executed if there is no noise
      let observed-player one-of other players
      if ([payoff] of observed-player) > payoff [
        set strategy ([strategy] of observed-player)
      ]
```

```
    ]
end
```

5.5. Complete code in the Code tab

The Code tab is ready!

```
globals [
  payoff-matrix
  n-of-strategies
  n-of-players
]

breed [players player]

players-own [
  strategy
  payoff
]

to setup
  clear-all
  setup-payoffs
  setup-players
  setup-graph
  reset-ticks
  update-graph
end

to setup-payoffs
  set payoff-matrix read-from-string payoffs
  set n-of-strategies length payoff-matrix
end

to setup-players
  let initial-distribution read-from-string n-of-players-for-each-strategy
  if length initial-distribution != length payoff-matrix [
    user-message (word "The number of items in\n"
      "n-of-players-for-each-strategy (i.e. "
      length initial-distribution "):\n"
      n-of-players-for-each-strategy
      "\nshould be equal to the number of rows\n"
      "in the payoff matrix (i.e. "
      length payoff-matrix "):\n"
      payoffs
    )
  ]
```

```
  let i 0
  foreach initial-distribution [ j ->
    create-players j [
      set payoff 0
      set strategy i
    ]
    set i (i + 1)
  ]
  set n-of-players count players
end

to setup-graph
  set-current-plot "Strategy Distribution"
  foreach (range n-of-strategies) [ i ->
    create-temporary-plot-pen (word i)
    set-plot-pen-mode 1
    set-plot-pen-color 25 + 40 * i
  ]
end

to go
  ask players [play]
  ask players [
    if (random-float 1 < prob-revision) [update-strategy]
  ]
  tick
  update-graph
end

to play
  let mate one-of other players
  set payoff item ([strategy] of mate) (item strategy payoff-matrix)
end

to update-strategy
  ifelse random-float 1 < noise
    [ set strategy (random n-of-strategies) ]
    [
      let observed-player one-of other players
      if ([payoff] of observed-player) > payoff [
        set strategy ([strategy] of observed-player)
      ]
    ]
end

to update-graph
  let strategy-numbers (range n-of-strategies)
  let strategy-frequencies map [ n ->
    count players with [strategy = n] / n-of-players ]
    strategy-numbers
```

```
  set-current-plot "Strategy Distribution"
  let bar 1
  foreach strategy-numbers [ n ->
    set-current-plot-pen (word n)
    plotxy ticks bar
    set bar (bar - (item n strategy-frequencies))
  ]
  set-plot-y-range 0 1
end
```

6. Sample run

Now that we have implemented the model, we can use it to answer the question posed above: Will adding a bit of noise change the dynamics of the Rock-Paper-Scissors game under the "imitate-the-better-realization" revision protocol? To do that, let us use the same setting as in the previous section, i.e. *payoffs* = [[0 -1 1][1 0 -1][-1 1 0]] and *prob-revision* = 0.1. To have 500 agents and initial conditions close to random, we can set *n-of-players-for-each-strategy* = [167 167 166]. Finally, let us use *noise* = 0.01. The following video shows a representative run with these settings.

A video element has been excluded from this version of the text. You can watch it online here: https://wisc.pb.unizin.org/agent-based-evolutionary-game-dynamics/?p=103

As you can see, noise dampens the amplitude of the cycles, so the monomorphic states where only one strategy is chosen by the whole population are not observed anymore.[1] Even if at some point one strategy went extinct, noise would bring it back into existence. Thus, the model with *noise* = 0.01 exhibits an everlasting pattern of cycles of varying amplitudes. This contrasts with the model without noise, which necessarily ends up in one of only three possible final states.

7. Exercises

You can use the following link to download the complete NetLogo model: nxn-imitate-if-better-noise.

1. In this model with noise, every state will be observed at some point if we wait for long enough, but long enough might be a really long time (e.g. centuries).

Exercise 1. Consider a Prisoner's Dilemma with payoffs [[2 4][1 3]] where strategy 0 is "Defect" and strategy 1 is "Cooperate". Set *prob-revision* to 0.1 and *noise* to 0. Set the initial number of players using each strategy, i.e. *n-of-players-for-each-strategy*, to [0 200], i.e., everybody plays "Cooperate". Press the setup button and run the model. While it is running, move the *noise* slider slightly rightward to introduce some small noise. Can you explain what happens?

Picture by Danielle MacInnes

Exercise 2. Consider a Rock-Paper-Scissors game with payoff matrix [[0 -1 1][1 0 -1][-1 1 0]]. Set *prob-revision* to 0.1 and *noise* to 0. Set the initial number of players using each strategy, i.e. *n-of-players-for-each-strategy*, to [100 100 100]. Press the setup button and run the model for a while. While it is running, click on the *noise* slider to set its value to 0.001. Can you explain what happens?

Exercise 3. Consider a game with payoff matrix [[1 1 0][1 1 1][0 1 1]]. Set *prob-revision* to 0.1, *noise* to 0.05, and the initial number of players using each strategy, i.e. *n-of-players-for-each-strategy*, to [500 0 500]. Press the setup button and run the model for a while (then press the setup button again to change the initial conditions). Can you explain what happens?

Exercise 4. Consider a game with *n* players and *s* strategies, with *noise* equal to 1. What is the infinite-horizon probability distribution of the number of players using each strategy?

CODE Exercise 5. Imagine that you'd like to run this model faster, and you are not interested in the plot. This is a common scenario when you want to conduct large-scale computational experiments. What lines of code could you comment out?

CODE Exercise 6. Note that you can modify the values of parameters *prob-revision* and *noise* at runtime with immediate effect on the dynamics of the model. How could you implement the possibility of changing the number of players in the population with immediate effect on the model?

1.3. Interactivity and efficiency

1. Goal

Our goal in this section is to improve the interactivity and the efficiency of our model.

By **interactivity** we mean the possibility of changing the value of parameters at runtime, with immediate effect on the dynamics of the model. This feature is very convenient for exploratory work. In this section, we will implement the necessary functionality to let the user change the number of agents in the population at runtime.

By **efficiency** we mean implementing the model in such a way that it can be executed using as little time and memory as possible. In this section, we will modify the code of our model slightly to make it run significantly faster.

Oftentimes there is a trade-off between interactivity and efficiency: making the model more interactive generally implies some loss of efficiency. Nonetheless, sometimes we can find ways of implementing a model more efficiently without compromising its interactivity.

It is also important to be aware that –most often– there is also a trade-off between efficiency and code readability. The changes required to make our model run faster will frequently make our code somewhat less readable too. Uri Wilensky –the creator of NetLogo– and William Rand do not recommend making such comprises:

> However, it is important that your code be readable, so others can understand it. In the end, computer time is cheap compared to human time. Therefore, it should be noted that, whenever there is a possibility of trade-off, clarity of code should be preferred over efficiency. Wilensky and Rand (2015, pp 219–20)

Our personal opinion is that this decision is best made case by case, taking into account the objectives and constraints of the whole modelling exercise in the specific context at hand. Our hope is that, after reading this book, you will be prepared to make these decisions by yourself in any specific situation you may encounter.

2. Motivation. Rock, paper, scissors

The dynamics of many evolutionary models strongly depend on the number of agents in the population. Can you guess how the population size affects the dynamics of the "imitate-the-better-realization" revision protocol with noise in the Rock-Paper-Scissors game? In this section we will implement the possibility of changing the population size at runtime, a feature that will greatly facilitate the exploration of this question.

3. Description of the model

We will not make any modification on the formal model our program implements. Thus, we refer to the previous section to read the description of the model. The only paragraph we add (about the program itself) is the following:

> The number of players in the simulation can be changed at runtime with immediate effect on the dynamics of the model, using parameter *n-of-players*:
>
> - If *n-of-players* is reduced, the necessary number of (randomly selected) players are killed.
> - If *n-of-players* is increased, the necessary number of (randomly selected) players are cloned.
>
> Thus, the proportions of agents playing each strategy remain the same on average (although the actual effect of this change is stochastic).

CODE 4. Skeleton of the code

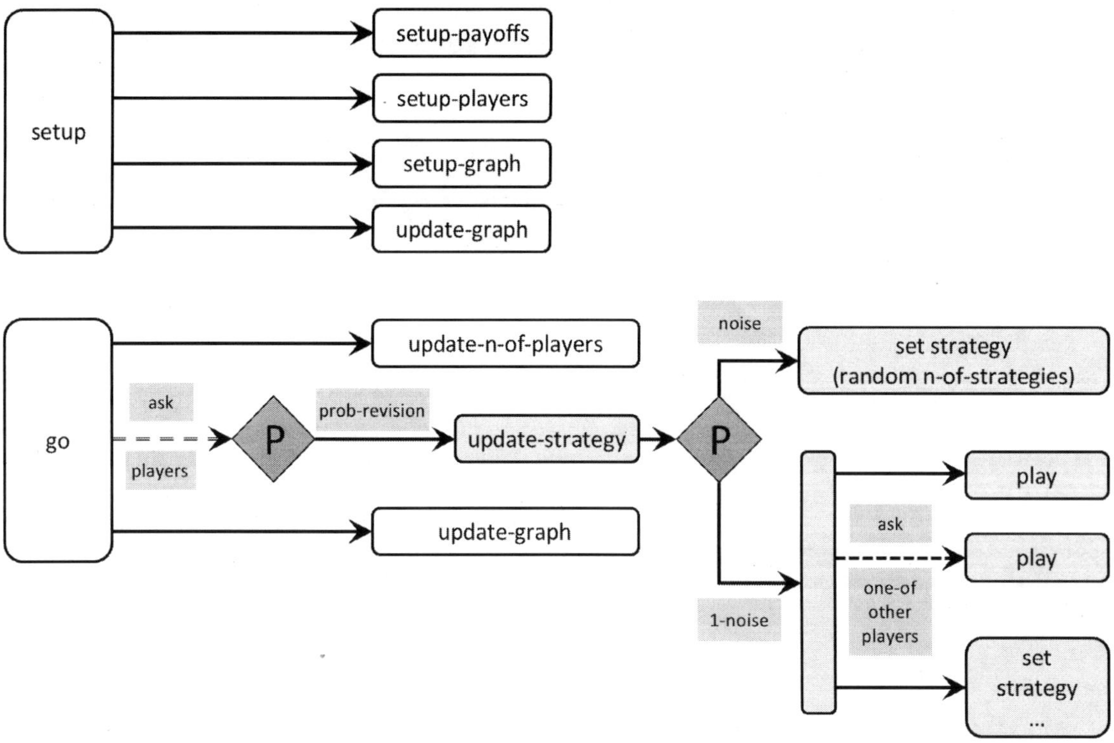

Figure 2. Skeleton of the code

CODE 5. Interactivity

Note that we can already modify the value of parameters *prob-revision* and *noise* at runtime, with immediate effect on the dynamics of the model. This is so because the values of these variables are used directly in the code. Parameter *prob-revision* is used only in procedure to go, in the following line:

```
if (random-float 1 < prob-revision) [update-strategy]
```

And parameter *noise* is used only in procedure to update-strategy, in the following line:

```
ifelse (random-float 1 < noise)
```

Whenever NetLogo reads the two lines of code above, it uses the current values of the two parameters. Because of this, we can modify the parameters' values on the fly and immediately see how that change affects the dynamics of the model.

By contrast, changing the value of parameter *n-of-players-for-each-strategy* at runtime will have no effect whatsoever. This is so because parameter *n-of-players-for-each-strategy* is only used in procedure to setup-players, which is executed at the beginning of the simulation –triggered by procedure to setup– and never again.

To enable the user to modify the population size at runtime, we should create a slider for the new parameter *n-of-players*. Before doing so, we have to remove the declaration of the global variable n-of-players in the Code tab, since the creation of the slider implies the definition of the variable as global.

```
globals [
  payoff-matrix
  n-of-strategies
  ;; n-of-players        <== We remove this line
]
```

After creating the slider for parameter *n-of-players*, we could also remove the monitor showing n-of-players from the interface, since it is no longer needed. Another option (see figure 1 below) is to use that same monitor to display the value of the ticks that have gone by since the beginning of the simulation. To do this, we just have to write the primitive `ticks` (instead of n-of-players) in the "Reporter" box of the monitor.

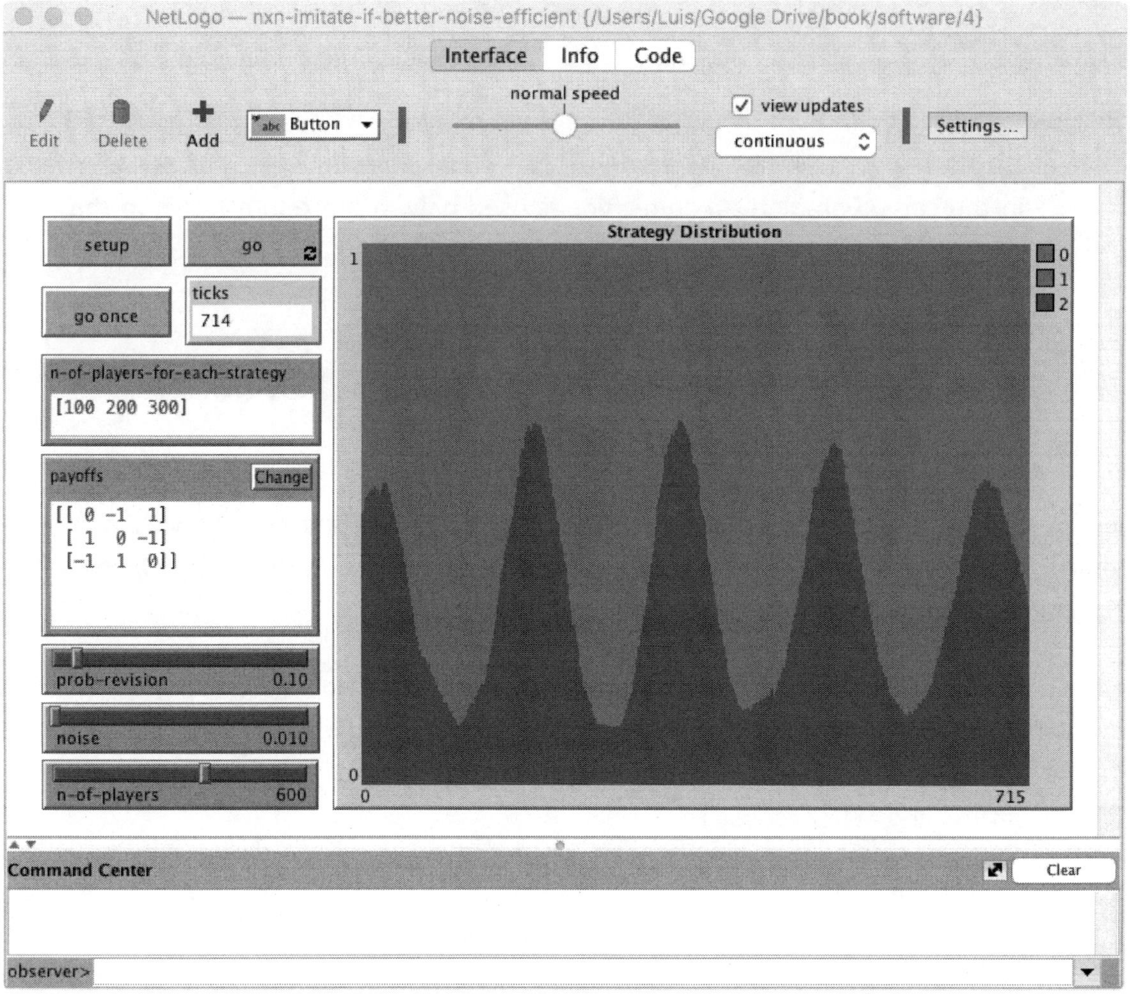

Figure 1. Interface design

The next step is to implement a separate procedure to check whether the value of parameter *n-of-players* differs from the current number of players in the simulation and, if it does, act accordingly. We find it natural to name this new procedure to update-n-of-players, and one possible implementation would be the following:

```
to update-n-of-players
  let diff (n-of-players - count players)

  if diff != 0 [
    ifelse diff > 0
    [ repeat diff [ ask one-of players [hatch-players 1] ] ]
    [ ask n-of (- diff) players [die] ]
  ]
end
```

Note the use of primitives `hatch-players` and `die` to clone and kill agents respectively. The difference between primitives `hatch-players` and `create-players` is important. Hatching is an action that only individual agents (i.e. "turtles" and breeds of "turtles", in NetLogo parlance) can execute. By contrast, only the observer can run `create-turtles` and `create-<breeds>` primitives.

Finally, we should include the call to the new procedure at the beginning of to go.

```
to go
  update-n-of-players          ;; <== New line
  ask players [play]
  ask players [
    if (random-float 1 < prob-revision) [update-strategy]
  ]
  tick
  update-graph
end
```

And with this, we're ready to go! Give it a try, and enjoy the good progress you are making!

CODE 6. Efficiency

Naturally, to make a model run faster, one can always untick the "view updates" box on the Interface tab.[1] This is a must in models that do not make use of the view, like the ones we are programming in this chapter, since it implies a significant speed-up at no cost. But beyond this simple piece of advice, in general, how can we know whether our model can run faster? A good first step is to try to identify inefficiencies in our code. These inefficiencies often take one of two possible forms:

- Computations that we conduct but we do not use at all.
- Computations that we conduct several times despite knowing that their outputs will not change.

Let us see an example of each of these inefficiencies in our current code.

6.1. Example of computations that we conduct but do not use

Can you identify computations that we perform in the current implementation but are not actually needed (i.e. the model would behave in the same way without carrying them out)?

Note that in this model we make all agents play in every tick, but we only use the payoffs obtained by the revising agents and by the agents they observe. Thus, we can make the model run faster by asking

1. This action is equivalent to pushing the speed slider –situated in the middle of the interface toolbar– to its rightmost position and can also be done via code using primitive `no-display`

only revising and observed agents to play. One way of implementing this efficiency improvement would be to modify the code of procedures to go and to update-strategy as follows:

```
to go
  update-n-of-players
  ;; ask players [play]       <== We remove this line
  ask players [
    if (random-float 1 < prob-revision) [update-strategy]
  ]
  tick
  update-graph
end

to update-strategy
  let observed-player one-of other players

  play                        ;; <== New line
  ask observed-player [play] ;; <== New line

  if ([payoff] of observed-player) > payoff [
    set strategy ([strategy] of observed-player)
  ]
end
```

These changes will make simulations with low *prob-revision* run much faster.[2]

6.2. Example of computations that we conduct several times when once would do

Let us now focus on the second type of inefficiency pointed out above. Can you identify a computation that we repeatedly conduct in every tick, even though its result does not change?

Note that we undertake the computation:

```
other players
```

several times in every tick, but we could conduct it just once for each agent in each simulation. To be sure, we conduct that operation every time an agent computes her payoff in to play:

2. Note, however, that the new model is not exactly the same as the old one. In the new –efficient– version of the model, agents switch strategies sequentially, since all relevant payoffs are computed just before any single revision takes place, using the strategy distribution at the time of the revision. In constrast, in the old version all revisions within the same tick made use of the payoffs computed at the beginning of the tick, using the strategy distribution at the beginning of the tick. It is not difficult to define an efficient and totally equivalent version of the old model by defining a new players-own variable to store players' strategy after the revision. We chose not to do so here for pedagogical reasons.

```
let mate one-of other players
```

And also every time an agent revises her strategy in to update-strategy:

```
let observed-agent one-of other players
```

This computation may not sound very expensive, but if the number of agents is large, it may well be (see exercise 3 below). To make the model run faster, we could create an individually-owned variable named e.g. other-players, as follows

```
players-own [
  strategy
  payoff
  other-players
]
```

And then we should set the new individually-owned variable other-players to the appropriate value only once at the beginning of each simulation (at the end of procedure to setup-agents).

```
ask players [ set other-players other players ]
```

Since we may change the number of players at runtime, we should also include the line above in the block of code where we clone or kill agents in procedure to update-n-of-agents, i.e.

```
to update-n-of-players
  let diff (n-of-players - count players)
  if diff != 0 [
    ifelse diff > 0
    [ repeat diff [ ask one-of players [hatch-players 1] ] ]
    [ ask n-of (- diff) players [die] ]
    ask players [set other-players other players]
  ]
end
```

Once we have done that, in the two lines of code where we had the code

```
other players
```

we should write other-players instead. These changes will make simulations with many players run faster.

6.3. Measuring execution speed of different parts of the code

There are two simple ways to measure execution speed in NetLogo. One is using primitives `reset-`

timer and timer. For instance, to time how long it takes to have every agent carry out the operation:

```
other players
```

we could write the following reporter:

```
to-report time-other-players
  reset-timer
  ask players [let temporary-var other players]
  report timer
end
```

A second –more advanced– way of measuring execution speed involves the Profiler Extension, which comes bundled with NetLogo. This extension allows us to see how many times each procedure in our model is called during a run and how long each call takes. The extension is simple to use and well documented here. To use it in our model, we should include the extension at the beginning of our code, as follows:

```
extensions [profiler]
```

Then we could execute the following procedure, borrowed from the Profiler Extension documentation page.

```
to show-profiler-report
  setup                   ;; set up the model
  profiler:start          ;; start profiling
  repeat 1000 [ go ]      ;; run something you want to measure
  profiler:stop           ;; stop profiling
  print profiler:report   ;; print the results
  profiler:reset          ;; clear the data
end
```

Once the procedure is implemented, you can run it by typing its name in the Command Center.

The profiler report includes the inclusive time and the exclusive time for each procedure. **Inclusive time** is the time the simulation spends running the procedure, i.e. since the procedure is entered until it finishes. **Exclusive time** is the time passed since the procedure is entered until it finishes, but does not include any time spent in other user-defined procedures which it calls. An example of the output printed by `show-profiler-report` follows:

```
BEGIN PROFILING DUMP
Sorted by Exclusive Time
```

```
Name                          Calls  Incl T(ms)  Excl T(ms)  Excl/calls
PLAY                         119130    2804.330    2804.330       0.024
UPDATE-STRATEGY               60131    4441.429    1637.099       0.027
UPDATE-GRAPH                   1000     231.718     231.718       0.232
GO                             1000    4823.320     147.693       0.148
UPDATE-N-OF-PLAYERS            1000       2.480       2.480       0.002

Sorted by Inclusive Time
GO                             1000    4823.320     147.693       0.148
UPDATE-STRATEGY               60131    4441.429    1637.099       0.027
PLAY                         119130    2804.330    2804.330       0.024
UPDATE-GRAPH                   1000     231.718     231.718       0.232
UPDATE-N-OF-PLAYERS            1000       2.480       2.480       0.002

Sorted by Number of Calls
PLAY                         119130    2804.330    2804.330       0.024
UPDATE-STRATEGY               60131    4441.429    1637.099       0.027
GO                             1000    4823.320     147.693       0.148
UPDATE-GRAPH                   1000     231.718     231.718       0.232
UPDATE-N-OF-PLAYERS            1000       2.480       2.480       0.002
END PROFILING DUMP
```

In the example above we can see –among other things– that:

- Simulations spend most of the time executing procedure to play (2804.330 ms) and procedure to update-strategy (1637.099 ms).
- The procedure that is called the greatest number of times is to play, which is called 119130 times. This makes sense, since there were 600 agents in this simulation, *prob-revision* was 0.1, a revision requires a play by the agent and by the opponent he observes, and we ran the model 1000 ticks (600 × 0.1 × 2 × 1000 = 120000).
- Our implementation to allow the user to modify the number of agents at runtime hardly takes any computing time (just 2.480 ms).

6.4. Other tips to improve the efficiency of NetLogo code

Railsback et al. (2017) give several guidelines to identify slow parts of NetLogo code and make them run faster, providing specific examples for agent-based models written in NetLogo.

CODE 7. Complete code in the Code tab

```
globals [
  payoff-matrix
  n-of-strategies
```

```
]

breed [players player]

players-own [
  strategy
  payoff
  other-players
]

to setup
  clear-all
  setup-payoffs
  setup-players
  setup-graph
  reset-ticks
  update-graph
end

to setup-payoffs
  set payoff-matrix read-from-string payoffs
  set n-of-strategies length payoff-matrix
end

to setup-players
  let initial-distribution read-from-string n-of-players-for-each-strategy
  if length initial-distribution != length payoff-matrix [
    user-message (word "The number of items in\n"
      "n-of-players-for-each-strategy (i.e. "
      length initial-distribution "):\n" n-of-players-for-each-strategy
      "\nshould be equal to the number of rows\n"
      "in the payoff matrix (i.e. "
      length payoff-matrix "):\n"
      payoffs
    )
  ]

  let i 0
  foreach initial-distribution [ j ->
    create-players j [
      set payoff 0
      set strategy i
    ]
    set i (i + 1)
  ]
  set n-of-players count players
  ask players [set other-players other players]
end

to setup-graph
  set-current-plot "Strategy Distribution"
```

```
]

breed [players player]

players-own [
  strategy
  payoff
  other-players
]

to setup
  clear-all
  setup-payoffs
  setup-players
  setup-graph
  reset-ticks
  update-graph
end

to setup-payoffs
  set payoff-matrix read-from-string payoffs
  set n-of-strategies length payoff-matrix
end

to setup-players
  let initial-distribution read-from-string n-of-players-for-each-strategy
  if length initial-distribution != length payoff-matrix [
    user-message (word "The number of items in\n"
      "n-of-players-for-each-strategy (i.e. "
      length initial-distribution "):\n" n-of-players-for-each-strategy
      "\nshould be equal to the number of rows\n"
      "in the payoff matrix (i.e. "
      length payoff-matrix "):\n"
      payoffs
    )
  ]

  let i 0
  foreach initial-distribution [ j ->
    create-players j [
      set payoff 0
      set strategy i
    ]
    set i (i + 1)
  ]
  set n-of-players count players
  ask players [set other-players other players]
end

to setup-graph
  set-current-plot "Strategy Distribution"
```

```
  foreach (range n-of-strategies) [ i ->
    create-temporary-plot-pen (word i)
    set-plot-pen-mode 1
    set-plot-pen-color 25 + 40 * i
   ]
end

to go
  update-n-of-players
  ask players [
    if (random-float 1 < prob-revision) [update-strategy]
  ]
  tick
  update-graph
end

to play
  let mate one-of other-players
  set payoff item ([strategy] of mate) (item strategy payoff-matrix)
end

to update-strategy
  ifelse (random-float 1 < noise)
    [ set strategy (random n-of-strategies) ]
    [
      let observed-player one-of other-players
      play
      ask observed-player [play]
      if ([payoff] of observed-player) > payoff [
        set strategy ([strategy] of observed-player)
      ]
    ]
end

to update-graph
  let strategy-numbers (range n-of-strategies)
  let strategy-frequencies map
    [n -> count players with [strategy = n] / n-of-players]
    strategy-numbers

  set-current-plot "Strategy Distribution"
  let bar 1
  foreach strategy-numbers [ n ->
    set-current-plot-pen (word n)
    plotxy ticks bar
    set bar (bar - (item n strategy-frequencies))
  ]
  set-plot-y-range 0 1
end

to update-n-of-players
```

```
  let diff (n-of-players - count players)

  if diff != 0 [
    ifelse diff > 0
    [ repeat diff [ ask one-of players [hatch-players 1] ] ]
    [ ask n-of (- diff) players [die] ]
    ask players [set other-players other players]
  ]
end
```

8. Sample run

Now that we can change the population size at runtime, we can easily explore the question posed above: How does population size affect the dynamics of the "imitate-the-better-realization" revision protocol with noise in the Rock-Paper-Scissors game? To do that, let us use the same setting as in the previous sections (i.e. *payoffs* = [[0 -1 1][1 0 -1][-1 1 0]] and *prob-revision* = 0.1), start with a small population of 60 agents (*n-of-players-for-each-strategy* = [20 20 20]), and then, increase *n-of-players* up to 2000 at runtime. The following video shows a representative run with these settings, where we increased the population size from 60 to 2000 at tick 4000.

A video element has been excluded from this version of the text. You can watch it online here: https://wisc.pb.unizin.org/agent-based-evolutionary-game-dynamics/?p=1061

As you can see, when the number of agents is small, the population consistently follows cycles of large amplitude among the three strategies. The cycles are so wide that sometimes one or even two strategies go extinct for a while. In stark contrast, when the population is large, the cycles get much smaller and the population tends to linger around the state where each strategy is used by approximately a third of the population.[3]

9. Exercises

You can use the following link to download the complete NetLogo model: nxn-imitate-if-better-noise-efficient.

3. The state where all strategies are equally represented is a globally asymptotically stable state of the mean dynamics of this model (which provides a good approximation for models with large populations). See solution to Exercise 1.2.2.

CODE Exercise 1. In this section we have improved both the interactivity and the efficiency of our model. Can you quantify how much faster the current version of the code runs compared to the previous one? For the sake of concreteness, use 1000-tick simulations with 600 agents and *prob-revision* 0.1.

Picture by Romain Peli

CODE Exercise 2. In this section we have reduced the number of times procedure to play is called (as long as *prob-revision* is less than 0.5). To illustrate this, compare the number of times this procedure is called in a 1000-tick simulation with 600 agents and *prob-revision* 0.1, before and after our efficiency improvement. Can you compute the number of times procedure to play is called in the general case?

CODE Exercise 3. In this section we have reduced the number of times the computation `other players` is conducted by creating an individually-owned variable (named other-players). To compare these two approaches, write a short NetLogo program where 10000 agents conduct this operation.

CODE Exercise 4. In this section we have reduced the number of times procedure to play is called (as long as *prob-revision* is less than 0.5). However, it is still possible that some players will execute procedure to play more than once in the same tick, specially if *prob-revision* is high. Can you think of a way to reduce the number of calls to procedure to play even further?

1.4. Analysis of these models

1. Two complementary approaches

Agent-based models are usually analyzed using computer simulation and/or mathematical analysis.

- The computer simulation approach consists in running many simulations –i.e. sampling the model many times– and then, with the data thus obtained, trying to infer general patterns and properties of the model.
- Mathematical approaches do not look at individual simulation runs, but instead analyze the rules that define the model directly, and try to derive their logical implications. Mathematical approaches use deductive reasoning only, so their conclusions follow with logical necessity from the assumptions embedded in the model (and in the mathematics employed).

These two approaches are complementary, in that they can provide fundamentally different insights on the same model. Furthermore, there are synergies to be exploited by using the two approaches together (see e.g. Izquierdo et al. (2013, 2019), Seri (2016), García and van Veelen (2016, 2018) and Hindersin et al. (2019)).

Here we provide several references to material that is helpful to analyze the agent-based models we have developed in this chapter of the book, and illustrate its usefulness with a few examples. Section 2 below deals with the computer simulation approach, while section 3 addresses the mathematical analysis approach.

2. Computer simulation approach

The task of running many simulation runs –with the same or different combinations of parameter values– is greatly facilitated by a tool named BehaviorSpace, which is included within NetLogo and is very well documented at NetLogo website. Here we provide an illustration of how to use it.

Consider a coordination game defined by payoffs [[1 0][0 2]], played by 1000 agents who sequentially revise their strategies with probability 0.01 in every tick following the imitate-the-better-realization rule without noise.[1] This model is stochastic and we wish to study how it *usually* behaves, departing from a situation where both strategies are equally represented. To that end, we could run several simulation runs (say 1000) and plot the average fraction of 1-strategists in every tick, together with

1. This is the model implemented in the previous section. It can be downloaded here. Note that in this model agents switch strategies sequentially, even when several revisions take place in the same tick. This is so because all relevant payoffs are computed just before any single revision takes place, using the strategy distribution at the time of the revision.

the minimum and the maximum values observed across runs in every tick. An illustration of this type of graph is shown in figure 1. Recall that strategies are labeled 0 and 1, so strategy 1 is the one that can get a payoff of 2.

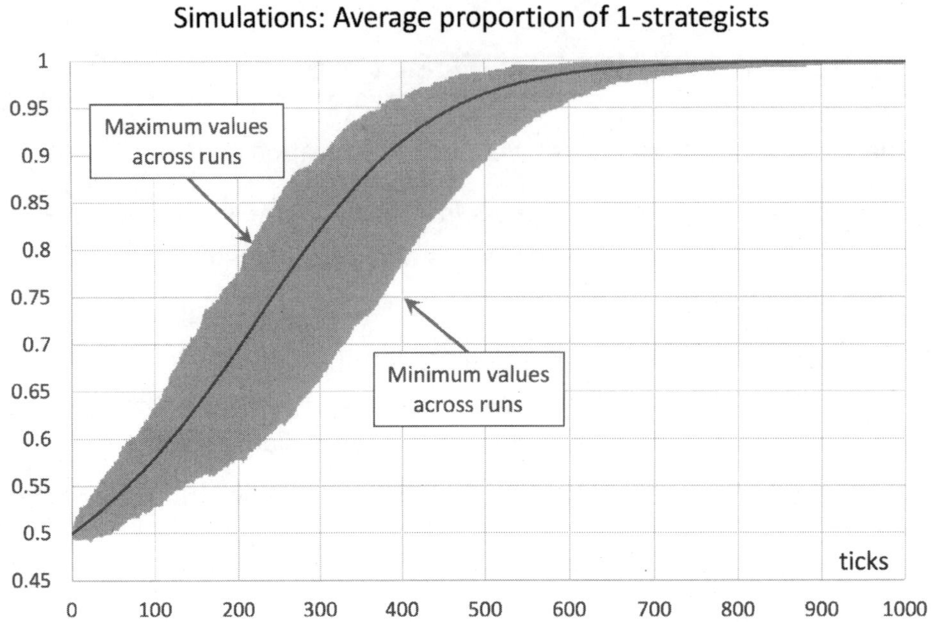

Figure 1. Average proportion of 1-strategists in an experiment of 1000 simulation runs. Orange error bars show the minimum and maximum values observed across the 1000 runs. Payoffs [[1 0][0 2]]; prob-revision 0.01; noise 0; initial conditions [500 500].

To set up the computational experiment that will produce the data required to draw figure 1, we just have to go to *Tools* (in the upper menu of NetLogo) and then click on *BehaviorSpace*. The new experiment can be set up as shown in figure 2.

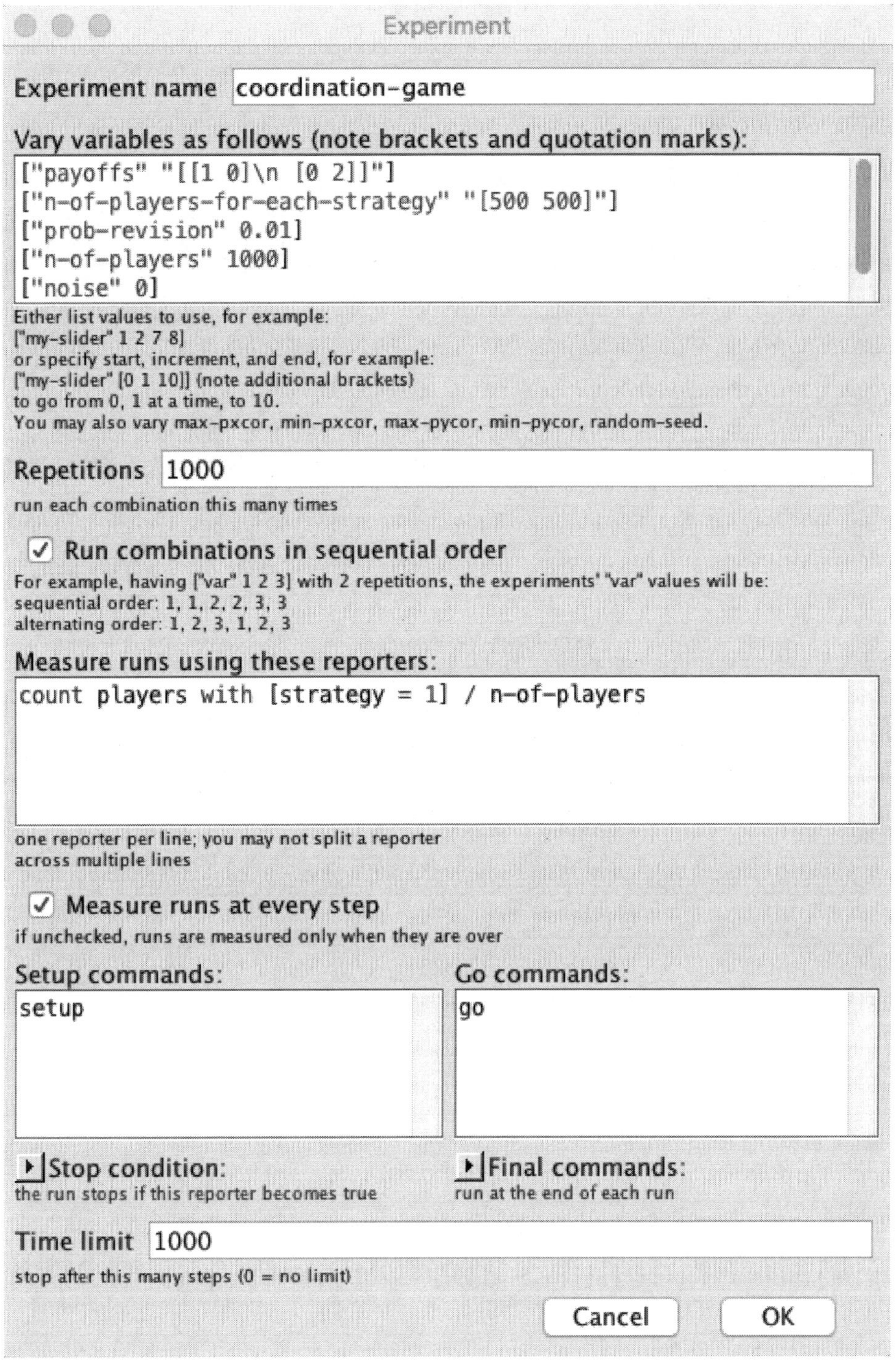

Figure 2. Experiment setup in BehaviorSpace

In this particular experiment, we are not changing the value of any parameter, but doing so is straightforward. For instance, if we wanted to run simulations with different values of *prob-revision* –say 0.01, 0.05 and 0.1–, we would just write:

```
[ "prob-revision" 0.01 0.05 0.1 ]
```

If, in addition, we would like to explore the values of *noise* 0, 0.01, 0.02 ... 0.1, we could use the syntax for loops, [*start increment end*], as follows:

```
[ "noise" [0 0.01 0.1] ] ;; note the additional brackets
```

If we made the two changes described above, then the new computational experiment would comprise 33000 runs, since NetLogo would run 1000 simulations for each combination of parameter values (i.e. 3 × 11).

The original experiment shown in figure 2, which consists of 1000 simulation runs only, takes a couple of minutes to run. Once it is completed, we obtain a *.csv* file with all the requested data, i.e. the fraction of 1-strategists in every tick for each of the 1000 simulation runs – a total of 1001000 data points. Then, with the help of a pivot table (within e.g. an Excel spreadsheet), it is easy to plot the graph shown in figure 1. A similar graph that can be easily plotted is one that shows the standard error of the average computed in every tick (see figure 3).[2]

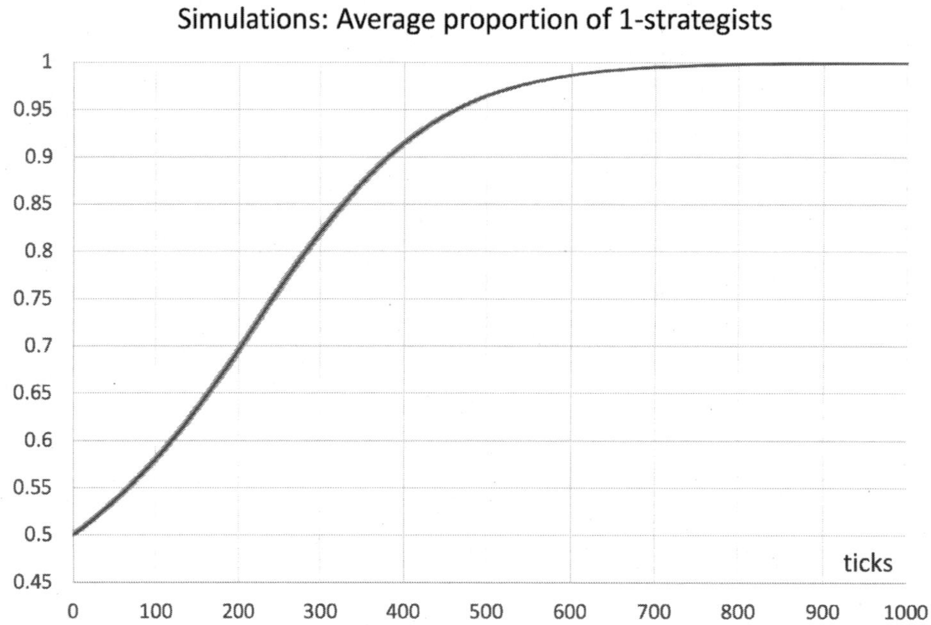

Figure 3. Average proportion of 1-strategists in an experiment of 1000 simulation runs. Orange error bars show the standard error. Payoffs: [[1 0][0 2]]; prob-revision: 0.01; noise 0; initial conditions [500 500].

3. Mathematical analysis approach. Markov chains

From a mathematical point of view, agent-based models can be usefully seen as time-homogeneous Markov chains (see Gintis (2013) and Izquierdo et al. (2009) for several examples). Doing so can make evident many features of the model that are not apparent before formalizing the model as a Markov chain. Thus, our first recommendation is to learn the basics of this theory. Karr (1990), Kulkarni (1995, chapters 2-4), Norris (1997), Kulkarni (1999, chapter 5), and Janssen and Manca (2006, chapter 3) are all excellent introductions to the topic.

All the models developed in this chapter can be seen as time-homogeneous Markov chains on

2. The standard error of the average equals the standard deviation of the sample divided by the square root of the sample size. In our example, the maximum standard error was well below 0.01.

the finite space of possible strategy distributions. This means that the number of agents that are following each possible strategy is all the information we need to know about the present -and the past- of the stochastic process in order to be able to -probabilistically- predict its future as accurately as it is possible. Thus, the number of possible states in these models is $\binom{N+s-1}{s-1}$, where N is the number of agents and s the number of strategies.[3]

In some simple cases, a full Markov analysis can be conducted by deriving the transition probabilities of the Markov chain and operating directly with them. Section 3.1 illustrates how this type of analysis can be undertaken on models with 2 strategies where agents revise their strategies sequentially.

However, in many other models a full Markov analysis is unfeasible because the exact formulas can lead to very cumbersome expressions, or may even be too complex to evaluate. This is often the case if the number of states is large.[4] In such situations, one can still take advantage of powerful approximation results, which we introduce in section 3.2.

3.1. Markov analysis of 2-strategy evolutionary processes where agents switch strategies sequentially

In this section we study 2-strategy evolutionary processes where agents switch strategies sequentially. For simplicity, we will asume that there is one revision per tick, but several revisions could take place in the same tick as long as they ocurred sequentially.[5] These processes can be formalized as birth-death chains, a special type of Markov chains for which various analytical results can be derived. An example of such a process is the one simulated in section 2 above.

3.1.1. Markov chain formulation

Consider a population of N agents who repeatedly play a symmetric 2-player 2-strategy game. The two possible strategies are labeled 0 and 1. In every tick, one random agent is given the opportunity to revise his strategy, and he does so according to a certain revision protocol (such as the imitate-the-better-realization protocol, the imitative pairwise-difference protocol or the best experienced payoff protocol).

Let X_k be the proportion of the population using strategy 1 at tick k. The evolutionary process described above induces a Markov chain $\{X_k\}$ on the state space $S^N = \{0, \frac{1}{N}, \ldots, 1\}$. We do not have to keep track of the proportion of agents using strategy 0 because there are only two strategies, so the two proportions must add up to one. Since there is only one revision per tick, note that there

---

3. This result can be easily derived using a "stars and bars" analogy.
4. As an example, in a 4-strategy game with 1000 players, the number of possible states (i.e. strategy distributions) is $\binom{1000+4-1}{4-1} = 167,668,501$.
5. Note that the implementation of procedure to update-strategy in the model implemented in the previous section implies that agents switch strategies sequentially. This is so because all relevant payoffs are computed just before any single revision takes place, using the strategy distribution at the time of the revision.

are only three possible transitions: one implies increasing X_k by $\frac{1}{N}$, another one implies decreasing X_k by $\frac{1}{N}$, and the other one leaves the state unchanged. Let us denote the transition probabilities as follows:

$$p(x) = \mathbb{P}(X_{k+1} = x + \tfrac{1}{N} \,|\, X_k = x)$$
$$q(x) = \mathbb{P}(X_{k+1} = x - \tfrac{1}{N} \,|\, X_k = x)$$

Thus, the probability of staying at the same state after one tick is:

$$\mathbb{P}(X_{k+1} = x \,|\, X_k = x) = 1 - p(x) - q(x)$$

This Markov chain has two important properties: the state space $S^N = \{0, \frac{1}{N}, \ldots, 1\}$ is endowed with a linear order and all transitions move the state one step to the left, one step to the right, or leave the state unchanged. These two properties imply that the Markov chain is a birth-death chain. Figure 4 below shows the transition diagram of this birth-death chain, ignoring the self-loops.

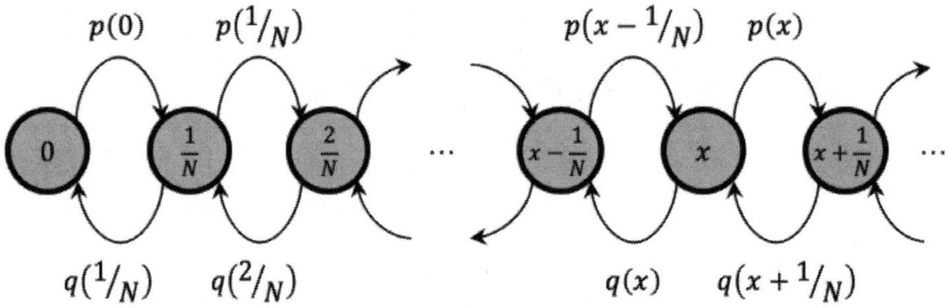

Figure 4. Transition diagram of a birth-death chain

The transition matrix P of a Markov chain gives us the probability of going from one state to another. In our case, the elements $P_{ij} = \mathbb{P}(X_{k+1} = \frac{j-1}{N} \,|\, X_k = \frac{i-1}{N})$ of the transition matrix are:

$$P = \begin{pmatrix} 1 - \sum\limits_{j\neq 1} P_{1j} & p(0) & 0 & 0 & \cdots & 0 \\ q(\frac{1}{N}) & 1 - \sum\limits_{j\neq 2} P_{2j} & p(\frac{1}{N}) & 0 & \cdots & 0 \\ 0 & q(\frac{2}{N}) & 1 - \sum\limits_{j\neq 3} P_{3j} & p(\frac{2}{N}) & \ddots & \vdots \\ \vdots & \ddots & \ddots & \ddots & \ddots & 0 \\ 0 & \cdots & 0 & q(\frac{N-1}{N}) & 1 - \sum\limits_{j\neq N} P_{Nj} & p(\frac{N-1}{N}) \\ 0 & \cdots & 0 & 0 & q(\frac{N}{N}) & 1 - \sum\limits_{j\neq N+1} P_{N+1\,j} \end{pmatrix}$$

In our evolutionary process, the transition probabilities $p(x)$ and $q(x)$ are determined by the revision protocol that agents use. Let us see how this works with a specific example. Consider the coordination game defined by payoffs [[1 0][0 2]], played by agents who sequentially revise their strategies according to the the imitate-the-better-realization rule (without noise). This is the model we have simulated in section 2 above.[6]

Let us derive $p(x) = \mathbb{P}(X_{k+1} = x + \frac{1}{N} \mid X_k = x)$. Note that the state increases by $\frac{1}{N}$ if and only if the revising agent is using strategy 0 and he switches to strategy 1. In the game with payoffs [[1 0][0 2]], this happens if and only if the following conditions are satisfied:

- the agent who is randomly drawn to revise his strategy is playing strategy 0 (an event which happens with probability $(1 - x)$),
- the agent that is observed by the revising agent is playing strategy 1 (an event which happens with probability $\frac{xN}{N-1}$; note that there are xN agents using strategy 1 and the revising agent observes *another* agent, thus the divisor $N - 1$), and
- the observed agent's payoff is 2, i.e. the observed agent –who is playing strategy 1– played with an agent who was also playing strategy 1 (an event which happens with probability $\frac{xN-1}{N-1}$; note that the observed agent plays with *another* agent who is also playing strategy 1).

Therefore:

$$p(x) = (1 - x)\frac{xN}{N-1}\frac{xN-1}{N-1}$$

Note that, in this case, the payoff obtained by the revising agent is irrelevant.

We can derive $q(x) = \mathbb{P}(X_{k+1} = x - \frac{1}{N} \mid X_k = x)$ in a similar fashion. Do you want to give it a try before reading the solution?

Computation of $q(x)$

Note that the state decreases by $\frac{1}{N}$ if and only if the revising agent is using strategy 1 and he switches to strategy 0. In the game with payoffs [[1 0][0 2]], this happens if and only if the following conditions are satisfied:

- the agent who is randomly drawn to revise his strategy is playing strategy 1 (an event which happens with probability x),
- the agent that is observed by the revising agent is playing strategy 0 (an event which

6. The only difference is that now we are asuming that there is exactly one revision per tick, while in the model simulated in section 2 agents sequentially revise their strategies with probability 0.01 in every tick. This difference is really just about what we decide to call "tick".

happens with probability $\frac{(1-x)N}{N-1}$; note that there are $(1-x)N$ 0-strategists and the revising agent observes *another* agent, thus the divisor $N-1$),

- the revising agent's payoff is 0, i.e. the revising agent played with an agent who was playing strategy 0 (an event which happens with probability $\frac{(1-x)N}{N-1}$; note that the revising agent plays with *another* agent, thus the divisor $N-1$).
- the observed agent's payoff is 1, i.e. the observed agent, who is playing strategy 0, played with an agent who was also playing strategy 0 (an event which happens with probability $\frac{(1-x)N-1}{N-1}$; note that the observed agent plays with *another* agent who is also playing strategy 0).

Therefore:

$$q(x) = x\frac{(1-x)N}{N-1}\frac{(1-x)N}{N-1}\frac{(1-x)N-1}{N-1}$$

With the formulas of $p(x)$ and $q(x)$ in place, we can write the transition matrix of this model for any given N. As an example, this is the transition matrix P for $N = 10$:

$$P = \begin{pmatrix}
1. & 0. & 0. & 0. & 0. & 0. & 0. & 0. & 0. & 0. & 0. \\
0.089 & 0.911 & 0. & 0. & 0. & 0. & 0. & 0. & 0. & 0. & 0. \\
0. & 0.123 & 0.857 & 0.020 & 0. & 0. & 0. & 0. & 0. & 0. & 0. \\
0. & 0. & 0.121 & 0.827 & 0.052 & 0. & 0. & 0. & 0. & 0. & 0. \\
0. & 0. & 0. & 0.099 & 0.812 & 0.089 & 0. & 0. & 0. & 0. & 0. \\
0. & 0. & 0. & 0. & 0.069 & 0.808 & 0.123 & 0. & 0. & 0. & 0. \\
0. & 0. & 0. & 0. & 0. & 0.040 & 0.812 & 0.148 & 0. & 0. & 0. \\
0. & 0. & 0. & 0. & 0. & 0. & 0.017 & 0.827 & 0.156 & 0. & 0. \\
0. & 0. & 0. & 0. & 0. & 0. & 0. & 0.004 & 0.857 & 0.138 & 0. \\
0. & 0. & 0. & 0. & 0. & 0. & 0. & 0. & 0 & 0.911 & 0.089 \\
0. & 0. & 0. & 0. & 0. & 0. & 0. & 0. & 0. & 0. & 1.
\end{pmatrix}$$

And here's a little *Mathematica*® script that can be used to generate the transition matrix for any N:

```
n = 10;
p[x_] := (1 - x) (x n/(n - 1)) ((x n - 1)/(n - 1))
q[x_] := x (((1 - x)n)/(n - 1))^2 ((1 - x)n - 1)/(n - 1)

P = SparseArray[{
```

```
    {i_, i_} -> (1 - p[(i - 1)/n] - q[(i - 1)/n]),
    {i_, j_} /; i == j - 1 -> p[(i - 1)/n],
    {i_, j_} /; i == j + 1 -> q[(i - 1)/n]
    }, {n + 1, n + 1}];

MatrixForm[P]
```

3.1.2. Transient dynamics

In this section, we use the transition matrix P we have just derived to compute the transient dynamics of our two-strategy evolutionary process, i.e. the probability distribution of X_k at a certain $k \geq 0$. Naturally, this distribution generally depends on initial conditions.

To be concrete, imagine we set some initial conditions, which we express as a (row) vector a_0 containing the initial probability distribution over the $N+1$ states of the system at tick $k=0$, i.e. $a_0 = \big(a_0(0), a_0(\frac{1}{N}), \ldots, a_0(\frac{N-1}{N}), a_0(1)\big)$, where $a_0(i) = \mathbb{P}(X_0 = i)$. If initial conditions are certain, i.e. if $X_0 = x_0$, then all elements of a_0 are 0 except for $a(x_0)$, which would be equal to 1.

Our goal is to compute the vector $a_k = (a_k(0), a_k(\frac{1}{N}), \ldots, a_k(\frac{N-1}{N}), a_k(1))$, which contains the probability of finding the process in each of the possible $N+1$ states at tick k (i.e. after k revisions), having started at initial conditions a_0. This a_k is a row vector representing the probability mass function of X_k.

To compute a_k, it is important to note that the t-step transition probabilities $\mathbb{P}(X_{k+t} = y \mid X_k = x)$ are given by the entries of the tth power of the transition matrix, i.e.:

$$(P^t)_{ij} = \mathbb{P}(X_{k+t} = \tfrac{j-1}{N} \mid X_k = \tfrac{i-1}{N})$$

Thus, we can easily compute the transient distribution a_k simply by multiplying the initial conditions a_0 by the kth power of the transition matrix P:

$$a_k = a_0 P^k$$

As an example, consider the evolutionary process we formalized as a Markov chain in the previous section, with $N = 100$ imitate-the-better-realization agents playing the coordination game [[1 0][0 2]]. Let us start at initial state $X_0 = 0.5$, i.e. $a_0 = (0, \ldots, 0, 1, 0, \ldots, 0)$, where the solitary 1 lies exactly at the middle of the vector a_0 (i.e. at position $(\frac{N}{2}+1)$). Figure 5 shows the distributions $a_{100}, a_{200}, a_{300}, a_{400}$ and a_{500}.

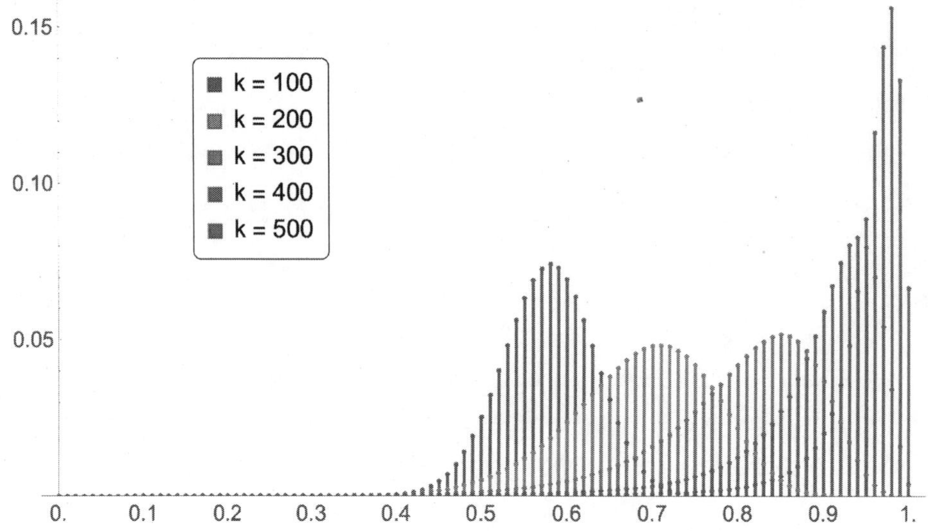

Figure 5. Probability mass function of X_k at different ticks. Number of agents $N = 100$. Initial conditions $X_0 = 0.5$.

To produce figure 5, we have computed the transition matrix with the previous *Mathematica*® script (having previously set the number of agents to 100) and then we have run the following two lines:

```
a0 = UnitVector[n + 1, 1 + n/2];
ListPlot[Table[a0.MatrixPower[N@P, i], {i, 100, 500, 100}], PlotRange -> All]
```

Looking at the probability distribution of X_{500}, it is clear that, after 500 revisions, the evolutionary process is very likely to be at a state where most of the population is using strategy 1. There is even a substantial probability (~6.66%) that the process will have reached the absorbing state where everyone in the population is using strategy 1. Note, however, that all the probability distributions shown in figure 5 have full support, i.e. the probability of reaching the absorbing state where no one uses strategy 1 after 100, 200, 300, 400 or 500 is very small, but strictly positive. As a matter of fact, it is not difficult to see that, given that $N = 100$ and $X_0 = 0.5$ (i.e. initially there are 50 agents using strategy 1), $a_k(0) = \mathbb{P}(X_k = 0 \,|\, X_0 = 0.5) > 0$ for any $k \geq 50$.

Finally, to illustrate the sensitivity of transient dynamics to initial conditions, we replicate the computations shown in figure 5, but with initial conditions $X_0 = 0.4$ (figure 6) and $X_0 = 0.3$ (figure 7).

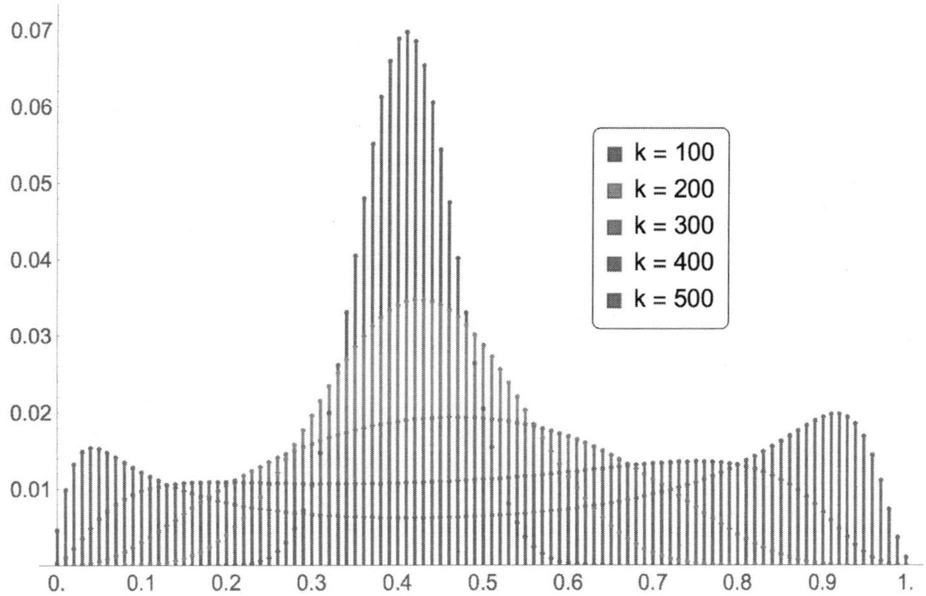

Figure 6. Probability mass function of X_k *at different ticks. Number of agents* $N = 100$. *Initial conditions* $X_0 = 0.4$.

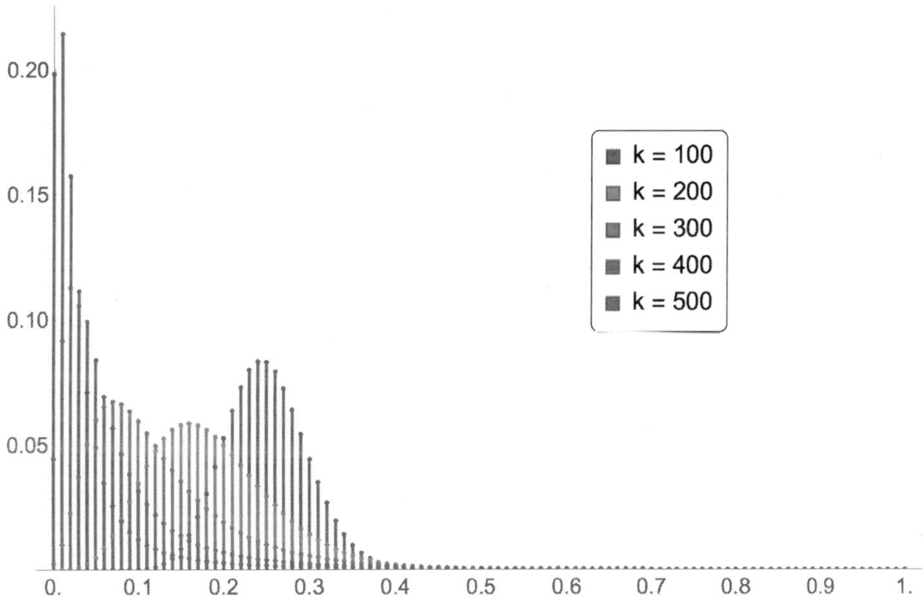

Figure 7. Probability mass function of X_k *at different ticks. Number of agents* $N = 100$. *Initial conditions* $X_0 = 0.3$.

Besides the probability distribution of X_k at a certain $k \geq 0$, we can analyze many other interesting properties of a Markov chain, such as the expected hitting time (or first passage time) of a certain state $i \in S$, which is the expected time at which the process first reaches state i. For general Markov chains, this type of results can be found in any of the references mentioned at the beginning of section 3. For birth-death chains specifically, Sandholm (2010, section 11.A.3) provides simple formulas to compute expected hitting times and hitting probabilities (i.e. the probability that the birth-death chain reaches state i before state j).

3.1.3. Infinite-horizon behavior

In this section we wish to study the infinite-horizon behavior of our evolutionary process, i.e. the distribution of X_k when the number of ticks k tends to infinity. This behavior generally depends on initial conditions, but we focus here on a specific type of Markov chain –i.e. irreducible and aperiodic– whose limiting behavior does not depend on initial conditions. To understand the concepts of irreducibility and aperiodicity, we recomend you read any of the references on Markov chains provided at the beginning of section 3. Here we just provide sufficient conditions that guarantee that a (time-homogeneous) Markov chain is irreducible and aperiodic:

Sufficient conditions for irreducibility and aperiodicity of time-homogeneous Markov chains

- If it is possible to go from any state to any other state in one single step ($P_{ij} > 0$ for all $i \neq j$) and there are more than 2 states, then the Markov chain is irreducible and aperiodic.
- If it is possible to go from any state to any other state in a finite number of steps, and there is at least one state in which the system may stay for two consecutive steps ($P_{ii} > 0$ for some i), then the Markov chain is irreducible and aperiodic.
- If there exists a positive integer m such that $(P^m)_{ij} > 0$ for all i and j, then the Markov chain is irreducible and aperiodic.

If one sees the transition diagram of a Markov chain (see e.g. Figure 4 above) as a directed graph (or network), the conditions above can be rewritten as:

- The network contains more than two nodes and there is a directed link from every node to every other node.
- The network is strongly connected and there is at least one loop.
- There exists a positive integer m such that there is at least one walk of length m from any node to every node (including itself).

The 2-strategy evolutionary process we are studying in this section is not necessarily irreducible if there is no noise. For instance, the coordination game played by imitate-the-better-realization agents analyzed in section 3.1.2 is not irreducible. That model will eventually reach one of the two absorbing states where all the agents are using the same strategy, and stay in that state forever. The probability of ending up in one or the other absorbing state depends on initial conditions (see Figure 8).[7]

7. These probabilities are sometimes called "fixation probabilities".

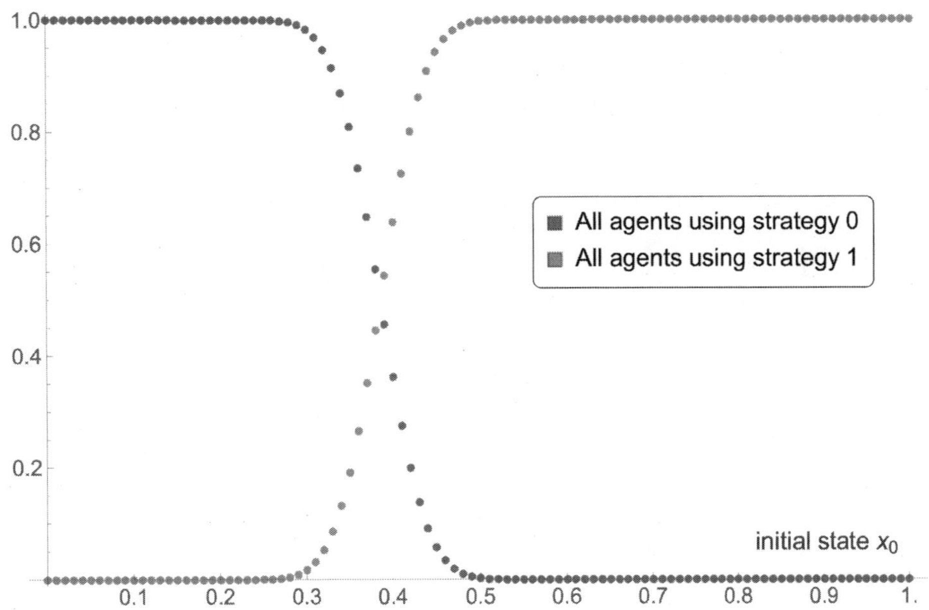

Figure 8. Probability of ending up in each of the two absorbing states for different initial states x_0, in the coordination game [[1 0][0 2]] played by $N = 100$ imitate-if-better agents.

However, if we add noise in the agents' revision protocol –so there is always the possibility that revising agents choose any strategy–, then it is easy to see that the second sufficient condition for irreducibility and aperiodicity above is fulfilled.[8]

Generally, in irreducible and aperiodic Markov chains $\{X_k\}$ with state space S (henceforth IAMCs), the probability mass function of X_k approaches a limit as k tends to infinity. This limit is called the limiting distribution, and is denoted here by μ, a vector with components $\mu(i)$ which denote the probability of finding the system in state $i \in S$ in the long run. Formally, in IAMCs the following limit exists and is unique (i.e. independent of initial conditions):

$$\lim_{k \to \infty} \mathbb{P}(X_k = i) = \mu(i) > 0 \text{ for all } i \in S.$$

Thus, in IAMCs the probability of finding the system in each of its states in the long run is strictly positive and independent of initial conditions. Importantly, in IAMCs the limiting distribution μ coincides with the occupancy distribution μ^*, which is the long-run fraction of the time that the IAMC spends in each state.[9] This means that we can estimate the limiting distribution μ of a IAMC using the computer simulation approach by running just one simulation for long enough (which enables us to estimate μ^*).

---

8. In terms of the transition probabilities $p(x)$ and $q(x)$, adding noise implies that $p(x) > 0$ for $x < 1$ (i.e. you can always move one step to the right unless x already equals 1), $q(x) > 0$ for $x > 0$ (i.e. you can always move one step to the left unless x already equals 0) and $p(x) + q(x) < 1$ for all $x \in [0, 1]$ (i.e. you can always stay where you are).
9. Formally, the occupancy of state i is defined as:

$$\mu^*(i) = \lim_{k \to \infty} \frac{\mathbb{E}(N_i(k))}{k+1}$$

where $N_i(k)$ denotes the number of times that the Markov chain visits state i over the time span $\{0, 1, \ldots, k\}$.

In any IAMC, the limiting distribution μ can be computed as the left eigenvector of the transition matrix P corresponding to eigenvalue 1.[10] Note, however, that computing eigenvectors is computationally demanding when the state space is large. Fortunately, for irreducible and aperiodic birth-death chains (such as our 2-strategy evolutionary process with noise), there is an analytic formula for the limiting distribution that is easy to evaluate:[11]

$$\mu(i) = \mu(0) \prod_{j=1}^{Ni} \frac{p(\frac{j-1}{N})}{q(\frac{j}{N})} \quad \text{for } i \in \{0, \frac{1}{N}, \ldots, 1\}$$

where the value of $\mu(0) = \left(\sum_{h=0}^{N} \prod_{j=1}^{h} \frac{p(\frac{j-1}{N})}{q(\frac{j}{N})} \right)^{-1}$ is derived by imposing that the elements of μ must add up to 1. This formula can be easily implemented in *Mathematica*®:

```
μ = Normalize[FoldList[Times, 1, Table[p[(j-1)/n]/q[j/n],{j, n}]], Total]
```

Note that the formula above is only valid for irreducible and aperiodic birth-death chains. An example of such a chain would be the model where a number of imitate-the-better-realization agents are playing the coordination game [[1 0][0 2]] with noise. Thus, for this model we can easily analyze the impact of noise on the limiting distribution. Figure 9 illustrates this dependency.

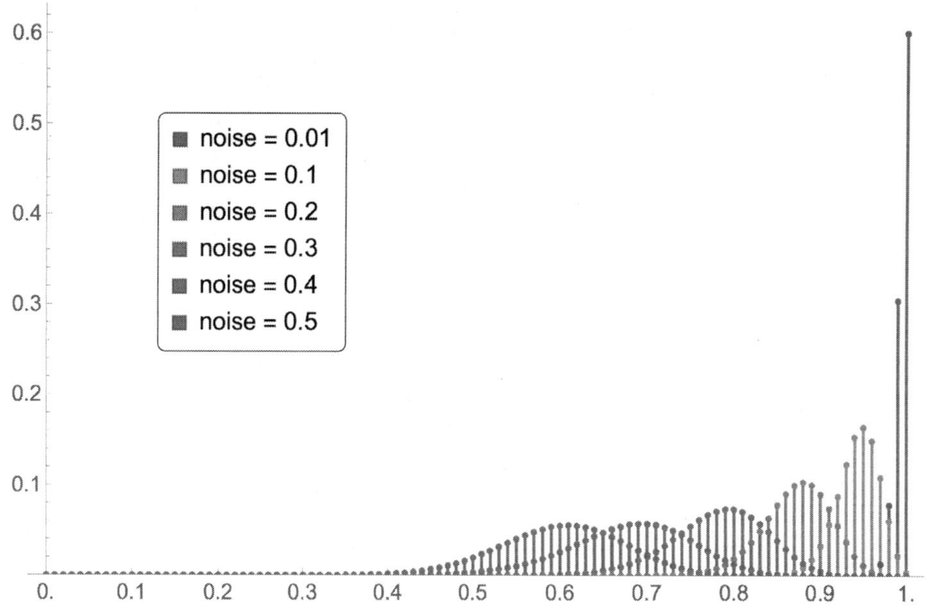

Figure 9. Limiting distribution μ for different values of noise in the coordination game [[1 0][0 2]] played by $N = 100$ imitate-the-better-realization agents.

---

10. The second-largest eigenvalue modulus of the transition matrix P determines the rate of convergence to the limiting distribution.
11. For the derivation of this formula, see e.g. Sandholm (2010, example 11.A.10, p. 443).

Figure 9 has been created by running the following *Mathematica*® script:

```
n = 100;

p[x_, noise_]:= (1-x)((1-noise)(x n/(n-1))((x n - 1)/(n-1)) + noise/2)
q[x_, noise_]:= x((1-noise)(((1-x)n)/(n-1))^2 ((1-x)n-1)/(n-1) + noise/2)

μs = Map[Normalize[
          FoldList[Times, 1, Table[p[(j-1)/n, #] / q[j/n, #], {j, n}]]
        , Total]&, {0.01, 0.1, 0.2, 0.3, 0.4, 0.5}];

ListPlot[μs, DataRange->{0, 1}, PlotRange->{0, All}, Filling -> Axis]
```

The limiting distribution of birth-death chains can be further characterized using results in Sandholm (2007).

3.2. Approximation results

In many models, a full Markov analysis cannot be conducted because the exact formulas are too complicated or because they may be too computationally expensive to evaluate. In such cases, we can still apply a variety of approximation results. This section introduces some of them.

3.2.1. Deterministic approximations of transient dynamics when the population is large. The mean dynamic

When the number of agents is sufficiently large, the mean dynamic of the process provides a good deterministic approximation to the dynamics of the stochastic evolutionary process over finite time spans. In this section we are going to analyze the behavior of our evolutionary process as the population size N becomes large, so we make this dependency on N explicit by using superscripts for X_k^N, $p^N(x)$ and $q^N(x)$.

Let us start by illustrating the essence of the mean dynamic approximation with our running example where N imitate-the-better-realization agents are playing the coordination game [[1 0][0 2]] without noise. Initially, half the agents are playing strategy 1 (i.e. $X_0^N = 0.5$). Figures 10, 11 and 12 show the expected proportion of 1-strategists $\mathbb{E}(X_k^N \mid X_0^N = 0.5)$ against the number of revisions k (scaled by N), together with the 95% band for X_k^N, for different population sizes.[12] Figure 10 shows the transient dynamics for $N = 100$, figure 11 for $N = 1000$ and figure 12 for $N = 10000$. These figures show exact results, computed as explained in section 3.1.2.

12. For each value of k, the band is defined by the smallest interval $\{i, j\}$ that leaves less than 2.5% probability at both sides, i.e. $\mathbb{P}(X_k^N < i \mid X_0^N = 0.5) < 0.025$ and $\mathbb{P}(X_k > j \mid X_0^N = 0.5) < 0.025$, with $i, j \in S^N$.

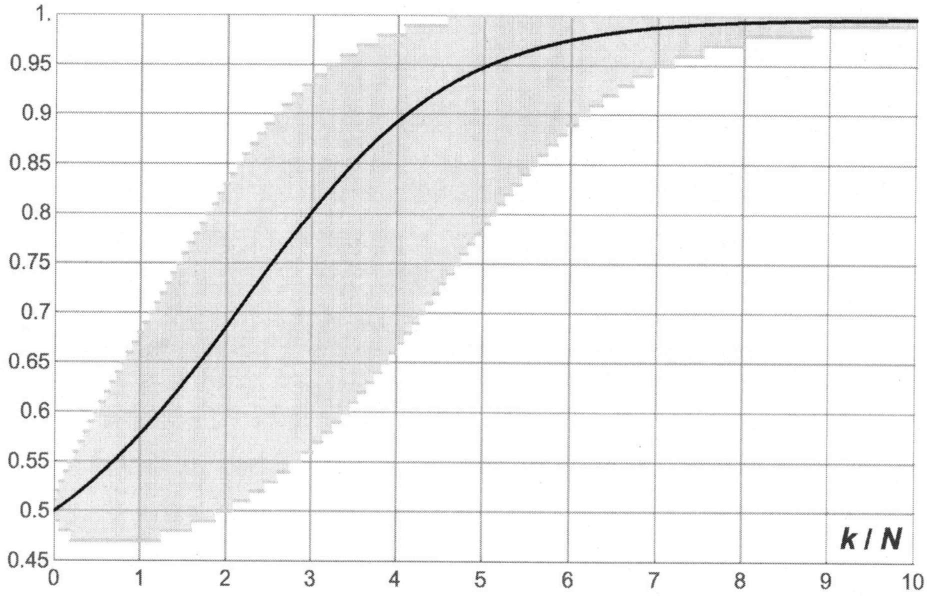

Figure 10. Expected proportion of agents playing strategy 1 and its 95% band (in yellow). Model: coordination game [[1 0][0 2]] played by $N = 100$ imitate-the-better-realization agents. Initially, half the population is using strategy 1.

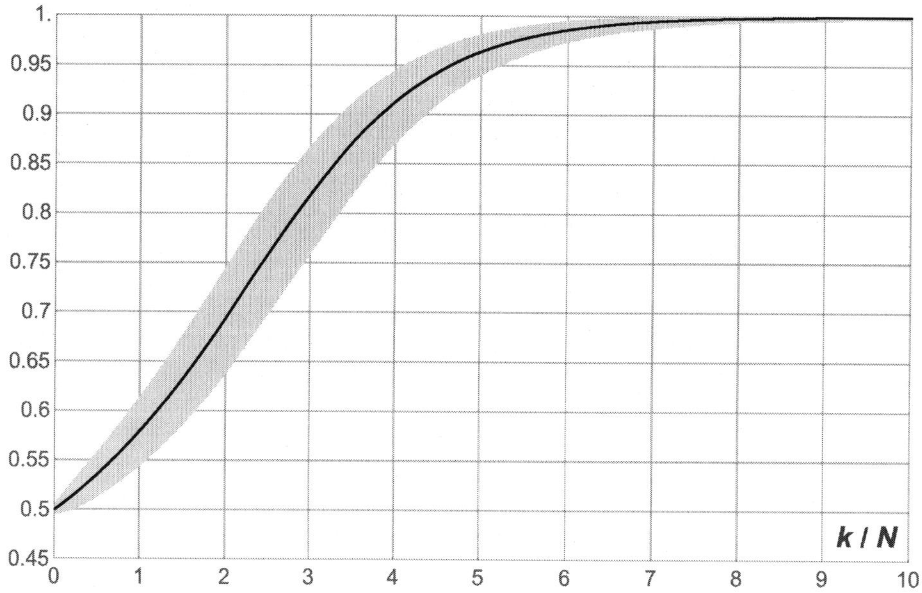

Figure 11. Expected proportion of agents playing strategy 1 and its 95% band (in yellow). Model: coordination game [[1 0][0 2]] played by $N = 1000$ imitate-the-better-realization agents. Initially, half the population is using strategy 1.

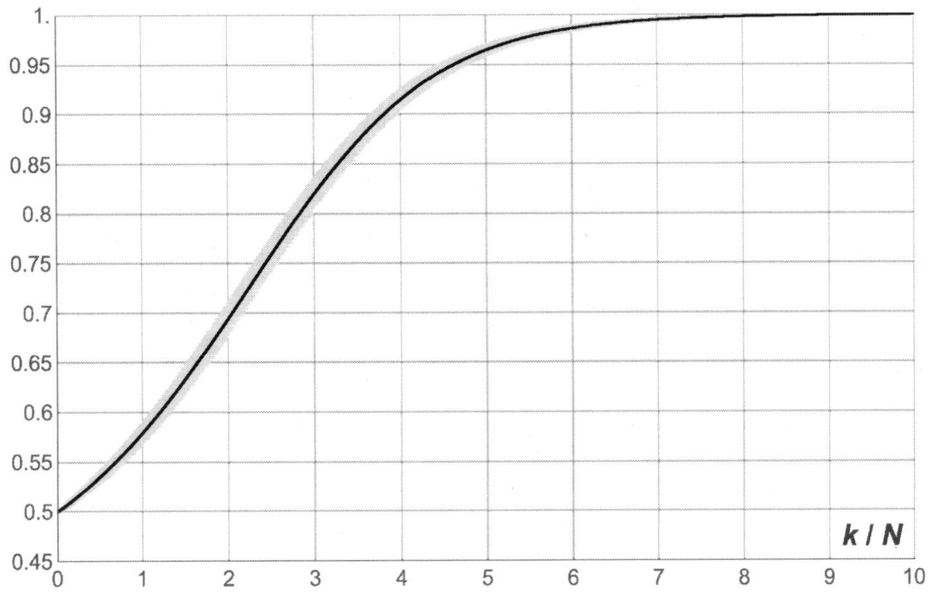

Figure 12. Expected proportion of agents playing strategy 1 and its 95% band (in yellow). Model: coordination game [[1 0][0 2]] played by $N = 10000$ imitate-the-better-realization agents. Initially, half the population is using strategy 1.

Looking at figures 10, 11 and 12 it is clear that, as the number of agents N gets larger, the stochastc evolutionary process $\{X_k^N\}$ gets closer and closer to its expected motion. The intuition is that, as the number of agents gets large, the fluctuations of the evolutionary process around its expected motion tend to average out. In the limit when N goes to infinity, the stochastic evolutionary process is very likely to behave in a nearly deterministic way, mirroring a solution trajectory of a certain ordinary differential equation called the *mean dynamic*.

To derive the mean dynamic of our 2-strategy evolutionary process, we consider the behavior of the process $\{X_k^N\}$ over the next dt time units, departing from state x. We define one unit of clock time as N ticks, i.e. the time over which every agent is expected to receive exactly one revision opportunity. Thus, over the time interval dt, the number of agents who are expected to receive a revision opportunity is Ndt. Of these Ndt agents who revise their strategies, $p^N(x)Ndt$ are expected to switch from strategy 0 to strategy 1 and $q^N(x)Ndt$ are expected to switch from strategy 1 to strategy 0. Hence, the expected change in the number of agents that are using strategy 1 over the time interval dt is $(p^N(x) - q^N(x))Ndt$. Therefore, the expected change in the proportion of agents using strategy 1, i.e. the expected change in state at x, is

$$dx = \frac{1}{N}(p^N(x) - q^N(x))Ndt = (p^N(x) - q^N(x))dt$$

Note that the transition probabilities $p^N(x)$ and $q^N(x)$ may depend on N. This does not represent a problem as long as this dependency vanishes as N gets large. In that case, to deal with that dependency, we take the limit of $p^N(x)$ and $q^N(x)$ as N goes to infinity since, after all, the mean dynamic approximation is only valid for large N. Thus, defining

$$p^\infty(x) = \lim_{N\to\infty} p^N(x)$$

and

$$q^{\infty}(x) = \lim_{N\to\infty} q^N(x)$$

we arrive at the mean dynamic equation:

$$\tfrac{d}{dt}x = \dot{x} = p^{\infty}(x) - q^{\infty}(x)$$

As an illustration of the usefulness of the mean dynamic to approximate transient dynamics, consider the simulations of the coordination game example presented in section 2. We already computed the transition probabilities $p^N(x)$ and $q^N(x)$ for this model in section 3.1.1:

$$p^N(x) = (1-x)\tfrac{xN}{N-1}\tfrac{xN-1}{N-1}$$

$$q^N(x) = x\tfrac{(1-x)N}{N-1}\tfrac{(1-x)N}{N-1}\tfrac{(1-x)N-1}{N-1}$$

Thus, the mean dynamic reads:

$$\dot{x} = p^{\infty}(x) - q^{\infty}(x) = (1-x)x^2 - x(1-x)^3 = x(x-1)\left(x^2 - 3x + 1\right)$$

where x stands for the fraction of 1-strategists. The solution of the mean dynamic with initial condition $x_0 = 0.5$ is shown in figure 13 below. It is clear that the mean dynamic provides a remarkably good approximation to the average transient dynamics plotted in figures 1 and 3.[13] And, as we have seen, the greater the number of agents, the closer the stochastic process will get to its expeted motion.

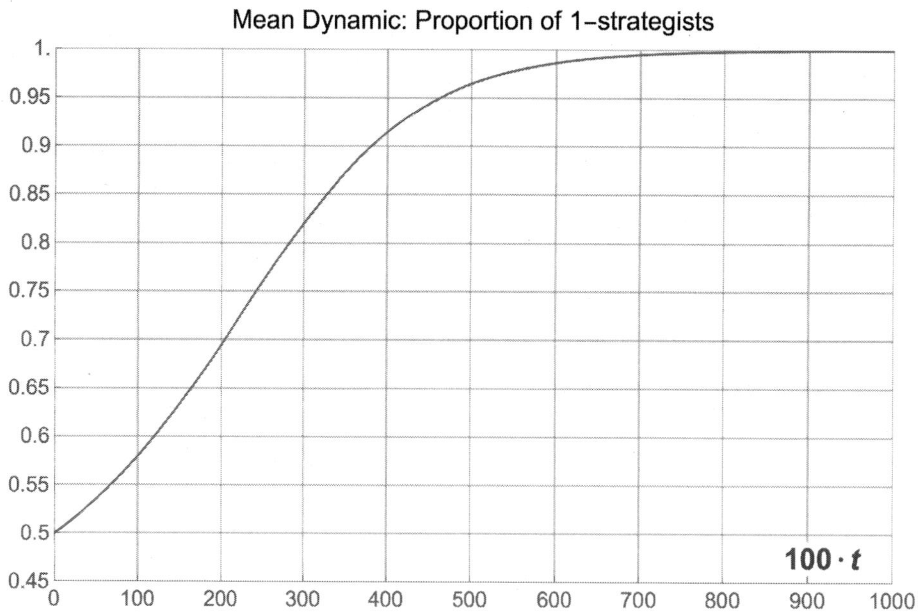

Figure 13. Trajectory of the mean dynamic of the example in section 2, showing the proportion of 1-strategists as a function of time (rescaled to match figures 1 and 3).

---

13. Note that one unit of clock time in the mean dynamic is defined in such a way that each player expects to receive one revision opportunity per unit of clock time. In the model simulated in section 2, *prob-revision* = 0.01, so one unit of clock time corresponds to 100 ticks (i.e. 1 / *prob-revision*).

Naturally, the mean dynamic can be solved for many different initial conditions, providing an overall picture of the transient dynamics of the model when the population is large. Figure 14 below shows an illustration, created with the following *Mathematica*® code:

```
Plot[
 Evaluate[
  Table[
   NDSolveValue[{x'[t] == x[t] (x[t] - 1) (x[t]^2 - 3 x[t] + 1),
      x[0] == x0}, x, {t, 0, 10}][ticks/100]
   , {x0, 0, 1, 0.01}]
 ], {ticks, 0, 1000}]
```

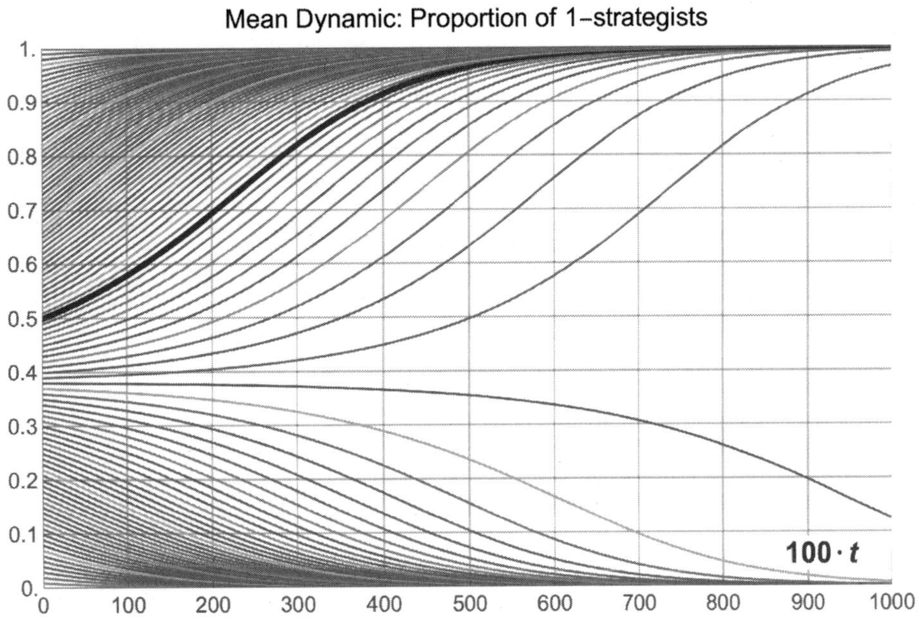

Figure 14. Trajectories of the mean dynamic of the example in section 2, showing the proportion of 1-strategists as a function of time (rescaled to match figures 1 and 3) for different initial conditions.

The cut-off point that separates the set of trajectories that go towards state $x = 1$ from those that will end up in state $x = 0$ is easy to derive, by finding the rest points of the mean dynamic:

$$\dot{x} = 0 = x(x - 1)\left(x^2 - 3x + 1\right)$$

The three solutions in the interval $[0, 1]$ are $x = 0$, $x = 1$ and $x = \frac{1}{2}\left(3 - \sqrt{5}\right) \approx 0.382$.

In this section we have derived the mean dynamic for our 2-strategy evolutionary process where agents switch strategies sequentially. Note, however, that the mean dynamic approximation is valid for games with any number of strategies and even for models where several revisions take place simultaneously (as long as the number of revisions is fixed as N goes to infinity or the probability of revision is $O(\frac{1}{N})$).

It is also important to note that, even though here we have presented the mean dynamic approximation in informal terms, the link between the stochastic process and its relevant mean dynamic rests on solid theoretical grounds (see Benaïm & Weibull (2003), Sandholm (2010, chapter 10) and Roth & Sandholm (2013)).

Finally, to compare agent-based simulations of the imitate-the-better-realization rule and its mean dynamics in 2×2 symmetric games, you may want to play with the purpose-built demonstration titled Expected Dynamics of an Imitation Model in 2×2 Symmetric Games. And to solve the mean dynamic of the imitate-the-better-realization rule in 3-strategy games, you may want to use this demonstration.

3.2.2. Diffusion approximations to characterize dynamics around equilibria

"Equilibria" in finite population dynamics are often defined as states where the expected motion of the (stochastic) process is zero. Formally, these equilibria correspond to the rest points of the mean dynamic of the original stochastic process. At some such equilibria, agents do not switch strategies anymore. Examples of such static equilibria would be the states where all agents are using the same strategy under the imitate-the-better-realization protocol. However, at some other equilibria, the expected flows of agents switching between different strategies cancel one another out (so the expected motion is indeed zero), but agents keep revising and changing strategies, potentially in a stochastic fashion. To characterize the dynamics around this second type of "equilibria", which are most often interior, the diffusion approximation is particularly useful.

As an example, consider a Hawk-Dove game with payoffs [[2 1][3 0]] and the imitate-the-better-realization revision rule without noise. The mean dynamic of this model is:

$$\dot{x} = x(1-x)(1-2x)$$

where x stands for the fraction of 1-strategists, i.e. "Hawk" agents.[14] Solving the mean dynamic reveals that most large-population simulations starting with at least one "Hawk" and at least one "Dove" will tend to approach the state where half the population play "Hawk" and the other play "Dove", and stay around there for long. Figure 15 below shows several trajectories for different initial conditions.

14. For details, see Izquierdo and Izquierdo (2013) and Loginov (2019).

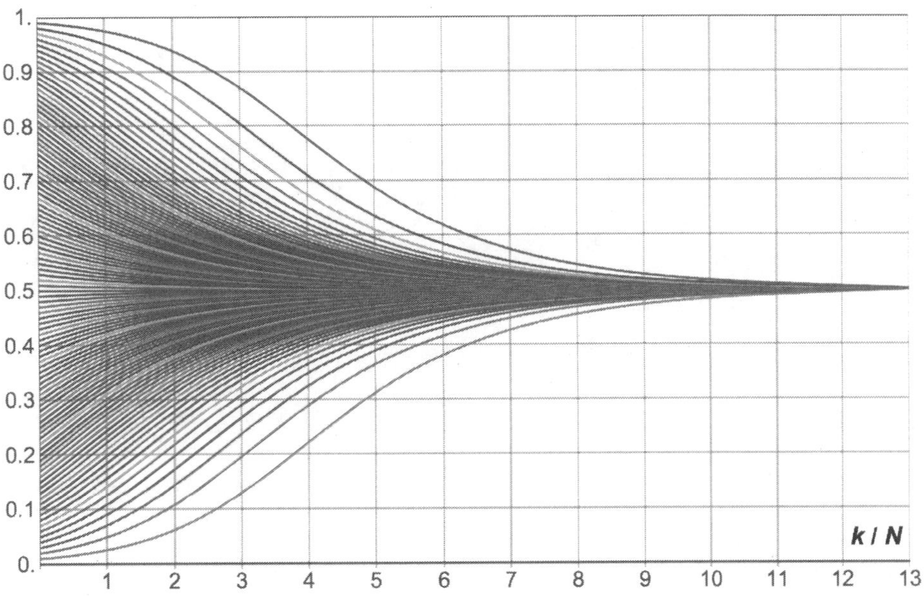

Figure 15. Trajectories of the mean dynamic of an imitate-the-better-realization Hawk-Dove game, showing the proportion of "Hawks" as a function of time for different initial conditions. One unit of time corresponds to N revisions.

Naturally, simulations do not get stuck in the half-and-half state, since agents keep revising their strategy in a stochastic fashion (see figure 16). To understand this stochastic flow of agents between strategies near equilibria, it is necessary to go beyond the mean dynamic. Sandholm (2003) shows that –under rather general conditions– stochastic finite-population dynamics near rest points can be approximated by a diffusion process, as long as the population size N is large enough. He also shows that the standard deviations of the limit distribution are of order $\frac{1}{\sqrt{N}}$.

To illustrate this order $\frac{1}{\sqrt{N}}$, we set up one simulation run starting with 10 agents playing "Hawk" and 10 agents playing "Dove". This state constitutes a so-called "Equilibrium", since the expected change in the strategy distribution is zero. However, the stochasticity in the revision protocol and in the matching process imply that the strategy distribution is in perpetual change. In the simulation shown in figure 16, we modify the number of players at runtime. At tick 10000, we increase the number of players by a factor of 10 up to 200 and, after 10000 more ticks, we set *n-of-players* to 2000 (i.e., a factor of 10, again). The standard deviation of the fraction of players using strategy "Hawk" (or "Dove") during each of the three stages in our simulation run was: 0.1082, 0.0444 and 0.01167 respectively. As expected, these numbers are related by a factor of approximately $\frac{1}{\sqrt{10}}$.

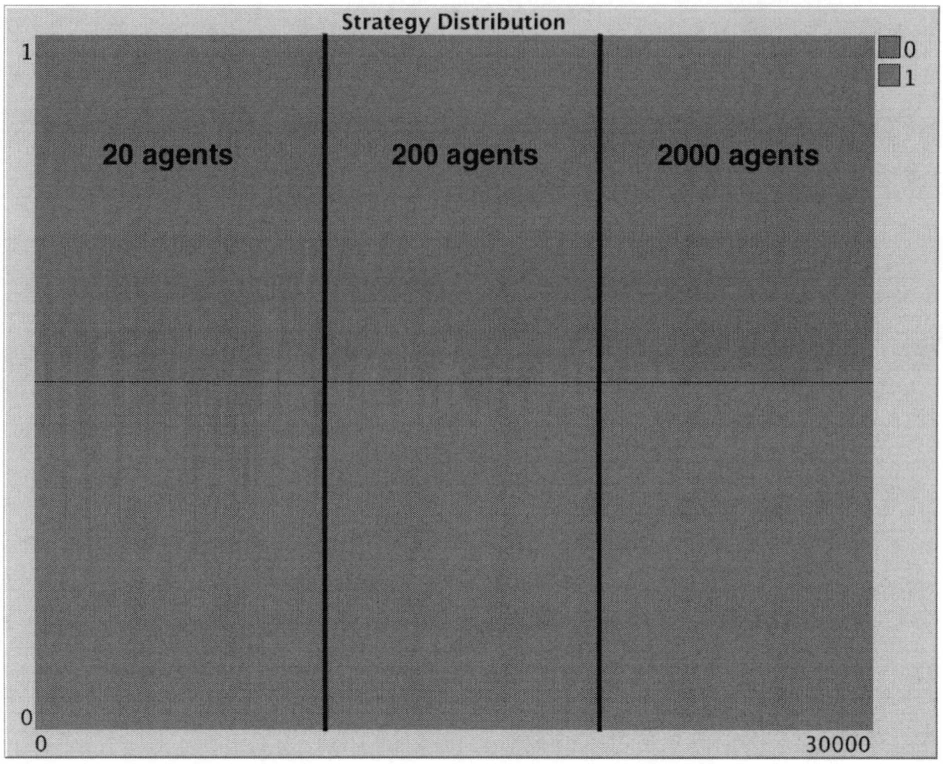

Figure 16. A simulation run of an imitate-the-better-realization Hawk-Dove game, set up with 20 agents during the first 10000 ticks, then 200 agents during the following 10000 ticks, and finally 2000 agents during the last 10000 ticks. Payoffs: [[2 1][3 0]]; prob-revision: 0.01; noise 0; initial conditions [10 10].

As a matter of fact, Izquierdo et al. (2019, example 3.1) use the diffusion approximation to show that in the large N limit, fluctuations of this process around its unique interior rest point $x = \frac{1}{2}$ are approximately Gaussian with standard deviation $\frac{1}{2\sqrt{N}}$.

3.2.3. Stochastic stability analyses

In the last model we have implemented in this chapter, if *noise* is strictly positive, the model's infinite-horizon behavior is characterized by a unique stationary distribution regardless of initial conditions (see section 3.1 above). This distribution has full support (i.e. all states will be visited infinitely often) but, naturally, the system will spend much longer in certain areas of the state space than in others. If the noise is sufficiently small (but strictly positive), the infinite-horizon distribution of the Markov chain tends to concentrate most of its mass on just a few states. Stochastic stability analyses are devoted to identifying such states, which are often called *stochastically stable states* (Foster and Young, 1990), and are a subset of the absorbing states of the process without noise.[15]

To learn about this type of analysis, the following references are particularly useful: Vega-Redondo (2003, section 12.6), Fudenberg and Imhof (2008), Sandholm (2010, chapters 11 and 12) and Wallace and Young (2015).

15. There are a number of different definitions of stochastic stability, depending on which limits are taken and in what order. For a discussion of different definitions, see Sandholm (2010, chapter 12).

To illustrate the applicability of stochastic stability analyses, consider our imitate-the-better-realization model where agents play the Hawk-Dove game analyzed in section 3.2.2 with some strictly positive *noise*. It can be proved that the only stochastically stable state in this model is the state where everyone chooses strategy Hawk.[16] This means that, given a certain population size, as *noise* tends to 0, the infinite-horizon dynamics of the model will concentrate on that single state.

An important concern in stochastic stability analyses is the time one has to wait until the prediction of the analysis becomes relevant. This time can be astronomically long, as the following example illustrates.

3.2.4 A final example

> A fundamental feature of these models, but all too often ignored in applications, is that the asymptotic behavior of the short-run deterministic approximation need have no connection to the asymptotic behavior of the stochastic population process. Blume (1997, p. 443)

Consider the Hawk-Dove game analyzed in section 3.2.2, played by $N = 30$ imitate-the-better-realization agents with noise = 10^{-10}, departing from an initial state where 28 agents are playing Hawk. Even though the population size is too modest for the mean dynamic and the diffusion approximations to be accurate, this example will clarify the different time scales at which each of the approximations is useful.

Let us review what we can say about this model using the three approximations discussed in the previous sections:

- **Mean dynamic.** Figure 15 shows the mean dynamic of this model without noise. The noise we are considering here is so small that the mean dynamic looks the same in the time interval shown in figure 15.[17] So, in our model with small noise, for large N, the process will tend to move towards state $x = 0.5$, a journey that will take about $13N$ revisions for our initial conditions $X_0 = \frac{28}{30} \approx 0.93$. The greater the N, the closer the stochastic process will be to the solution trajectory of its mean dynamic.
- **Diffusion approximation.** Once in the vicinity of the unique interior rest point $x = 0.5$, the diffusion approximation tells us that –for large N– the dynamics are well approximated by a Gaussian distribution with standard deviation $\frac{1}{2\sqrt{N}}$.

---

16. To be precise, here we are considering stochastic stability *in the small noise limit*, where we fix the population size and take the limit of *noise* to zero (Sandholm, 2010, section 12.1.1). The proof can be conducted using the concepts and theorems put forward by Ellison (2000). Note that the radius of the state where everyone plays Hawk is 2 (i.e. 2 mutations are needed to leave its basin of attraction), while its coradius is just 1 (one mutation is enough to go from the state where everyone plays Dove to the state where everyone plays Hawk).
17. The only difference is that, in the model with noise, the two trajectories starting at the monomorphic states eventually converge to the state $x = 0.5$, but this convergence cannot be appreciated in the time interval shown in figure 15.

- **Stochastic stability**. Finally, we also know that, for a level of noise low enough (but strictly positive), the limiting distribution is going to place most of its mass on the unique stochastically stable state, which is $x = 1$. So, *eventually*, the dynamics will approach its limiting distribution, which –assuming the noise is low enough– places most of its mass on the monomorphic state $x = 1$.[18]

Each of these approximations refers to a different time scale. In this regard, we find the classification made by Binmore and Samuelson (1994) and Binmore et al. (1995) very useful (see also Samuelson (1997) and Young (1998)). These authors distinguish between the short run, the medium run, the long run and the ultralong run:

> By the short run, we refer to the initial conditions that prevail when one begins one's observation or analysis. By the ultralong run, we mean a period of time long enough for the asymptotic distribution to be a good description of the behavior of the system. The long run refers to the time span needed for the system to reach the vicinity of the first equilibrium in whose neighborhood it will linger for some time. We speak of the medium run as the time intermediate between the short run *[i.e. initial conditions]* and the long run, during which the adjustment to equilibrium is occurring. Binmore et al. (1995, p. 10)

Let us see these different time scales in our Hawk-Dove example. The following video shows the exact transient dynamics of this model, computed as explained in section 3.1.2. Note that the video shows all the revisions up until $k = 400$, but then it moves faster and faster. The blue progress bar indicates the number of revisions already shown.

A video element has been excluded from this version of the text. You can watch it online here: https://wisc.pb.unizin.org/agent-based-evolutionary-game-dynamics/?p=105

Transient dynamics of a model where $N = 30$ imitate-the-better-realization agents are playing a Hawk-Dove game, with noise=10^{-10}. Each iteration corresponds to one revision.

In the video we can distinguish the different time scales:

- The short run, which is determined by the initial conditions $X_0 = \frac{28}{30} \approx 0.93$.
- The medium run, which in this case spans roughly from $k = 0$ to $k \approx 13N = 390$. The dynamics of this adjustment process towards the equilibrium $x = 0.5$ can be characterized by the mean dynamic, especially for large N.
- The long run, which in this case refers to the dynamics around the equilibrium $x = 0.5$, spanning roughly from $k \approx 13N = 390$ to $k \approx 10^7$. These dynamics are well described by

18. Using the analytic formula for the limiting distribution of irreducible and aperiodic birth-death chains provided in section 3.1.3, we have checked that $\mu(1) > 0.9$ for $N = 30$ and noise = 10^{-10}.

the diffusion approximation, especially for large N.

- The ultra long run, which in this case is not really reached until $k \gtrsim 10^{10}$. It is not until then that the limiting distribution becomes a good description of the dynamics of the model.

It is remarkable how long it takes for the infinite horizon prediction to hold force. Furthermore, the wait grows sharply as N increases and also as the level of noise decreases.[19] These long waiting times are typical of stochastic stability analyses, so care must be taken when applying the conclusions of these analyses to real world settings.

In summary, as N grows, both the mean dynamic and the difussion approximations become better. For any fixed N, eventually, the behavior of the process will be well described by its limiting distribution. If the noise is low enough (but strictly positive), the limiting distribution will place most of its mass on the unique stochastically stable state $x = 1$. But note that, as N grows, it will take exponentially longer for the infinite-horizon prediction to kick in (see Sandholm and Staudigl (2018)).

Note also that for the limiting distribution to place most of its mass on the stochastically stable state, the level of noise has to be sufficiently low, and if the population size N increases, the maximum level of noise at which the limiting distribution concentrates most of its mass on the stochastically stable state decreases. As an example, consider the same setting as the one shown in the video, but with $N = 50$. In this case, the limiting distribution is completely different (see figure 17). A noise level of 10^{-10} is not enough for the limiting distribution to place most of its mass on the stochastically stable state when $N = 50$.

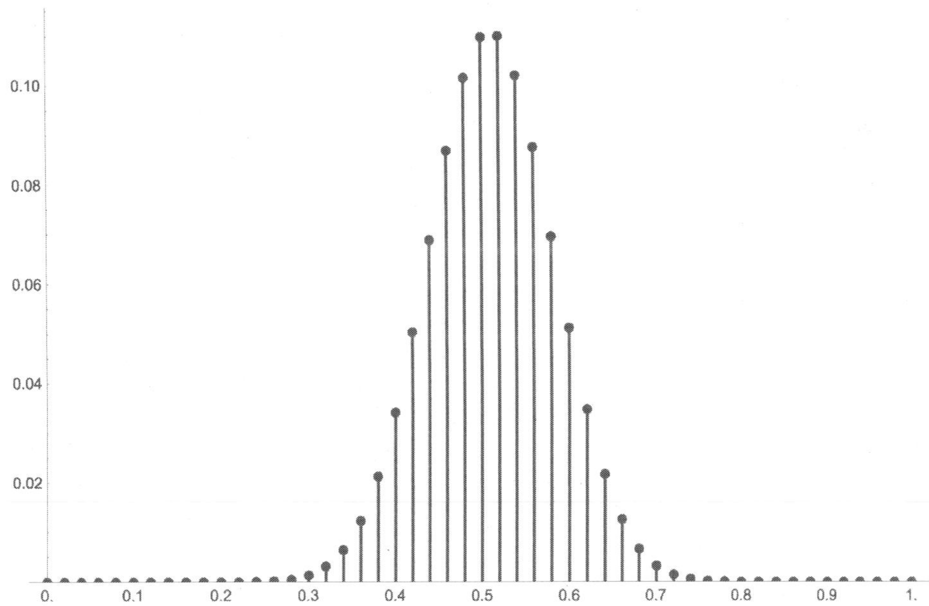

Figure 17. Limiting distribution of a model where $N = 50$ imitate-the-better-realization agents are playing a Hawk-Dove game, with noise = 10^{-10}.

19. Using tools from large deviations theory, Sandholm and Staudigl (2018) show that –for large population sizes N– the time required to reach the boundary is of an exponential order in N.

Figure 17 has been created by running the following *Mathematica*® script:

```
n = 50;
noise = 10.^-10;

p[x_, noise_] := (1-x)((1-noise)* ((x n)/(n-1))((1-x)n/(n-1)) + noise/2)
q[x_, noise_] := x((1-noise)(((1-x)n)/(n-1))(x n - 1)/(n-1) + noise/2)

μ = Normalize[
      FoldList[Times, 1, Table[p[(j-1)/n, noise] / q[j/n, noise], {j, n}]]
    , Total];

ListPlot[μ, DataRange->{0, 1}, PlotRange->{0, All}, Filling -> Axis]
```

4. Exercises

Exercise 1. Consider the evolutionary process analyzed in section 3.1.2. Figure 5 shows that, if we start with half the population using each strategy, the probability that the whole population will be using strategy 1 after 500 revisions is about 6.66%. Here we ask you to use the NetLogo model implemented in the previous section to estimate that probability. To do that, you will have to set up and run an experiment using BehaviorSpace.

Exercise 2. Derive the mean dynamic of a Prisoner's Dilemma game for the imitate-the-better-realization protocol.

Exercise 3. Derive the mean dynamic of the coordination game discussed in section 0.1 (with payoffs [[1 0][0 2]]) for the imitative pairwise-difference protocol.

Exercise 4. Derive the mean dynamic of the coordination game discussed in section 0.1 (with payoffs [[1 0][0 2]]) for the best experienced payoff protocol.

2. SPATIAL INTERACTIONS ON A GRID

2.0. Spatial chaos in the Prisoner's Dilemma

1. Goal

The goal of this chapter is to learn how to build agent-based models with *spatial structure*. In models with spatial structure, agents do not interact with all other agents with the same probability, but they interact preferentially with those who are nearby.[1]

More generally, populations where some pairs of agents are more likely to interact with each other than with others are called *structured* populations. This contrasts with the *random matching* models developed in the previous chapter, where all members of the population were equally likely to interact with each other.[2] The dynamics of an evolutionary process under random matching can be very different from the dynamics of the same process in a structured population. In social dilemmas in particular, population structure can play a crucial role (Gotts et al. (2003), Hauert (2002,[3] 2006), Roca et al. (2009a, 2009b)).[4]

2. Motivation. Cooperation in spatial settings

In the previous chapter, we saw that if agents play the Prisoner's Dilemma under random matching, defection prevails. Here we want to explore whether adding spatial structure may affect that observation. Could cooperation be sustained if we removed the unrealistic assumption that all members of the population are equally likely to interact with each other? To shed some light on this question, in this section we will implement a model analyzed by Nowak and May (1992, 1993).

3. Description of the model

In this model, there is a population of agents arranged on a 2-dimensional lattice of "patches". There is one agent in each patch. The size of the lattice, i.e. the number of patches in each of the two

---

1. Note that in most evolutionary models there are two types of neighborhoods for each individual agent A:
    - the set of agents with whom agent A plays the game, and
    - the set of agents that agent A may observe at the time of revising his strategy.

   Most often these two sets coincide for each individual agent, but that is not necessarily the case (see e.g. Ohtsuki et al. (2007a, b).
2. Populations where all members are equally likely to interact with each other are sometimes called *well-mixed populations*.
3. See Roca et al. (2009b) for an important and illuminating discussion of this paper.
4. Christoph Hauert has an excellent collection of interactive tutorials on this topic at his site EvoLudo (Hauert 2018).

dimensions, can be set by the user. Each patch has eight neighboring patches (i.e. the eight cells which surround it), except for the patches at the boundary, which have five neighbors if they are on a side, or three neighbors if they are at one of the four corners.

Agents repeatedly play a symmetric 2-player 2-strategy game, where the two possible strategies are labeled C (for Cooperate) and D (for Defect). The payoffs of the game are determined using four parameters: *CC-payoff*, *CD-payoff*, *DC-payoff*, and *DD-payoff*, where *XY-payoff* denotes the payoff obtained by an X-player who meets a Y-player.

The initial percentage of C-players in the population is *initial-%-of-C-players*, and they are randomly distributed in the grid. From then onwards, the following sequence of events –which defines a tick– is repeatedly executed:

1. Every agent plays the game with all his neighbors (once with each neighbor) and with himself (Moore neighborhood). The total payoff for the player is the sum of the payoffs in these encounters.
2. All agents *simultaneously* revise their strategy according to the **"imitate the best neighbor"** revision protocol, which reads as follows:

> Consider the set of all your neighbors plus yourself; then adopt the strategy of one of the agents in this set who has obtained the greatest payoff. If there is more than one agent with the greatest payoff, choose one of them at random to imitate.

CODE 4. Interface design

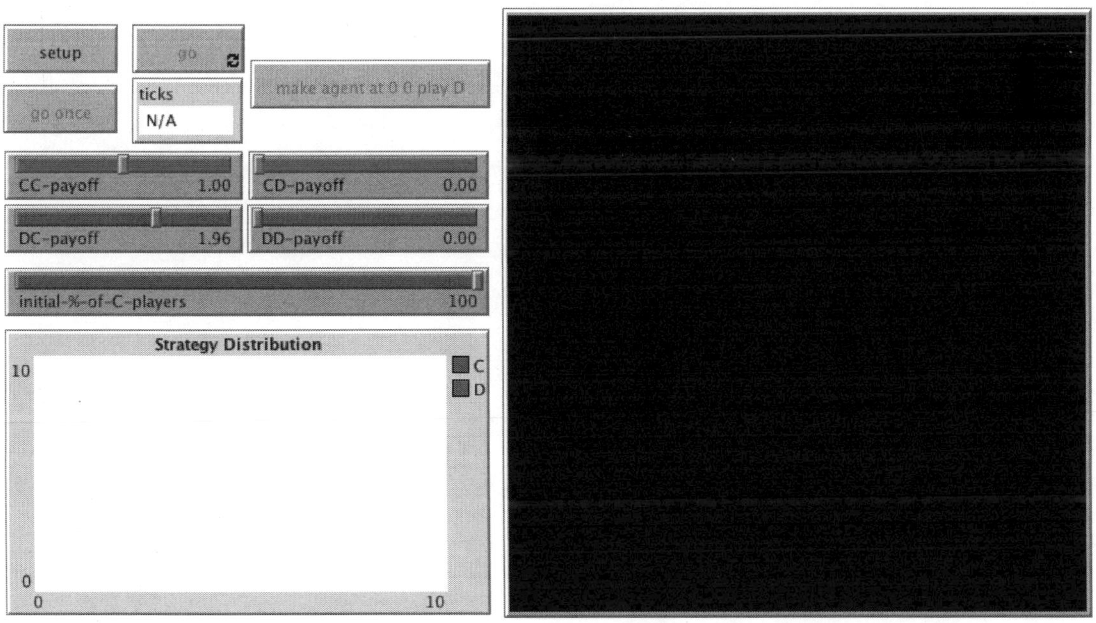

Figure 1. Interface design.

To define each agent's neighborhood, in this chapter we will use the 2-dimensional grid already built in NetLogo, often called "the world". This will make our code simpler and the visualizations nicer.

The interface (see figure 1 above) includes:

- The 2D view of the NetLogo world (i.e. the large black square in the interface), which is made up of patches. This view is already on the interface by default when creating a new NetLogo model.

> Choose the dimensions of the world by clicking on the "Settings…" button on the top bar, or by right-clicking on the 2D view and choosing *Edit*. A window will pop up, which allows you to choose the number of patches by setting the values of min-pxcor, max-pxcor, min-pycor and max-pycor. You can also determine the patches' size in pixels, and whether the grid wraps horizontally, vertically, both or none (see Topology section). You can choose these parameters as in figure 2 below:
>
> 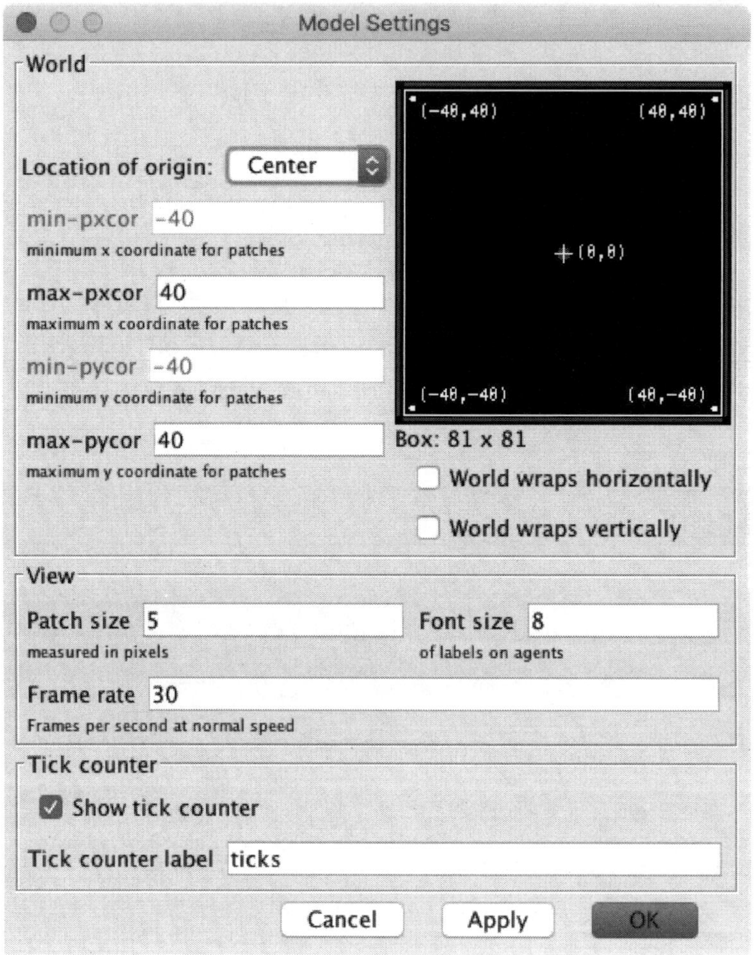
>
>
> *Figure 2. Model settings.*

- Three buttons:
  1. One button named setup, which runs the procedure to setup.
  2. One button named go once, which runs the procedure to go.
  3. One button named go, which runs the procedure to go indefinitely.

> In the Code tab, write the procedures to setup and to go, without including any code inside for now.

Then, create the buttons, just like we did in the previous chapter.

Note that the interface in figure 1 has an extra button labeled make agent at 0 0 play D. You may wish to include it now. The code that goes inside this button is proposed as Exercise 2.

- Four sliders, to choose the payoffs for each possible outcome (CC, CD, DC, DD).

Create the four sliders with global variable names *CC-payoff*, *CD-payoff*, *DC-payoff*, and *DD-payoff*. Remember to choose a range, an interval and a default value for each of them. You can choose minimum 0, maximum 2 and increment 0.01.

- A slider to let the user select the initial percentage of C-players.

Create a slider for global variable *initial-%-of-C-players*. You can choose limit values 0 (as the minimum) and 100 (as the maximum), and an increment of 1.

- A plot that will show the evolution of the number of agents playing each strategy.

Create a plot and name it Strategy Distribution.

CODE 5. Code

5.1. Skeleton of the code

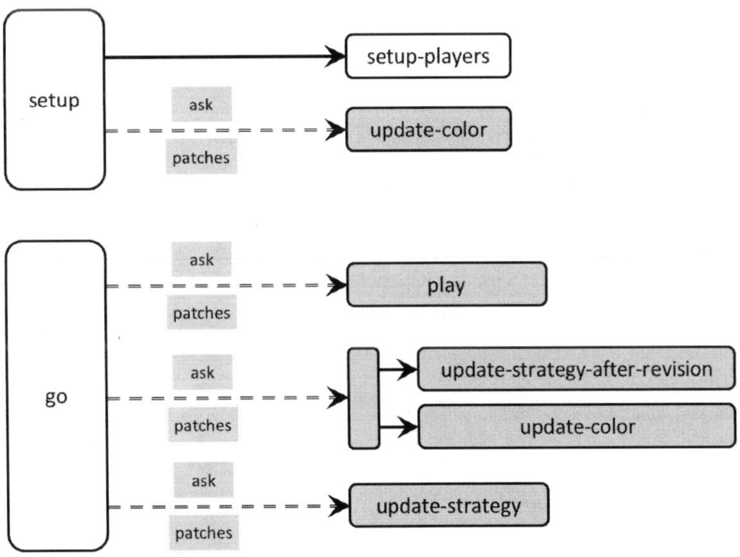

Figure 3. Skeleton of the code

5.2. Global variables and individually-owned variables

We will not need any global variables besides those defined with the sliders in the interface.

Note that in this model there is a one-to-one correspondence between our immobile players and the patches they live in. Thus, there is no need to create any turtles (i.e. NetLogo mobile agents) in our model. We can work only with patches, and our code will be much simpler and readable.

Thus, we can make the built-in "patches" be the players, identifying each patch with one player. These patches already exist in NetLogo, making up the world, so we do not need to create them. Having said that, we do need to associate with each patch all the information that we want it to carry. This information will be:

- Whether the patch is a C-player or D-player. For efficiency and code readability we can use a boolean variable to this end, which we can call C-player? and which will take the value true or false.
- Whether the patch will be a C-player or a D-player after its revision. For this purpose, we may use the boolean variable C-player?-after-revision. This is needed because we want to model *synchronous* updating, i.e. we want all patches to change their strategy at the same time. To do this, first we will ask all patches to compute the strategy they will adopt after the revision and, once all patches have computed their next strategy, we will ask them all to switch to it at the same time.
- The total payoff obtained by the patch playing with its neighbours. We can call this variable payoff.
- For efficiency, it will also be useful to endow each patch with the set of neighbouring patches plus itself. The reason is that this set will be used many times, and it never changes, so it can be computed just once at the beginning and stored in memory. We will store this set in a variable named my-nbrs-and-me.
- The following variable is also defined for efficiency reasons. Note that the payoff of a patch depends on the number of C-players and D-players in its set my-nbrs-and-me. To spare the operation of counting D-players, we can calculate it as the number of players in my-nbrs-and-me (which does not change in the whole simulation) minus the number of C-players. To this end, we can store the number of players in the set my-nbrs-and-me of each patch as an individually-owned variable that we naturally name n-of-my-nbrs-and-me.

Thus, this part of the code looks as follows:

```
patches-own [
  C-player?
  C-player?-after-revision
  payoff
  my-nbrs-and-me
  n-of-my-nbrs-and-me
]
```

5.3. Setup procedures

In the setup procedure we will:

1. Clear everything up, so we initialize the model afresh, using the primitive `clear-all`:

```
clear-all
```

2. Set initial values for the variables that we have associated to each patch. We can set the payoff to 0,[5] and both C-player? and C-player-last? to false (later we will ask some patches to set these values to true). To set the value of my-nbrs-and-me, NetLogo primitives `neighbors` and `patch-set` are really handy.

```
ask patches [
  set payoff 0
  set C-player? false
  set C-player?-after-revision false
  set my-nbrs-and-me (patch-set neighbors self)
  set n-of-my-nbrs-and-me (count my-nbrs-and-me)
]
```

3. Ask a certain number of randomly selected patches to be C-players. That number depends on the percentage *initial-%-of-C-players* chosen by the user and on the total number of patches, and it must be an integer, so we can calculate it as:

```
round (initial-%-of-C-players * count patches / 100)
```

   To randomly select a certain number of agents from an agentset (such as patches), we can use the primitive `n-of` (which reports another –usually smaller– agentset). Thus, the resulting instruction will be:

```
ask n-of (round (initial-%-of-C-players * count patches / 100)) patches [
  set C-player? true
  set C-player?-after-revision true
]
```

4. Color patches according to the four possible combinations of values of C-player? and C-player?-after-revision. The color of a patch is controled by the NetLogo built-in patch variable `pcolor`. A first (and correct) implementation of this task could look like:

5. By default, user-defined variables in NetLogo are initialized with the value 0, so there is no actual need to explicitly set the initial value of individually-owned variables to 0, but it does no harm either.

```
ask patches [
  ifelse C-player?-after-revision
  [
    ifelse C-player?
    [set pcolor blue]
    [set pcolor lime]
  ]
  [
    ifelse C-player?
    [set pcolor yellow]
    [set pcolor red]
  ]
]
```

However, the following implementation, which makes use of NetLogo primitive `ifelse-value` is more readable, as one can clearly see that the only thing we are doing is to set the patch's `pcolor`.

```
ask patches [
  set pcolor
    ifelse-value C-player?-after-revision
     [ifelse-value C-player? [blue] [lime]]
     [ifelse-value C-player? [yellow] [red]]
]
```

5. Reset the tick counter using `reset-ticks`.

Note that:

- Points 2 and 3 above are about setting up the players, so, to keep our code nice and modular, we could group them into a new procedure called to setup-players. This will make our code more elegant, easier to understand, easier to debug and easier to extend, so let us do it!
- The operation described in point 4 above will be conducted every tick, so we should create a separate procedure to this end that we can call to update-color, to be run by individual patches. Since this procedure is rather secondary (i.e. our model could run without this), we have a slight preference to place it at the end of our code, but feel free to do it as you like, since the order in which NetLogo procedures are written in the Code tab is immaterial.

Thus, the code up to this point should be as follows:

```
patches-own [
  C-player?
  C-player?-after-revision
  payoff
```

```
  my-nbrs-and-me
  n-of-my-nbrs-and-me
]

to setup
  clear-all
  setup-players
  ask patches [update-color]
  reset-ticks
end

to setup-players
  ask patches [
    set payoff 0
    set C-player? false
    set C-player?-after-revision false
    set my-nbrs-and-me (patch-set neighbors self)
    set n-of-my-nbrs-and-me (count my-nbrs-and-me)
  ]
  ask n-of (round (initial-%-of-C-players * count patches / 100)) patches [
    set C-player? true
    set C-player?-after-revision true
  ]
end

to go

end

to update-color
  set pcolor
    ifelse-value C-player?-after-revision
     [ifelse-value C-player? [blue] [lime]]
     [ifelse-value C-player? [yellow] [red]]
end
```

5.4. Go procedure

The procedure to go contains all the instructions that will be executed in every tick. In this particular model, we will ask each player (i.e. patch):

1. To play with its neighbours in order to calculate its payoff. For modularity and clarity purposes, we should do this in a new procedure named to play.
2. To compute the value of its next strategy and store it in the variable C-player?-after-revision. In this way, the variable C-player? will keep the strategy with which the current payoff has been obtained, and we can update the value of C-player?-after-revision without losing that information, which will be required by neighboring players when they compute their next strategy. To keep our code nice and modular, we will do this computation in a new procedure

called to update-strategy-after-revision.

3. To update its color according to their C-player? and C-player?-after-revision values, using the procedure to update-color.
4. To update its strategy (i.e. the value of C-player?). We will do this in a separate new procedure called to update-strategy.

We should also mark the end of the round, or tick, after all players have updated their strategies, using the primitive tick, which increases the tick counter by one, and updates the graph on the interface. Thus, by now the code of procedure to go should look as follows:

```
to go
  ask patches [ play ]
  ask patches [
    update-strategy-after-revision
      ;; here we are not updating the agent's strategy yet
    update-color
  ]
  ask patches [ update-strategy ]
    ;; now we update every agent's strategy at the same time
  tick
end
```

5.5 Other procedures

to play

In procedure to play we want patches to calculate their payoff. This payoff will be the number of C-players in the set my-nbrs-and-me times the payoff obtained with a C-player, plus the number of D-players in the set times the payoff obtained with a D-player.

We will store the number of C-players in the set my-nbrs-and-me in a local variable that we can name n-of-C-players. The number can be computed as follows:

```
let n-of-C-players count my-nbrs-and-me with [C-player?]
```

Note that if the calculating patch is a C-player, the payoff obtained when playing with another C-player is *CC-payoff*, and if the calculating patch is a D-player, the payoff obtained when playing with a C-player is *DC-payoff*. Thus, in general, the payoff obtained when playing with a C-player can then be obtained using the following code:

```
ifelse-value C-player? [CC-payoff] [DC-payoff]
```

Similarly, the payoff obtained when playing with a D-player is:

```
ifelse-value C-player? [CD-payoff] [DD-payoff]
```

Taking all this into account, we can implement procedure to play as follows:[6]

```
to play
  let n-of-C-players count my-nbrs-and-me with [C-player?]
  set payoff n-of-C-players *
                  (ifelse-value C-player? [CC-payoff] [DC-payoff]) +
             (n-of-my-nbrs-and-me - n-of-C-players) *
                  (ifelse-value C-player? [CD-payoff] [DD-payoff])
end
```

to update-strategy-after-revision

In this procedure, which will be run by individual patches, we want the patch to compute its next strategy, which will be the strategy used by one of the patches with the maximum payoff in the set my-nbrs-and-me. To select one of these maximum-payoff patches, we may use primitives `one-of` and `with-max` as follows:

```
one-of (my-nbrs-and-me with-max [payoff])
```

Now remember that strategy updating in this model is *synchronous*, i.e. every player revises his strategy at the same time. Thus, we want each patch to adopt the strategy that was used by the selected maximum-payoff patch when it played the game, i.e. before any strategy revision may have taken place. This strategy is stored in variable C-player?. With this, we conclude the code of procedure to update-strategy-after-revision.

```
to update-strategy-after-revision
  set C-player?-after-revision [C-player?] of one-of my-nbrs-and-me with-max
[payoff]
end
```

Another (equivalent) implementation of this procedure, which makes use of primitive `max-one-of` is the following.

```
to update-strategy-after-revision
  set C-player?-after-revision [C-player?] of max-one-of my-nbrs-and-me [payoff]
end
```

6. The parentheses around the first `ifelse-value` block are necessary since NetLogo 6.1.0 (see https://ccl.northwestern.edu/netlogo/docs/transition.html#changes-for-netlogo-610).

to update-strategy

This is a very simple procedure where the patch just updates its strategy (stored in variable C-player?) with the value of C-player?-after-revision. This update is not conducted right after having computed the value of C-player?-after-revision to make the strategy updating *synchronous*.

```
to update-strategy
  set C-player? C-player?-after-revision
end
```

5.6. Complete code in the Code tab

The Code tab is ready!

```
patches-own [
  C-player?
  C-player?-after-revision
  payoff
  my-nbrs-and-me
  n-of-my-nbrs-and-me
]

to setup
  clear-all
  setup-players
  ask patches [update-color]
  reset-ticks
end

to setup-players
  ask patches [
    set payoff 0
    set C-player? false
    set C-player?-after-revision false
    set my-nbrs-and-me (patch-set neighbors self)
    set n-of-my-nbrs-and-me (count my-nbrs-and-me)
  ]
  ask n-of (round (initial-%-of-C-players * count patches / 100)) patches [
    set C-player? true
    set C-player?-after-revision true
  ]
end

to go
  ask patches [ play ]
  ask patches [
    update-strategy-after-revision
```

```
      ;; here we are not updating the agent's strategy yet
    update-color
  ]
  ask patches [ update-strategy ]
    ;; now we update every agent's strategy at the same time
  tick
end

to play
  let n-of-C-players count my-nbrs-and-me with [C-player?]
  set payoff n-of-C-players * (ifelse-value C-player? [CC-payoff] [DC-payoff]) +
       (n-of-my-nbrs-and-me - n-of-C-players) * (ifelse-value C-player? [CD-
payoff] [DD-payoff])
end

to update-strategy-after-revision
  set C-player?-after-revision [C-player?] of one-of my-nbrs-and-me with-max
[payoff]
end

to update-strategy
  set C-player? C-player?-after-revision
end

to update-color
  set pcolor
    ifelse-value C-player?-after-revision
     [ifelse-value C-player? [blue] [lime]]
     [ifelse-value C-player? [yellow] [red]]
end
```

5.7. Code in the plots

We will use blue color for the number of C-players and red for the number of D-players.

To complete the Interface tab, edit the graph and create the pens as in the image below:

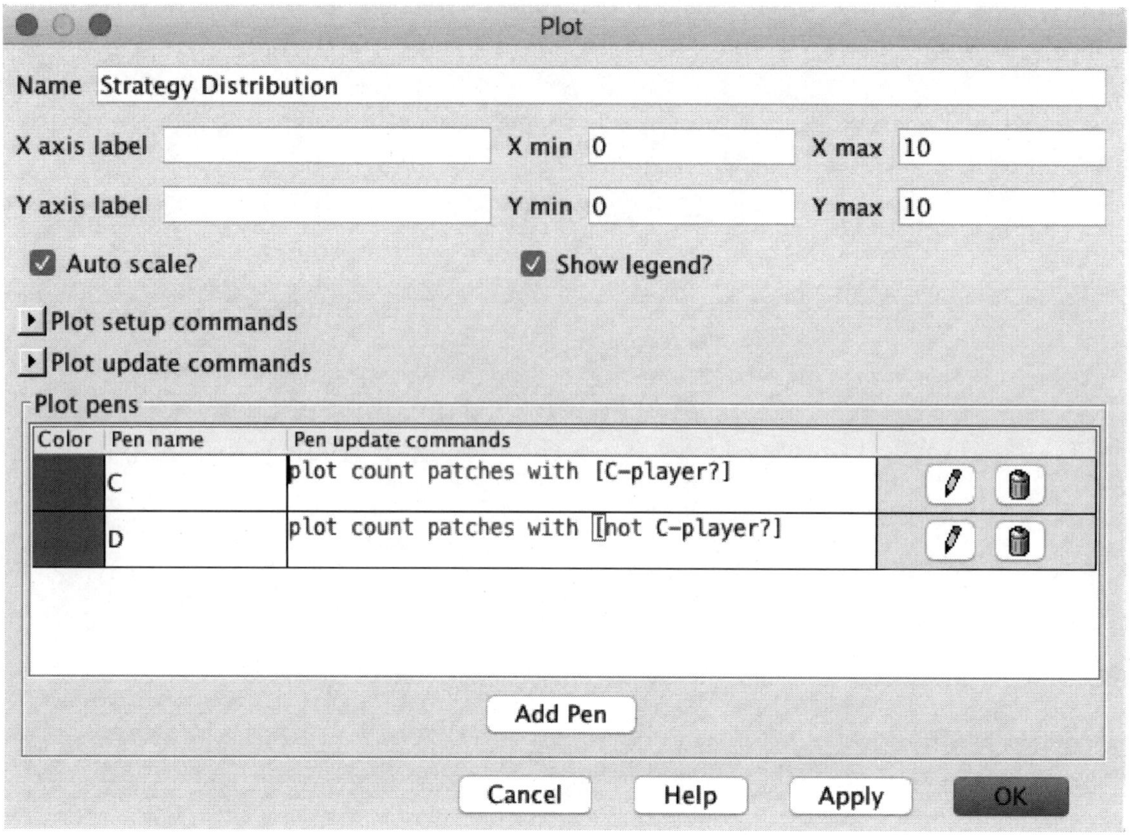

Figure 4. Plot settings.

6. Sample runs

We can use the model we have implemented to shed some light on the question that we posed at the motivation above. We will use the same parameter values as Nowak and May (1992), so we can replicate their results: *CD-payoff* = *DD-payoff* = 0, *CC-payoff* = 1, *DC-payoff* = 1.85, and *initial-%-of-C-players* = 90.[7] An illustration of the sort of patterns that this model generates is shown in the video below.

A video element has been excluded from this version of the text. You can watch it online here: https://wisc.pb.unizin.org/agent-based-evolutionary-game-dynamics/?p=108

As you can see, both C-players and D-players coexist in this spatial environment, with clusters of both

7. Some authors make *CD-payoff* = *DD-payoff*, so they can parameterize the game with just one parameter, i.e. *DC-payoff*. Note, however, that the resulting game lies at the border between a Prisoner's Dilemma and a Hawk-Dove (aka Chicken or Snowdrift) game. Making *CD-payoff* = *DD-payoff* is by no means a normalization of the Prisoner's Dilemma, but a restriction which reduces the range of possibilities that can be studied.

types of players expanding, colliding and fragmenting. The overall fraction of C-players fluctuates around 0.318 for most initial conditions (Nowak and May, 1992). Thus, we can see that adding spatial structure can make cooperation be sustained even in a population where agents can only play C or D (i.e. they cannot condition their actions on previous moves).

Incidentally, this model is also useful to see that a simple 2-player 2-strategy game in a two-dimensional spatial setting can generate chaotic and kaleidoscopic patterns (Nowak and May, 1993). To illustrate this, let us use the same payoff values as before, but let us start with all agents playing C, i.e. *initial-%-of-C-players* = 100.

When you click on setup, the whole world should look blue, since all agents are C-players. If you now click on go, nothing should happen, since all agents are playing the same strategy and the strategy updating is imitative. To make things interesting, let us ask the agent at the center to play D. You can do this by typing the following code at the Command Center (i.e. the line at the bottom of the NetLogo screen) *after* clicking on setup:

```
ask patch 0 0 [set C-player? false]
```

If you now click on go, you should see the following beautiful patterns:

A video element has been excluded from this version of the text. You can watch it online here: https://wisc.pb.unizin.org/agent-based-evolutionary-game-dynamics/?p=108

7. Exercises

You can use the following link to download the complete NetLogo model: 2×2-imitate-best-nbr.

Exercise 1. Let us run a (weak) Prisoner's Dilemma game with payoffs *DD-payoff* = *CD-payoff* = 0, *CC-payoff* = 1 and *DC-payoff* = 1.7. Set the *initial-%-of-cooperators* to 90. Run the model and observe the evolution of the system as you gradually increase the value of *DC-payoff* from 1.7 to 2. If at any point all the players adopt the same strategy, press the setup button again to start a new simulation. Compare your observations with those in fig. 1 of Nowak and May (1992). Note: To use the same dimensions as Nowak and May (1992), you can change the location of the NetLogo world's origin to the bottom left corner, and set both the max-pxcor and the max-pycor to 199. You may also want to change the patch size to 2.

CODE Exercise 2. Create a button to make the patch at 0 0 be a D-player. You may want to label it make agent at 0 0 play D. This button will be useful to replicate some of the experiments in Nowak and May (1992, 1993).

Exercise 3. Replicate the experiment shown in figure 3 of Nowak and May (1992). Note that you will have to make the NetLogo world be a 99 × 99 square lattice.

CODE Exercise 4. Implement the following extension to Nowak and May (1992)'s model, proposed by Mukherji et al. (1996):

> With a small probability ε, each player errs and chooses evenly between strategies C and D; with probability 1-ε, the player follows the Nowak and May update rule.

You may wish to rerun the sample run above with a small value for ε. You may also want to replicate the experiment shown in Mukherji et al. (1996, fig. 1).

CODE Exercise 5. Implement the following extension to Nowak and May (1992)'s model, proposed by Mukherji et al. (1996):

> During each period, players fail to update their previous strategy with a small probability, θ.

You may wish to rerun the sample run above with a small value for θ. You may also want to replicate the experiment shown in Mukherji et al. (1996, fig. 1).

CODE Exercise 6. Implement the following extension to Nowak and May (1992)'s model, proposed by Mukherji et al. (1996):

> After following the Nowak and May update rule, each cooperator has a small independent probability, ϕ, of cheating by switching to defection.

You may wish to rerun the sample run above with a small value for ϕ. You may also want to replicate the experiment shown in Mukherji et al. (1996, fig. 1).

2.1. Robustness and fragility

1. Goal

Our goal in this section is to extend the model we have created in the previous section by adding three features that will prove very useful:

- Noise, i.e. the possibility that revising agents select a strategy at random with a small probability.
- Self-matching, i.e. the possibility to choose whether agents are matched with themselves to play the game or not.
- Asynchronous strategy updating, i.e. the possibility that agents revise their strategies *sequentially* –rather than *simultaneously*– within the same tick.[1]

These three features will allow us to assess the robustness of our previous computational results.

2. Motivation. Robustness of cooperation in spatial settings

In the previous section, we saw that spatial structure can induce significant levels of cooperation in the Prisoner's Dilemma, at least for some parameter settings. In particular, we saw that with *CD-payoff* = *DD-payoff* = 0, *CC-payoff* = 1, *DC-payoff* = 1.85, the overall fraction of C-players fluctuates around 0.318 for most initial conditions (Nowak and May, 1992). Here we wonder how robust this result is to changes in some of the model assumptions. In particular, we would like to study what happens...

- if we add a bit of noise,
- if agents do not play the game with themselves,
- if strategy updating is asynchronous, rather than synchronous, or
- if we use *DD-payoff* = 0.1 (rather than *DD-payoff* = 0), making the game a true Prisoner's Dilemma.

1. There are different ways one can implement asynchronicity. Here we implement what Cornforth et al. (2005) call "Random Asynchronous Order". Under this scheme, at each tick all agents revise their strategy in a random order.

3. Description of the model

The model we are going to develop here is a generalization of the model implemented in the previous section. In particular, we are going to add the following three parameters:

- *noise*. With probability *noise*, the revising agent will adopt a random strategy; and with probability (1 – *noise*), the revising agent will choose her strategy following the "imitate the best neighbor" protocol. Thus, if *noise* = 0, we recover the model implemented in the previous section.
- *self-matching?*. If *self-matching?* is true, agents play the game with themselves, just like before. On the other hand, if *self-matching?* is false, agents do not play the game with themselves.
- *synchronous-updating?*. If *synchronous-updating?* is true, agents update their strategies *simultaneously*, just like before. On the other hand, if *synchronous-updating?* is false, agents play and update their strategies *sequentially*, i.e. one after another. In this latter case, all agents revise their strategies in every tick in a random order.

Everything else stays as described in the previous section.

CODE 4. Interface design

We depart from the model we developed in the previous section (so if you want to preserve it, now is a good time to duplicate it).

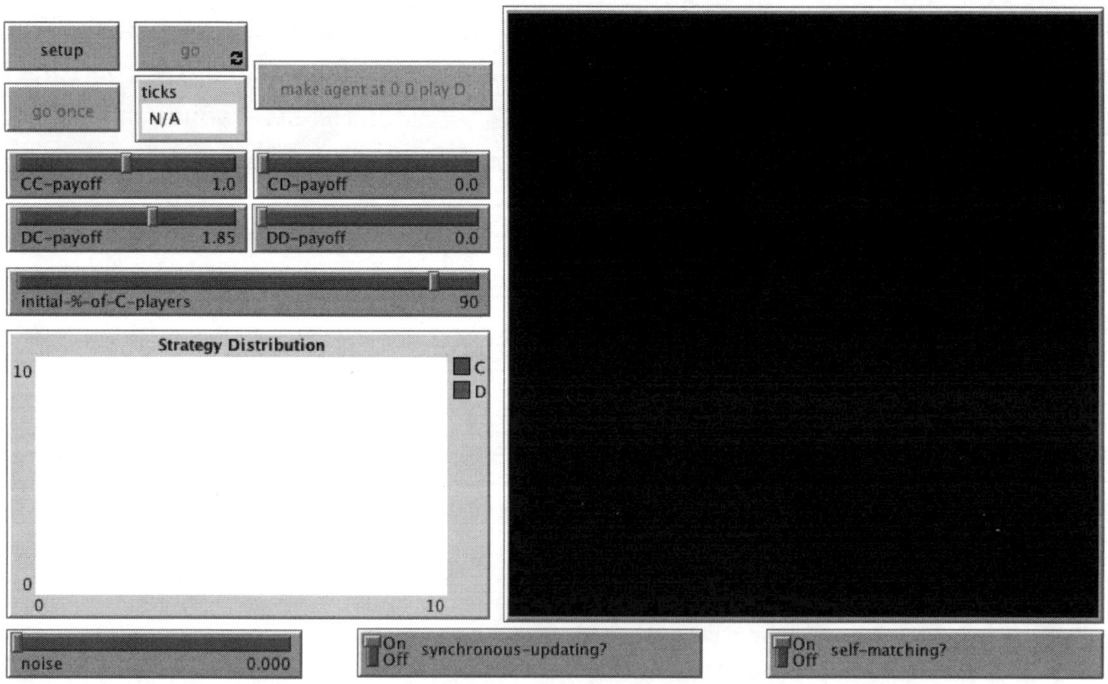

Figure 1. Interface design.

In the new interface (see figure 1 above), we just have to add one slider for the new parameter *noise*, and two switches: one for parameter *synchronous-updating?* and another one for parameter *self-matching?*. We have added these elements at the bottom of the interface, but feel free to place them wherever you like.

CODE 5. Code

5.1. Skeleton of the code

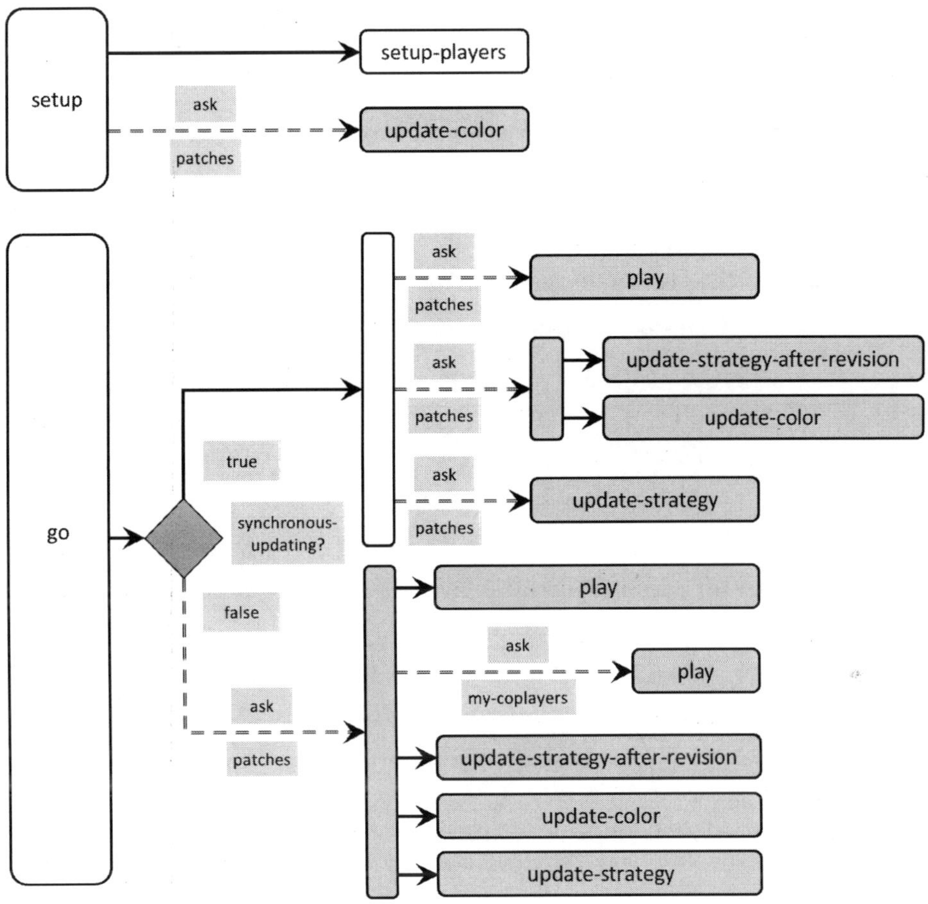

Figure 2. Skeleton of the code

5.2. Extension I. Adding noise to the revision protocol

Recall that the implementation of the revision protocol is conducted in procedure to update-strategy-after-revision. At present, the code of this procedure looks as follows:

```
to update-strategy-after-revision
  set C-player?-after-revision [C-player?] of one-of my-nbrs-and-me with-max
[payoff]
end
```

To implement the choice of a random strategy with probability *noise* by revising agents, we can use NetLogo primitive ifelse-value as follows:[2]

```
to update-strategy-after-revision
  set C-player?-after-revision ifelse-value (random-float 1 < noise)
    [ one-of [true false] ] ;; this is run with probability noise
    [ [C-player?] of one-of (my-nbrs-and-me with-max [payoff]) ]
end
```

The noise extension is now ready, so you may want to explore the impact of noise in this model.

5.3. Extension II. Playing the game with yourself or not

> Whether it is natural to include self-interactions in the theory depends on the biological assumptions underlying the model. In general, if each cell is viewed as being occupied by a single individual adopting a given strategy then it is natural to exclude self-interaction. However, if each cell is viewed as being occupied by a population, all of whose members are adopting a given strategy, then it may be more natural to include self-interaction. Killingback and Doebeli (1996, p. 1136)

In our model, agents will play the game with themselves or not depending on the value of the new parameter *self-matching?*. To implement this extension elegantly, we find it convenient to define a new patch variable named my-coplayers, which will store the agentset with which the patch will play. Thus, if *self-matching?* is true, my-coplayers will include the patch's neighbors plus the patch itself, while if *self-matching?* is false, my-coplayers will include only the patch's neighbors.

It will also be convenient to define another patch variable named n-of-my-coplayers, which will store the cardinality of my-coplayers for each patch. This is just for the same (efficiency) reasons we defined n-of-my-nbrs-and-me in the previous model. Now that we have variables my-coplayers and n-of-my-coplayers, patch variable n-of-my-nbrs-and-me will no longer be needed. Thus, the definition of patch-own variables in the Code tab will look as follows:

```
patches-own [
  C-player?
  C-player?-after-revision
  payoff
```

---

2. We could also implement the noise extension using the NetLogo primitive ifelse, but the use of ifelse-value makes it clear that the only thing we are doing in this procedure is to set the value of the patch variable C-player?-after-revision.

```
    my-nbrs-and-me
    my-coplayers            ;; <== new variable
    n-of-my-coplayers       ;; <== new variable
    ;; n-of-my-nbrs-and-me     <== not needed anymore
  ]
```

Now we have to set the value of the two new patch-own variables. Since these values will not change during the course of the simulation and they pertain to the individual players, the natural place to set them is in procedure to setup-players.

```
to setup-players
  ask patches [
    set payoff 0
    set C-player? false
    set C-player?-after-revision false
    set my-nbrs-and-me (patch-set neighbors self)

    ;; set n-of-my-nbrs-and-me (count my-nbrs-and-me)    <== not needed anymore

    ;; the following two lines are new
    set my-coplayers ifelse-value self-matching? [my-nbrs-and-me] [neighbors]
    set n-of-my-coplayers (count my-coplayers)
  ]

  ask n-of (round (initial-%-of-C-players * count patches / 100)) patches [
    set C-player? true
    set C-player?-after-revision true
  ]
end
```

Finally, we have to modify procedure to play so patches play with agentset my-coplayers, rather than with agentset my-nbrs-and-me.

```
to play
  let n-of-C-players count my-coplayers with [C-player?]
  set payoff n-of-C-players * (ifelse-value C-player? [CC-payoff] [DC-payoff]) +
       (n-of-my-coplayers - n-of-C-players) * ifelse-value C-player? [CD-payoff]
[DD-payoff]
end
```

Note also that we have to replace the variable n-of-my-nbrs-and-me with n-of-my-coplayers when computing the payoff. You can now explore the consequences of not forcing agents to play the game with themselves!

5.4. Extension III. Asynchronous strategy updating

To implement asynchronous updating we will have to modify procedure to go. If *synchronous-updating?* is true, updating takes place just like before, so we can wrap the code we had in to go within an `ifelse` statement whose condition is the boolean variable *synchronous-updating?* , i.e.:

```
to go
  ifelse synchronous-updating?
    [
      ask patches [ play ]
      ask patches [
        update-strategy-after-revision
          ;; here we are not updating the agent's strategy yet
        update-color
      ]
      ask patches [ update-strategy ]
        ;; now we update every agent's strategy at the same time
    ]
    [
      ;; this is where we have to place the code
      ;; for asynchronous strategy updating
    ]
  tick
end
```

The implementation of sequential updating requires that every patch (in a random order) goes through the whole cycle of playing and updating its strategy without being interrupted. Note that, at the time of revising the strategy, agents will compare their payoff with their coplayers' payoffs, so before calling procedure update-strategy-after-revision we have to make sure that all these payoffs have been properly computed, i.e. we must ask the revising agent and her coplayers to play the game. So basically, each patch, in sequential order, must:

- play the game,
- ask its coplayers to play the game (so their payoffs are updated),
- run update-strategy-after-revision to compute its next strategy (C-player?-after-revision),
- update its color (now that we have access both to the current strategy C-player? and to the next strategy C-player?-after-revision)
- update its strategy, i.e. set the value of C-player? to C-player?-after-revision. This is done in procedure update-strategy.

Taking all this into account, the code in the procedure to go looks as follows:

```
to go
  ifelse synchronous-updating?
    [
```

```
      ask patches [ play ]
      ask patches [
        update-strategy-after-revision
          ;; here we are not updating the agent's strategy yet
        update-color
      ]
      ask patches [ update-strategy ]
        ;; now we update every agent's strategy at the same time
    ]
    [
      ask patches [
        play
        ask my-coplayers [ play ]
           ;; since your coplayers' strategies or
           ;; your coplayers' coplayers' strategies
           ;; could have changed since the last time
           ;; your coplayers played
        update-strategy-after-revision
        update-color
        update-strategy
      ]
    ]
  tick
end
```

5.5. Complete code in the Code tab

The Code tab is ready! Congratulations! You have implemented three important generalizations of the model in very little time.

```
patches-own [
  C-player?
  C-player?-after-revision
  payoff
  my-nbrs-and-me
  my-coplayers
  n-of-my-coplayers
]

to setup
  clear-all
  setup-players
  ask patches [update-color]
  reset-ticks
end

to setup-players
```

```
  ask patches [
    set payoff 0
    set C-player? false
    set C-player?-after-revision false
    set my-nbrs-and-me (patch-set neighbors self)
    set my-coplayers ifelse-value self-matching? [my-nbrs-and-me] [neighbors]
    set n-of-my-coplayers (count my-coplayers)
  ]
  ask n-of (round (initial-%-of-C-players * count patches / 100)) patches [
    set C-player? true
    set C-player?-after-revision true
  ]
end

to go
  ifelse synchronous-updating?
    [
      ask patches [ play ]
      ask patches [
        update-strategy-after-revision
          ;; here we are not updating the agent's strategy yet
        update-color
      ]
      ask patches [ update-strategy ]
        ;; now we update every agent's strategy at the same time
    ]
    [
      ask patches [
        play
        ask my-coplayers [ play ]
           ;; since your coplayers' strategies or
           ;; your coplayers' coplayers' strategies
           ;; could have changed since the last time
           ;; your coplayers played
        update-strategy-after-revision
        update-color
        update-strategy
      ]
    ]
  tick
end

to play
  let n-of-cooperators count my-coplayers with [C-player?]
  set payoff n-of-cooperators * (ifelse-value C-player? [CC-payoff] [DC-payoff]) +
      (n-of-my-coplayers - n-of-cooperators) * ifelse-value C-player? [CD-
payoff] [DD-payoff]
end

to update-strategy-after-revision
  set C-player?-after-revision ifelse-value (random-float 1 < noise)
```

```
      [ one-of [true false] ]
      [ [C-player?] of one-of (my-nbrs-and-me with-max [payoff]) ]
end

to update-strategy
  set C-player? C-player?-after-revision
end

to update-color
  set pcolor
    ifelse-value C-player?-after-revision
     [ifelse-value C-player? [blue] [lime]]
     [ifelse-value C-player? [yellow] [red]]
end
```

6. Sample runs

Now that we have implemented the extended model, we can use it to answer the questions posed in the motivation above. Let us see how the simulation we ran in the previous section (with *CD-payoff* = *DD-payoff* = 0, *CC-payoff* = 1, *DC-payoff* = 1.85, and *initial-%-of-C-players* = 90 in a 81×81 grid) is affected by each of the changes outlined in the motivation, one by one. We will refer to this parameterization as *the baseline setting*.

What happens if we add a bit of noise?

If you run the model with noise, you will see that the level of cooperation diminishes drastically. Using BehaviorSpace, we have estimated that the percentage of cooperators in the regime where cooperators and defectors coexist drops from ~32% in the model without noise to ~15% if *noise* = 0.04. If *noise* = 0.05, the long-run fraction of cooperation is just ~3%, so nearly all cooperation is coming from the random strategy updates (which accounts for 2.5% of the cooperation).[3] The influence of noise in the baseline setting was pointed out by Mukherji et al. (1996).

3. The model with low noise seems to have two regimes, one where most agents are defecting and another one where cooperators and defectors coexist. Simulations that start with a low percentage of initial cooperators tend to move first to the mostly-defection regime, while simulations that start with higher proportions of initial cooperators tend to move to the coexistence regime. Note, however, that transitions from one regime to the other are always possible with noise, and therefore they will occur if we wait for long enough. Having said that, the time we would have to wait to actually see these transitions may be extremely long in some settings. Note also that the model with noise can be seen as an irreducible and aperiodic Markov chain (see sufficient conditions for irreducibility and aperiodicity). This means that the long-run dynamics of this model are independent of initial conditions.

What happens if agents do not play the game with themselves?

The impact of *self-matching?* is also clear. When agents do not play the game with themselves, no cooperation can emerge in the baseline setting. If the initial fraction of cooperators is high, some small clusters of initial cooperators may survive, but these clusters disappear if we add a tiny bit of noise. As an illustration, the video below shows a simulation with *self-matching?* = false, *initial-%-of-C-players* = 99 and *noise* = 0.01.

> *A video element has been excluded from this version of the text. You can watch it online here: https://wisc.pb.unizin.org/agent-based-evolutionary-game-dynamics/?p=110*

Therefore, it turns out that playing with oneself is a necessary condition to obtain some cooperation in the baseline setting.

What happens if strategy updating is asynchronous, rather than synchronous?

The impact of *synchronous-updating?* on cooperation is also clear. If agents update their strategies sequentially, rather than simultaneously, no cooperation whatsoever can be sustained in the baseline setting. This observation was pointed out by Huberman and Glance (1993). As a matter of fact, to eliminate cooperation in this setting, it is sufficient that only a small fraction of the population (~15%) do not synchronize (Mukherji et al., 1996).[4]

What happens if we use *DD-payoff* = 0.1?

Increasing the value of *DD-payoff* to 0.1 (so the game becomes a real Prisoner's Dilemma) also eliminates the emergence of cooperation. If the initial fraction of cooperators is high, some small clusters of initial cooperators may survive, but these clusters disappear if we add some noise.[5] As an illustration, the video below shows a simulation with *DD-payoff* = 0.1, *initial-%-of-C-players* = 99 and *noise* = 0.01.

> *A video element has been excluded from this version of the text. You can watch it online here: https://wisc.pb.unizin.org/agent-based-evolutionary-game-dynamics/?p=110*

Discussion

In this section we have discovered that the emergence of cooperation observed in the sample run of the previous section is not robust at all. Any of the four modifications we have explored is sufficient to destroy cooperation altogether. Having said that, the emergence of cooperation in the spatially embedded Prisoner's Dilemma is much more robust for lower values of *DC-payoff* (see

---

4. Newth and Cornforth (2009) analyze various other updating schemes in this model.
5. If DD-payoff $\geq$ 0.58, no clusters of initial cooperators can survive, even in the absence of noise.

Nowak et al. (1994a, 1994b, 1996)). As an example, consider a simulation with *DC-payoff* = 1.3, where we include the four modifications we have investigated, i.e. *noise* = 0.05, *self-matching?* = false, *synchronous-updating?* = false, and *DD-payoff* = 0.1. The other parameter values are the same as in our baseline simulation, i.e. *CD-payoff* = 0, *CC-payoff* = 1, and the grid is 81×81. Cooperation in this setting can indeed emerge and be sustained. The video below shows an illustrative run with initial conditions *initial-%-of-C-players* = 25. The long-run proportion of cooperators in this setting is greater than 50%.

> *A video element has been excluded from this version of the text. You can watch it online here: https://wisc.pb.unizin.org/agent-based-evolutionary-game-dynamics/?p=110*

In section 2.3 we will see that there is another assumption in this model that has a very important (positive) influence in the emergence of cooperation: the use of the "imitate the best neighbor" protocol. But for now, let us take a step back and think about what we have learned in this section in general terms, i.e. beyond the specifics of this particular model.

In this section we have learned that assumptions that may seem irrelevant at first sight can actually play a crucial role in the dynamics of our models. Furthermore, there are often complex interactions between the effects of different assumptions. We have also learned that small changes in one parameter can lead to big changes in the dynamics of our models (see exercise 1 below for a striking example). Unfortunately, this sensitivity to seemingly small details is not the exception but the rule in agent-based models. For this reason, it is of utmost importance to always check the robustness of our computational results, to explore the parameter space adequately, and to keep our conclusions within the scope of what we have actually investigated, not beyond.

7. Exercises

You can use the following link to download the complete NetLogo model: 2×2-imitate-best-nbr-extended.

Exercise 1. Roca et al. (2009a, fig. 10; 2009b, fig. 2) report a counterintuitive singularity that we can replicate with our model. To do so, modify the baseline setting (*CD-payoff* = *DD-payoff* = 0, *CC-payoff* = 1) by choosing *self-matching?* = false, make the world 100×100 with periodic (or 'wrap-around') boundaries, and set initial conditions *initial-%-of-C-players* = 50. Now compare the long-run fraction of cooperators for values of *DC-payoff* equal to 1.3999, 1.4 and 1.4001. What do you observe?

Photo by Tyler Easton on Unsplash

To understand this curious phenomenon, you may also want to run simulations with initial conditions *initial-%-of-C-players* = 100 and make use of our button labeled make agent at 0 0 play D.

P.S. One may wonder whether this singularity could be an artifact due to floating-point errors, since (1.4 + 1.4 + 1.4 + 1.4 + 1.4) ≠ 7 in the IEEE754 floating-point standard (which is the standard used in most programming languages, and in NetLogo in particular).[6] You can check that the singularity is not due to floating-point errors choosing an equivalent parameterization that is not prone to floating-point errors. Can you come up with an equivalent parameterization that uses only integers when computing payoffs?

Exercise 2. Consider the simulation run from the previous section which produced the beautiful kaleidoscopic patterns. How does each of the four modifications outlined in the motivation affect its dynamics?

Exercise 3. How can we parameterize our model to replicate the results shown in figure 2 of Killingback and Doebeli (1996, p. 1138)?

CODE Exercise 4. What changes should we make in the code to be able to replicate figure 3 of Killingback and Doebeli (1996, p. 1139)? Note that in the model used to produce that figure, individual patches do not update their strategy with 5% probability.

CODE Exercise 5. In section "Sample runs", when we added some noise to the baseline setting, we

---

6. Note that in our implementation of procedure to play we do not add individual payoffs but we multiply them, so we would not compute (1.4 + 1.4 + 1.4 + 1.4 + 1.4) but instead 5*1.4, which is indeed exactly equal to 7 in IEEE754 floating-point arithmetic. For more on the potential impact of floating-point errors on agent-based models, see Polhill et al. (2006) and Izquierdo and Polhill (2006).

stated that the percentage of cooperators in the regime where cooperators and defectors coexist is about ~15% if *noise* = 0.04. Try to corroborate this estimation using BehaviorSpace.

CODE Exercise 6. In our model, changing the value of *noise* has an immediate effect on the dynamics of the model at runtime. The same occurs with *synchronous-updating?*, but not with *self-matching?*. How can you make the model respond immediately to changes in *self-matching?* ? Try to do it in a way that does not affect the execution speed.

2.2. Extension to any number of strategies

1. Goal

Our goal here is to extend the model we have created in the previous section –which accepted games with 2 strategies only– to model (2-player symmetric) games with any number of strategies.

2. Motivation. Spatial Hawk-Dove-Retaliator

The model we are going to develop in this section will allow us to explore games with any number of strategies. Thus, we will be able to model games like the classical Hawk-Dove-Retaliator (Maynard Smith (1982, pp. 17-18), which is an extension of the Hawk-Dove game, with the additional strategy *Retaliator*. Retaliators are just like Doves, except in contests against Hawks. When playing against Hawks, Retaliators behave like Hawks. A possible payoff matrix for this symmetric game is the following:

	Hawk (H)	Dove (D)	Retaliator (R)
Hawk (H)	-1	2	-1
Dove (D)	0	1	1
Retaliator (R)	-1	1	1

Let us consider the population game where agents are matched to play the normal form game with payoffs as above.[1] The only Evolutionarily Stable State (ESS; see Thomas (1984) and Sandholm (2010, section 8.3)) of this population game is the state (½H + ½D), with half the population playing Hawk and the other half playing Dove (Maynard Smith (1982, appendix E), Binmore (2013)). Also, note that Retaliators are weakly dominated by Doves: they get a strictly lower expected payoff than Doves in any situation, except in those population states with no Hawks whatsoever (at which retaliators get exactly the same payoff as Doves).

Figure 1 below shows the best response correspondence of this game. Population states are represented in a simplex, and the color at any population state indicates the strategy that provides the highest expected payoff at that state: orange for Hawk, green for Dove, and blue for Retaliator. As an example, the population state where the three strategies are equally present, i.e. (⅓H + ⅓D +⅓R), which lies at the barycenter of the simplex, is colored in green, denoting that the strategy that provides the highest expected payoff at that state is Dove.

1. The payoff function of the associated population game is $F(x) = Ax$, where x denotes the population state and A denotes the payoff matrix of the normal form game. This population game can be obtained by assuming that every agent plays with every other agent.

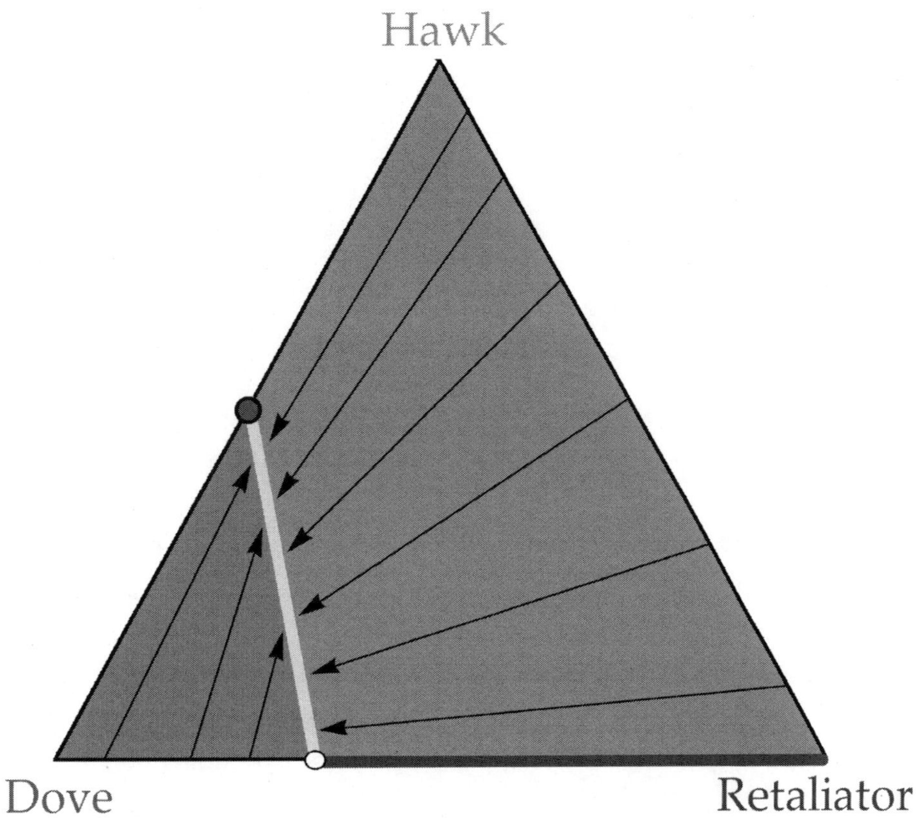

Fig. 1. Best response correspondence for the Hawk-Dove-Retaliator game. Color indicates the strategy with the highest expected payoff at each population state. Arrows are just a visual aid that indicate the direction of the best response. The yellow line indicates that both Dove and Hawk are best response. The purple line indicates that both Dove and Retaliator are best response. All three strategies are best response at the white circle at (⅔D +⅓R). Finally, the unique ESS (½H + ½D) is indicated with a red circle.

We would like to study the dynamic stability of the unique ESS (½H + ½D) in spatial contexts. In unstructured populations, ESSs are asymptotically stable under a wide range of revision protocols (see e.g. Sandholm (2010, theorem 8.4.7)), and in particular under the best response protocol. Therefore, one might be tempted to think that in our spatial model with the "imitate the best neighbor" protocol (including some noise to allow for the occasional entry of any strategy), simulations will tend to spend most of the time around the unique (½H + ½D) and Retaliators would hardly be observed. This hypothesis may be further supported by the fact that the area around the unique ESS where Retaliators are suboptimal is quite sizable. In no situation can Retaliators obtain a higher expected payoff than Doves, and departing from the unique ESS, at least one half of the population would have to be replaced (i.e. all the Hawks) for Retaliators to get the same expected payoff as Doves.

Having seen all this, it may come as no surprise that if we simulate this game with the random-matching model we implemented in the previous chapter, retaliators tend to disappear from any interior population state. The following video shows an illustrative simulation starting from a situation where all agents are retaliators (and including some noise to allow for the entry of any strategy).[2]

2. The fact that the simulation tends to linger around the ESS is a coincidence, since the imitate-the-better-realization

> A video element has been excluded from this version of the text. You can watch it online here: https://wisc.pb.unizin.org/agent-based-evolutionary-game-dynamics/?p=112

So, will space give Retaliators any chance of survival? Let's build a model to explore this question!

3. Description of the model

The model we are going to develop here is a generalization of the model implemented in the previous section. The new model will have a new parameter, *payoffs*, that the user can use to input a payoff matrix of the form [[A_{00} A_{01} ... A_{0n}] [A_{10} A_{11} ... A_{1n}] ... [A_{n0} A_{n1} ... A_{nn}]], containing the payoffs A_{ij} that an agent playing strategy *i* obtains when meeting an agent playing strategy *j* ($i, j \in \{0, 1, ..., n\}$). The number of strategies will be inferred from the number of rows in the payoff matrix.

The user will also be able to set any initial conditions using parameter *n-of-players-for-each-strategy*, which will be a list of the form [a_0 a_1 ... a_n], where item a_i is the initial number of agents playing strategy *i*. Naturally, the sum of all the elements in this list should equal the number of patches in the world.

Everything else stays as described in the previous section.

CODE 4. Interface design

We depart from the model we developed in the previous section (so if you want to preserve it, now is a good time to duplicate it).

---

protocol depends only on ordinal properties of the payoffs. What is not a coincidence is that Retaliators (which are weakly dominated by Doves) are eliminated in the absence of noise (Loginov, 2019).

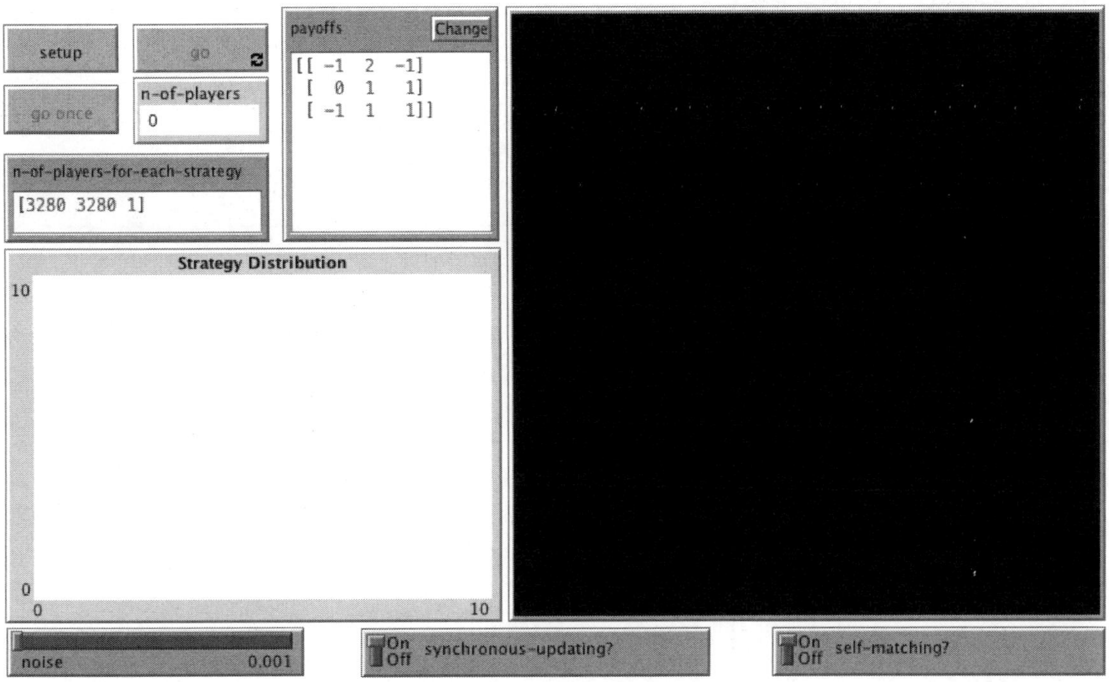

Fig. 2. Interface design

The new interface (see figure 2 above) requires the following modifications:

- Remove the sliders for parameters *CC-payoff*, *CD-payoff*, *DC-payoff*, *DD-payoff*, and *initial-%-of-C-players*. Since these sliders were our way of declaring the corresponding global variables, you will now get all sorts of errors, but don't panic, we will sort them out later.
- Remove the button labeled make agent at 0 0 play D. Yes, more errors, but let us do our best to stay calm; we will fix them in a little while.
- Add an input box for parameter *payoffs*.

> Create an input box with associated global variable *payoffs*. Set the input box type to "String (reporter)" and tick the "Multi-Line" box. Note that the content of *payoffs* will be a string (i.e. a sequence of characters) from which we will have to extract the payoff numeric values.

- Create an input box to let the user set the initial number of players using each strategy.

> Create an input box with associated global variable *n-of-players-for-each-strategy*. Set the input box type to "String (reporter)".

- Remove the "pens" in the Strategy Distribution plot. Since the number of strategies is unknown until the payoff matrix is read, we will need to create the required number of "pens" in the Code tab.

> Edit the Strategy Distribution plot and delete both pens.

- We have also modified the monitor. Before it showed the ticks and now it shows the number of players (i.e. the value of a global variable named n-of-players, to be defined shortly). You may want to do this or not, as you like.

CODE 5. Code

5.1. Skeleton of the code

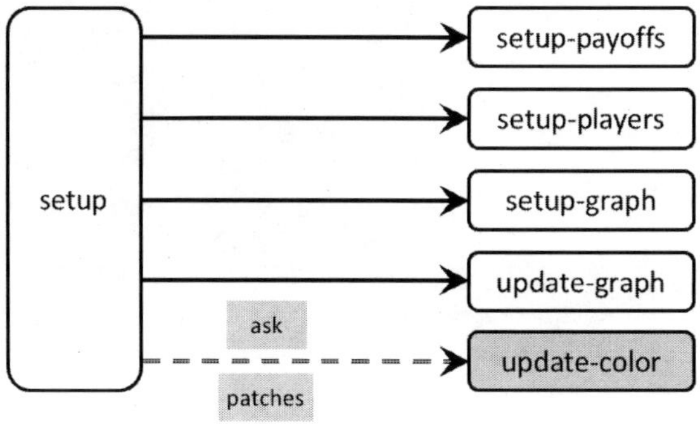

Figure 3. Skeleton of the setup procedure

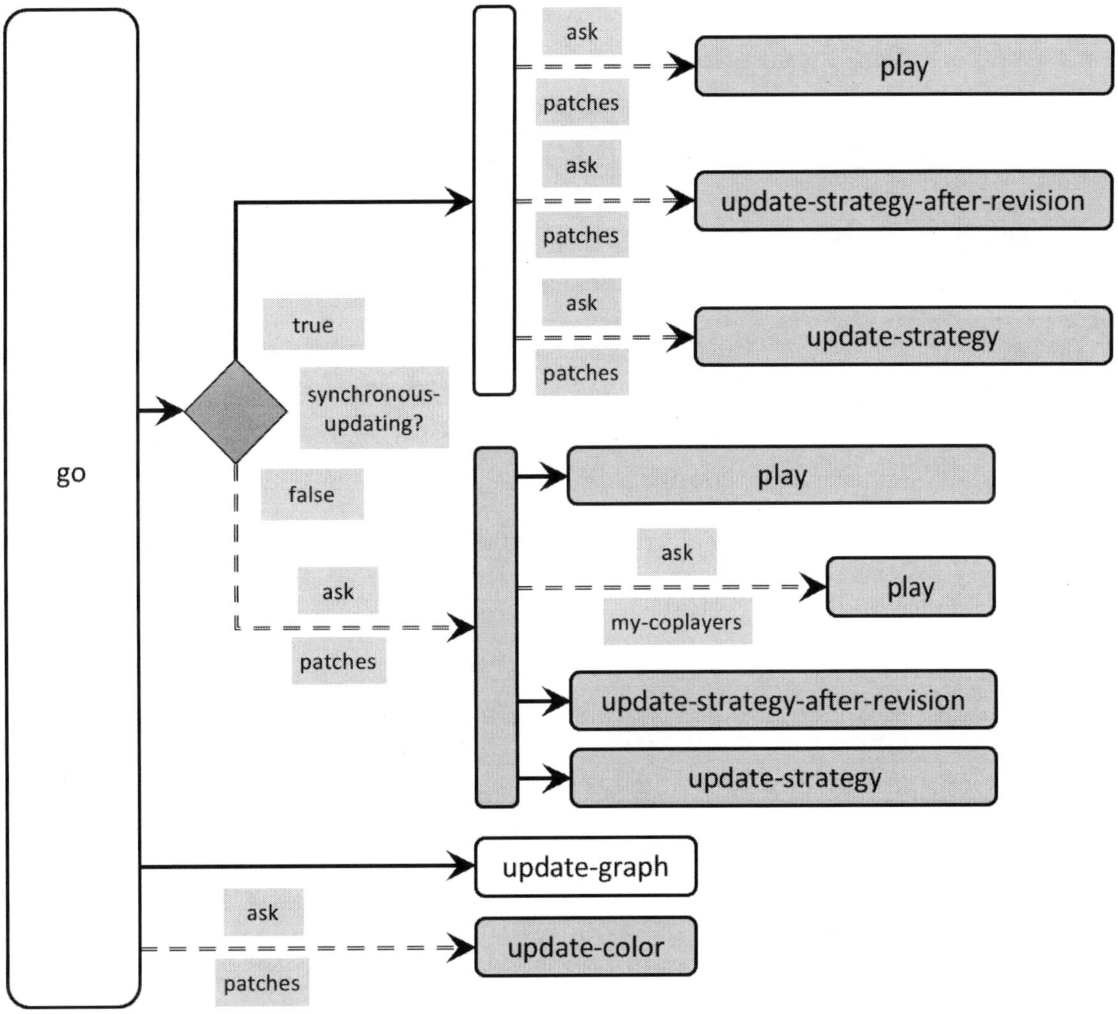

Figure 4. Skeleton of the go procedure

5.2. Global variables and individually-owned variables

First of all, we declare the global variables that we are going to use and we have not already declared in the interface. We will be using a global variable named payoff-matrix to store the payoff values on a list. It will also be handy to have a variable store the number of strategies and another variable store the number of players. Since this information will likely be used in various procedures and will not change during the course of a simulation, it makes sense to define the new variables as global. The natural names for these two variables are n-of-strategies and n-of-players:

```
globals [
  payoff-matrix
  n-of-strategies
  n-of-players
]
```

Now we focus on the patches-own variables. We are going to need each individual patch to store its strategy and its strategy-after-revision. These two variables replace the previous C-player? and C-player?-after-revision. Thus, the code for patches-own variables looks as follows now:

```
patches-own [
  ;; C-player?                    <== no longer needed
  ;; C-player?-after-revision     <== no longer needed
  strategy                     ;; <== new variable
  strategy-after-revision      ;; <== new variable
  payoff
  my-nbrs-and-me
  my-coplayers
  n-of-my-coplayers
]
```

5.3. Setup procedures

The current setup procedure looks as follows:

```
to setup
  clear-all
  setup-players
  ask patches [update-color]
  reset-ticks
end
```

Clearly we will have to keep this code, but additionally we will have to set up the payoffs and set up the graph (since the number of pens to be created depends on the payoff matrix now). To do this elegantly, we should create separate procedures for each set of related tasks; to setup-payoffs and to setup-graph are excellent names for these new procedures. Thus, the code of procedure to setup should include calls to these new procedures:

```
to setup
  clear-all
  setup-payoffs      ;; <== new line
  setup-players
  setup-graph        ;; <== new line
  reset-ticks

  update-graph       ;; <== new line
  ask patches [update-color]
end
```

Note that we have also included a call to another new procedure named to update-graph, to plot the initial conditions.[3] The code of procedure to setup in this model looks almost identical to the code of the same procedure in the model we developed in the previous chapter. As a matter of fact, we will be able to reuse much of the code we wrote for that model. Let us now implement procedures to setup-payoffs, to setup-graph and to update-graph. We will also have to modify procedures to setup-players and to update-color.

to setup-payoffs

The procedure to setup-payoffs will include the instructions to read the payoff matrix, and will also set the value of the global variable n-of-strategies. Looking at the implementation of the same procedure in the model we developed in the previous chapter, can you implement procedure to setup-payoffs for our new model?

Implementation of procedure to setup-payoffs.

Yes, well done! We can use exactly the same code!

```
to setup-payoffs
  set payoff-matrix read-from-string payoffs
  set n-of-strategies length payoff-matrix
end
```

to setup-players

The current procedure to setup-players looks as follows:

```
to setup-players
  ask patches [
    set payoff 0
    set C-player? false
    set C-player?-after-revision false
    set my-nbrs-and-me (patch-set neighbors self)
    set my-coplayers ifelse-value self-matching? [my-nbrs-and-me] [neighbors]
    set n-of-my-coplayers (count my-coplayers)
  ]
```

3. There is some flexibility in the order of the lines within procedure to setup. For instance, the call to procedure setup-graph could be made before or after executing `reset-ticks`.

```
  ask n-of (round (initial-%-of-C-players * count patches / 100)) patches [
    set C-player? true
    set C-player?-after-revision true
  ]
end
```

This procedure will have to be modified substantially. In particular, the lines in bold in the code above include variables that do not exist anymore. But don't despair! Once again, to modify procedure to setup-players appropriately, the implementation of the same procedure in the model we developed in the previous chapter will be invaluable. Using that code, can you try to implement procedure to setup-players in our new model?

Implementation of procedure to setup-players.

The lines marked in bold below are the only modifications we have to make to the implementation of this procedure from the previous chapter.

```
to setup-players
  let initial-distribution read-from-string n-of-players-for-each-strategy
  if length initial-distribution != length payoff-matrix [
    user-message (word "The number of items in\n"
      "n-of-players-for-each-strategy (i.e. "
      length initial-distribution "):\n" n-of-players-for-each-strategy
      "\nshould be equal to the number of rows\n"
      "in the payoff matrix (i.e. "
      length payoff-matrix "):\n"
      payoffs
    )
  ]

  ask patches [set strategy false]
  let i 0
  foreach initial-distribution [ j ->
    ask n-of j (patches with [strategy = false]) [
      set payoff 0
      set strategy i
      set my-nbrs-and-me (patch-set neighbors self)
      set my-coplayers ifelse-value self-matching?
         [my-nbrs-and-me] [neighbors]
      set n-of-my-coplayers (count my-coplayers)
    ]
    set i (i + 1)
  ]
```

```
  set n-of-players count patches
end
```

Finally, it would be a nice touch to warn the user if the total number of players in list *n-of-players-for-each-strategy* is not equal to the number of patches. One possible way of doing this is to include the code below, right before setting the patches' strategies to false.

```
if sum initial-distribution != count patches [
  user-message (word "The total number of agents in\n"
    "n-of-agents-for-each-strategy (i.e. "
    sum initial-distribution "):\n" n-of-players-for-each-strategy
    "\nshould be equal to the number of patches (i.e. "
    count patches ")"
  )
]
```

to setup-graph

The procedure to setup-graph will create the required number of pens –one for each strategy– in the Strategy Distribution plot. Looking at the implementation of the same procedure in the model we developed in the previous chapter, can you implement procedure to setup-graph for our new model?

Implementation of procedure to setup-graph.

Yes, well done! We can use exactly the same code!

```
to setup-graph
  set-current-plot "Strategy Distribution"
  foreach (range n-of-strategies) [ i ->
    create-temporary-plot-pen (word i)
    set-plot-pen-mode 1
    set-plot-pen-color 25 + 40 * i
  ]
end
```

to update-graph

Procedure to update-graph will draw the strategy distribution using a stacked bar chart, just like in the model we implemented in the previous chapter (see figure 3 in section 1.1). This procedure is called at the end of setup to plot the initial distribution of strategies, and will also be called at the end of procedure to go, to plot the strategy distribution at the end of every tick.

Looking at the implementation of the same procedure in the model we developed in the previous chapter, can you implement procedure to update-graph for our new model?

Implementation of procedure to update-graph.

Yes, well done! We only have to replace the word **players** in the previous code with **patches** in the current code.

```
to update-graph
  let strategy-numbers (range n-of-strategies)
  let strategy-frequencies map [ n ->
        count patches with [strategy = n] / n-of-players
     ] strategy-numbers

  set-current-plot "Strategy Distribution"
  let bar 1
  foreach strategy-numbers [ n ->
    set-current-plot-pen (word n)
    plotxy ticks bar
    set bar (bar - (item n strategy-frequencies))
  ]
  set-plot-y-range 0 1
end
```

to update-color

Note that in the previous model, patches were colored according to the four possible combinations of values of C-player? and C-player?-after-revision. Now that there can be many strategies, it seems more natural to use one color for each strategy. It also makes sense to use the same color legend as in the Strategy Distribution plot (see procedure to setup-graph). Can you try and implement the new version of to update-color?

Implementation of procedure to update-color.

Here we go!

```
to update-color
  set pcolor 25 + 40 * strategy
end
```

5.4. Go procedure

The current go procedure looks as follows:

```
to go
  ifelse synchronous-updating?
    [
      ask patches [ play ]
      ask patches [
        update-strategy-after-revision
          ;; here we are not updating the agent's strategy yet
        update-color
      ]
      ask patches [ update-strategy ]
        ;; now we update every agent's strategy at the same time
    ]
    [
      ask patches [
        play
        ask my-coplayers [ play ]
           ;; since your coplayers' strategies or
           ;; your coplayers' coplayers' strategies
           ;; could have changed since the last time
           ;; your coplayers played
        update-strategy-after-revision
        update-color
        update-strategy
      ]
    ]
  tick
end
```

In the previous version of the model, the call to update-color had to be done in between the calls to update-strategy-after-revision and update-strategy. Now that the patches' color only depends on their (updated) strategy, we should ask patches to run update-color at the end of procedure to go, after every patch has updated its strategy.

Finally, recall that we also have to run update-graph at the end of procedure to go, to plot the strategy distribution at the end of every tick. Thus, the code of procedure to go will be as follows:

```
to go
  ifelse synchronous-updating?
    [
      ask patches [ play ]
      ask patches [ update-strategy-after-revision ]
        ;; here we are not updating the agent's strategy yet
      ask patches [ update-strategy ]
        ;; now we update every agent's strategy at the same time
    ]
    [
      ask patches [
        play
        ask my-coplayers [ play ]
           ;; since your coplayers' strategies or
           ;; your coplayers' coplayers' strategies
           ;; could have changed since the last time
           ;; your coplayers played
        update-strategy-after-revision
        update-strategy
      ]
    ]
  tick
  update-graph                   ;; <== new line
  ask patches [update-color]     ;; <== new line
end
```

5.5. Other procedures

to play

In procedure to play the patch has to compute its payoff. For that, the patch must count how many of its coplayers are using each of the possible strategies. We can count the number of coplayers that are using strategy $i \in \{0, 1, ..., (\text{n-of-strategies} - 1)\}$ as:

```
count my-coplayers with [strategy = i]
```

Thus, we just have to run this little function for each value of $i \in \{0, 1, ..., (\text{n-of-strategies} - 1)\}$. This can be easily done using primitive n-values:

```
n-values n-of-strategies [ i -> count my-coplayers with [strategy = i] ]
```

The code above produces a list with the number of coplayers that are using each strategy. Let us store this list in local variable n-of-coplayers-with-strategy-?:

```
let n-of-coplayers-with-strategy-? n-values n-of-strategies [ i ->
     count my-coplayers with [strategy = i] ]
```

Now note that the relevant row of the payoff-matrix is the one at position strategy. We store this row in local variable my-payoffs:

```
let my-payoffs (item strategy payoff-matrix)
```

Finally, the payoff that the patch will get for each coplayer playing strategy *i* is the *i*-th element of the list my-payoffs, so we only have to multiply the two lists (my-payoffs and n-of-coplayers-with-strategy-?) element by element, and add up all the elements in the resulting list. To multiply the two lists element by element we use primitive map:

```
sum (map * my-payoffs n-of-coplayers-with-strategy-?)
```

With this, we have finished the code in procedure to play.

```
to play
  let n-of-coplayers-with-strategy-? n-values n-of-strategies [ i ->
    count my-coplayers with [strategy = i] ]
  let my-payoffs (item strategy payoff-matrix)
  set payoff sum (map * my-payoffs n-of-coplayers-with-strategy-?)
end
```

to update-strategy-after-revision

Right now, procedure to update-strategy-after-revision is implemented as follows:

```
to update-strategy-after-revision
  set C-player?-after-revision ifelse-value (random-float 1 < noise)
    [ one-of [true false] ]
    [ [C-player?] of one-of (my-nbrs-and-me with-max [payoff]) ]
end
```

What changes do we have to make in this procedure?

Implementation of procedure to update-strategy-after-revision.

The only changes we have to make are highlighted in bold below:

```
to update-strategy-after-revision
  set strategy-after-revision ifelse-value (random-float 1 < noise)
    [ random n-of-strategies ]
    [ [strategy] of one-of (my-nbrs-and-me with-max [payoff]) ]
end
```

to update-strategy

Right now, procedure to update-strategy is implemented as follows:

```
to update-strategy
  set C-player? C-player?-after-revision
end
```

What changes do we have to make in this procedure?

Implementation of procedure to update-strategy.

Keep up the excellent work!

```
to update-strategy
  set strategy strategy-after-revision
end
```

5.6. Complete code in the Code tab

The Code tab is ready!

```
globals [
  payoff-matrix
  n-of-strategies
  n-of-players
]
```

```
patches-own [
  strategy
  strategy-after-revision
  payoff
  my-nbrs-and-me
  my-coplayers
  n-of-my-coplayers
]

to setup
  clear-all
  setup-payoffs
  setup-players
  setup-graph
  reset-ticks
  update-graph
  ask patches [update-color]
end

to setup-payoffs
  set payoff-matrix read-from-string payoffs
  set n-of-strategies length payoff-matrix
end

to setup-players
  let initial-distribution read-from-string n-of-players-for-each-strategy
  if length initial-distribution != length payoff-matrix [
    user-message (word "The number of items in\n"
      "n-of-players-for-each-strategy (i.e. "
      length initial-distribution "):\n" n-of-players-for-each-strategy
      "\nshould be equal to the number of rows\n"
      "in the payoff matrix (i.e. "
      length payoff-matrix "):\n"
      payoffs
    )
  ]

  if sum initial-distribution != count patches [
    user-message (word "The total number of agents in\n"
      "n-of-agents-for-each-strategy (i.e. "
      sum initial-distribution "):\n" n-of-players-for-each-strategy
      "\nshould be equal to the number of patches (i.e. "
      count patches ")"
    )
  ]

  ask patches [set strategy false]
  let i 0
  foreach initial-distribution [ j ->
    ask n-of j (patches with [strategy = false]) [
      set payoff 0
```

```
      set strategy i
      set my-nbrs-and-me (patch-set neighbors self)
      set my-coplayers ifelse-value self-matching?
        [my-nbrs-and-me] [neighbors]
      set n-of-my-coplayers (count my-coplayers)
    ]
    set i (i + 1)
  ]
  set n-of-players count patches
end

to setup-graph
  set-current-plot "Strategy Distribution"
  foreach (range n-of-strategies) [ i ->
    create-temporary-plot-pen (word i)
    set-plot-pen-mode 1
    set-plot-pen-color 25 + 40 * i
  ]
end

to go
  ifelse synchronous-updating?
    [
      ask patches [ play ]
      ask patches [ update-strategy-after-revision ]
        ;; here we are not updating the agent's strategy yet
      ask patches [ update-strategy ]
        ;; now we update every agent's strategy at the same time
    ]
    [
      ask patches [
        play
        ask my-coplayers [ play ]
           ;; since your coplayers' strategies or
           ;; your coplayers' coplayers' strategies
           ;; could have changed since the last time
           ;; your coplayers played
        update-strategy-after-revision
        update-strategy
      ]
    ]
  tick
  update-graph
  ask patches [update-color]
end

to play
  let n-of-coplayers-with-strategy-? n-values n-of-strategies [ i ->
    count my-coplayers with [strategy = i] ]
  let my-payoffs (item strategy payoff-matrix)
  set payoff sum (map * my-payoffs n-of-coplayers-with-strategy-?)
```

```
end

to update-strategy-after-revision
  set strategy-after-revision ifelse-value (random-float 1 < noise)
    [ random n-of-strategies ]
    [ [strategy] of one-of my-nbrs-and-me with-max [payoff] ]
end

to update-strategy
  set strategy strategy-after-revision
end

to update-graph
  let strategy-numbers (range n-of-strategies)
  let strategy-frequencies map [ n ->
    count patches with [strategy = n] / n-of-players ] strategy-numbers

  set-current-plot "Strategy Distribution"
  let bar 1
  foreach strategy-numbers [ n ->
    set-current-plot-pen (word n)
    plotxy ticks bar
    set bar (bar - (item n strategy-frequencies))
  ]
  set-plot-y-range 0 1
end

to update-color
  set pcolor 25 + 40 * strategy
end
```

5.7. Code inside the plots

Note that we take care of all plotting in the update-graph procedure. Thus there is no need to write any code inside the plot. We could instead have written the code of procedure to update-graph inside the plot, but given that it is somewhat lengthy, we find it more convenient to group it with the rest of the code in the Code tab.

6. Sample runs

Now that we have implemented the model we can explore the dynamics of the spatial Hawk-Dove-Retaliator game! Will Retaliators survive in a spatial context? Let us explore this question using the parameter values shown in figure 2 above. Get ready... because the results are going to blow your mind!

A video element has been excluded from this version of the text. You can watch it online here: https://wisc.pb.unizin.org/agent-based-evolutionary-game-dynamics/?p=112

Unbelievable! Retaliators do not only survive, but they are capable of taking over about half the population. Is this observation robust? If you modify the parameters of the model you will see that indeed it is. The following video shows an illustrative run with *noise* = 0.05, *synchronous-updating?* = false and *self-matching?* = false.

A video element has been excluded from this version of the text. You can watch it online here: https://wisc.pb.unizin.org/agent-based-evolutionary-game-dynamics/?p=112

The greater level of *noise* means that more Hawks appear by chance. This harms Retaliators more than it harms Doves, but Retaliators still manage to stay the most prevalent strategy in the population. How can this be?

First, note that even though the state where the whole population is choosing Retaliator is not an ESS, it is a Neutrally Stable State (Sandholm, 2010, p. 82). And, crucially, it is the only pure state that is Nash (i.e. the only pure strategy that is best response to itself). Note that in spatial contexts neighbors face similar situations when playing the game (since their neighborhoods overlap). Because of this, it is often the case that neighbors choose the same strategy, and therefore clusters of agents using the same strategy are common. In the Hawk-Dove-Retaliator game, clusters of Retaliators are more stable than clusters of Doves (which are easily invadable by Hawks) and also more stable than clusters of Hawks (which are easily invadable by Doves). This partially explains the amazing success of Retaliators in spatial contexts, even though they are weakly dominated by Doves.

7. Exercises

You can use the following link to download the complete NetLogo model: nxn-imitate-best-nbr.

Exercise 1. Killingback and Doebeli (1996, pp. 1140-1) explore the spatial Hawk-Dove-Retaliator-Bully game, with payoff matrix:

```
[[ -1  2 -1 2]
 [  0  1  1 0]
 [ -1  1  1 2]
 [  0  2  0 1]]
```

Do Retaliators still do well in this game?

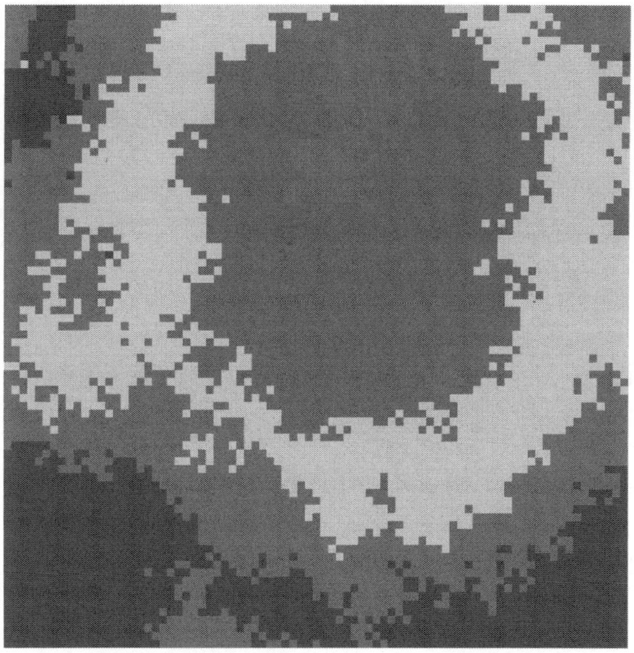

Snapshot of a simulation run of a spatial monocyclic game with noise = 0.001, synchronous-updating? = false and self-matching? = true.

Exercise 2. Explore the beautiful dynamics of the following monocyclic game (Sandholm, 2010, example 9.2.2, pp. 329-30):

```
[[ 0 -1  0  0  1]
 [ 1  0 -1  0  0]
 [ 0  1  0 -1  0]
 [ 0  0  1  0 -1]
 [-1  0  0  1  0]]
```

Compare simulations with balanced initial conditions (i.e. all strategies approximately equally present) and with unbalanced initial conditions (e.g. only one strategy present at the beginning of the simulation). What do you observe?

Exercise 3. How can we parameterize our model to replicate the results shown in figure 4 of Killingback and Doebeli (1996, p. 1141)?

CODE Exercise 4. In procedure to play we compute the list with the number of coplayers that are using each strategy as follows:

```
n-values n-of-strategies [ i -> count my-coplayers with [strategy = i] ]
```

Can you implement the same functionality using the primitive `map` instead of `n-values`?

CODE Exercise 5. Reimplement the procedure to update-strategy-after-revision so the revising agent uses the imitative pairwise-difference protocol adapted to networks, i.e. the revising agent looks at a random neighbor and copies her strategy only if the observed agent's average payoff is higher than the revising agent's average payoff; in that case, the revising agent switches with probability proportional to the payoff difference.

2.3. Other types of neighborhoods and other revision protocols

1. Goal

Our goal in this section is to extend the model we have created in the previous section by adding two features that are crucial to assess the impact of space on evolutionary models:

- The possibility to model different types of neighborhoods of arbitrary size. Besides Moore neighborhoods, we will implement Von Neumann neighborhoods, and both of them of any size.
- The possibility to model other revision protocols besides the "imitate the best neighbor" protocol. In particular, we will implement the imitative pairwise-difference protocol, the imitative positive-proportional protocol, and the imitative logit protocol.[1]

2. Motivation. Robustness of cooperation in spatial settings

In section 2.1 we explored the impact of different assumptions on the robustness of cooperation in spatial settings. However, one assumption we did not change was the revision protocol (aka update rule). Roca et al. (2009a, 2009b) conducted an impressive simulation study of the effect of spatial structure in 2×2 games, and discovered that the revision protocol can play a major role. In particular, they found that the "imitate the best neighbor" protocol (which Roca et al. (2009a, 2009b) call "unconditional imitation") favors cooperation in the Prisoner's Dilemma more than any other revision protocol they studied.

> In what concerns the Prisoner's Dilemma, the above results also prove that the promotion of cooperation in this game is not robust against changes in the update rule, because the beneficial effect of spatial lattices practically disappears for rules different from unconditional imitation, when seen in the wider scope of the ST plane. Roca et al. (2009b, p. 9)

In this section we are going to implement several revision protocols. This will allow us to replicate Roca et al.'s (2009a, 2009b) results… and many others (see the proposed exercises).

1. The names given to the different protocols follow Izquierdo et al. (2019).

3. Description of the model

The model we are going to develop here is a generalization of the model implemented in the previous section. In particular, we are going to add the following four parameters:

- *neighborhood-type*. This parameter is used to define the agents' neighborhood (both for playing and for strategy updating).[2] The parameter can have two possible values: "*Moore*" for a Moore neighborhood, or "*Von Neumann*" for a Von Neumann neighborhood.
- *neighborhood-range*. This parameter determines the range of the neighborhood. A patch's Moore neighborhood of range *r* consists of the patches within Chebyshev distance *r*. A patch's Von Neumann neighborhood of range *r* is composed of the patches within Manhattan distance *r*. Note that in our descriptions of revision protocols below, we do not consider a patch to be a neighbor of itself unless otherwise stated.
- *protocol*. This parameter determines the revision protocol that agents will follow. It will be implemented with a chooser, with four possible values:
    - "*best-neighbor*" (Nowak and May, 1992, 1993). This is the "imitate the best neighbor" protocol, already implemented in our model.[3]
    - "*imitative-pairwise-difference*" (Hauert 2002,[4] 2006). This is the imitative pairwise-difference protocol we saw in section 0.1 adapted to networks. Under this protocol, the revising agent looks at a random neighbor and considers copying her strategy only if the observed neighbor's average payoff is higher than the revising agent's average payoff; in that case, the revising agent switches with probability proportional to the payoff difference.[5]
    - "*imitative-positive-proportional-m*" (Nowak et al., 1994a, b). Under this revision protocol, the revising agent copies the strategy of one of her neighbors (including herself, in this case) with probability proportional to their total payoff raised to parameter *m*.[6] Parameter *m* controls the intensity of selection (see below). We do not allow for negative payoffs when using this protocol.[7]

2. Recall that the set of patches that a patch plays with also depends on the value of *self-matching?*.
3. Roca et al. (2009a, 2009b) call this revision protocol "unconditional imitation" and Hauert (2002) calls it "best takes over". Also, note that Hauert (2002) resolves ties differently.
4. See Roca et al. (2009b) for an important and illuminating discussion of this paper.
5. Roca et al. (2009a, 2009b) call this revision protocol "replicator rule or proportional imitation rule", though their implementation is not exactly the same as ours. They use total payoffs and we use average payoffs. The two implementations differ only if it is possible that two agents have different number of neighbors (e.g. as with non-periodic boundary conditions). Note, however, that Roca et al. (2009a, 2009b)'s experiments have periodic boundary conditions, i.e. all agents have the same number of neighbors, so for all these cases the two implementations are equivalent. Hauert (2002) calls this revision protocol "imitate the better".
6. It may make more sense to use *average* rather than *total* payoffs. We use total payoffs here to be able to replicate Nowak et al.'s (1994a, b) experiments. To use average payoffs, the change in the code is minimal.
7. Roca et al. (2009a, 2009b) call this revision protocol with $m = 1$ "Moran rule". Their implementation is not exactly the same as ours, since they do allow for negative payoffs by introducing a constant. Note, however, that the two implementations are equivalent if payoffs are non-negative. Hauert (2002) calls this revision protocol with $m =$

- "*imitative-logit-m*" (Weibull, 1995, p. 161; Szabó and Tőke, 1998). Under this revision protocol, the revising agent i looks at one of her neighbors j at random and copies her strategy with probability $\frac{e^{m\pi_j}}{e^{m\pi_i}+e^{m\pi_j}}$, where π_z denotes agent z's average payoff and $m \geq 0$.[8] Parameter *m* controls the intensity of selection (see below).

- *m*. This is a parameter that controls the intensity of selection in revision protocols "*imitative-positive-proportional-m*" and "*imitative-logit-m*" (see above). High values of *m* imply that selection is strongly based on payoffs, i.e. the agents with the highest payoffs will be chosen with very high probability. Lower values of *m* mean that the sensitivity of selection to payoffs is weak (e.g. if *m* = 0, selection among agents is random, i.e. independent of their payoffs).

Everything else stays as described in the previous section.

CODE 4. Interface design

We depart from the model we developed in the previous section (so if you want to preserve it, now is a good time to duplicate it).

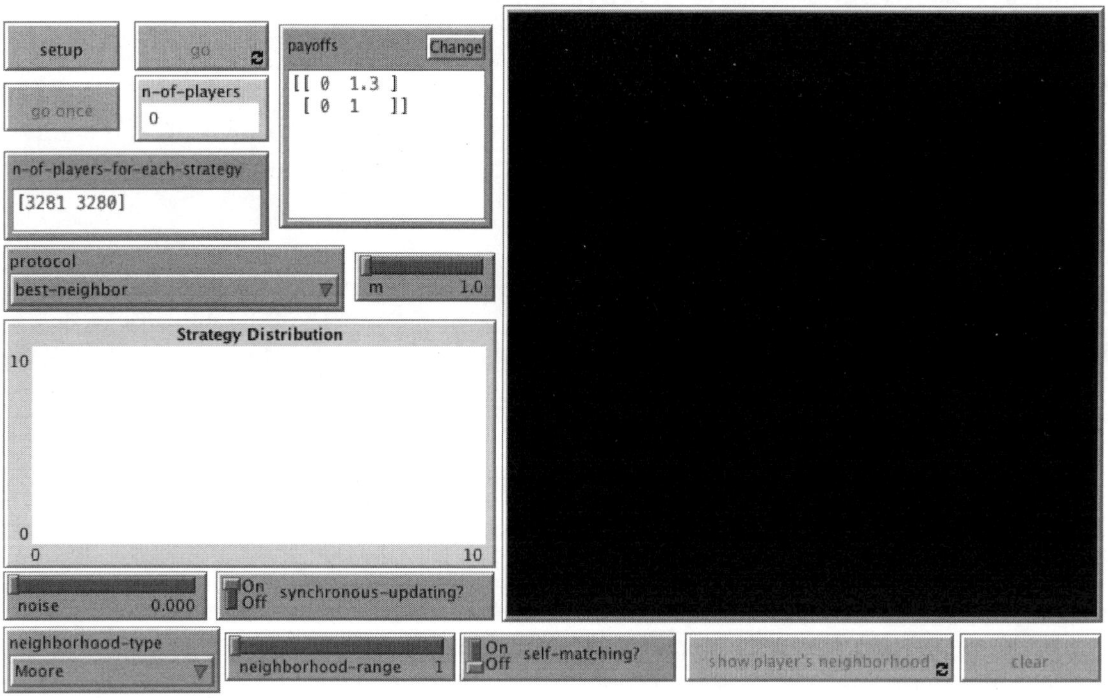

Figure 1. Interface design.

In the new interface (see figure 1 above), we have to add:

1 "proportional update".

8. Roca et al. (2009a, 2009b) and other authors (see e.g. Traulsen and Hauert (2009), Perc and Szolnoki (2010) and Adami et al. (2016)) call this revision protocol the "Fermi rule". Note also that some authors (e.g. Szabó and Tőke (1998)) use *total* payoffs rather than *average* payoffs.

- One chooser for new parameter *neighborhood-type* (with possible values "*Moore*" and "*Von Neumann*"), and a slider for parameter *neighborhood-range* (with *minimum* = 1 and *increment* = 1).
- One chooser for new parameter *protocol* (with possible values "*best-neighbor*", "*imitative-pairwise-difference*", "*imitative-positive-proportional-m*" and "*imitative-logit-m*"), and a slider for parameter *m* (with *minimum* = 0 and *increment* = 0.1).

We have also added a button (labeled show player's neighborhood) to see any patch's neighborhood on the 2D view and another button (labeled clear) to clear the display of the neighborhood.

CODE 5. Code

5.1. Skeleton of the code

The skeleton of the code for procedures to setup and to go is the same as in the previous model. In this section we will modify mainly the following two procedures:

- procedure to setup-players, to set the players' neighborhoods according to parameters *neighborhood-type* and *neighborhood-range* (see figure 2).

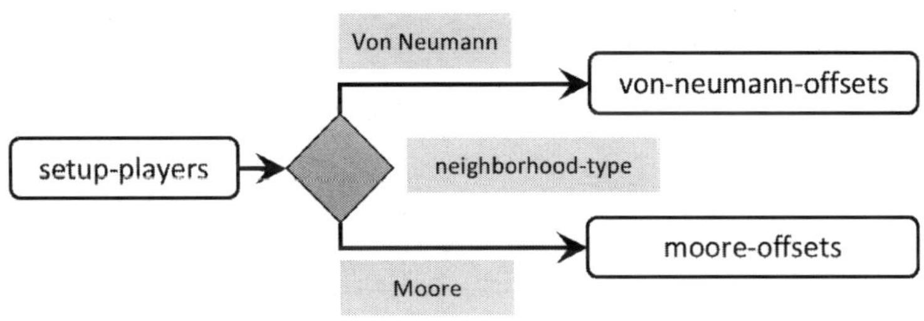

Figure 2. Calls to other procedures from procedure to setup-players.

- procedure to update-strategy-after-revision, to run the revision protocol indicated in parameter *protocol* (see figure 3).

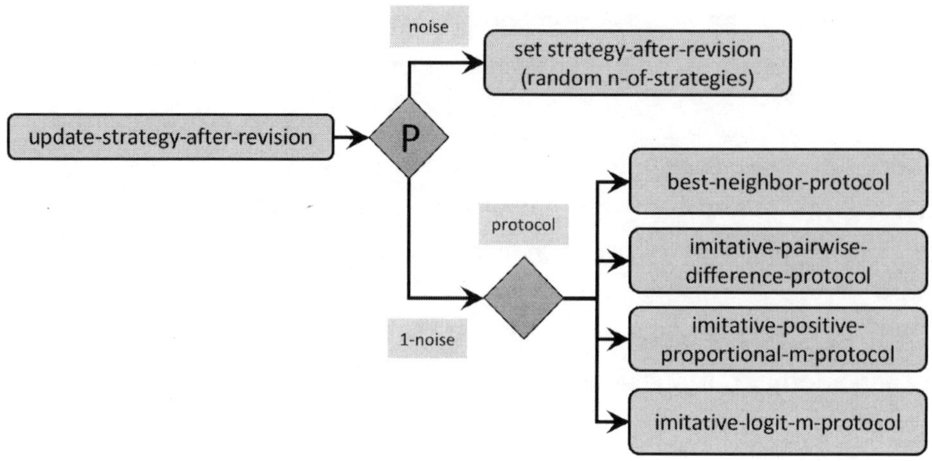

Figure 3. Calls to other procedures from procedure to update-strategy-after-revision.

5.2. Extension I. Implementation of different neighborhoods

Recall that patches have the following two individually owned variables:

- my-coplayers, which contains the set of agents with whom the patch plays the game (and is affected by parameter *self-matching?*), and
- my-nbrs-and-me, which is the set of agents the player considers when revising its strategy.

These two agentsets are the same if *self-matching?* is true, and differ only in the focal patch if *self-matching?* is false. We will keep this distinction for any type of neighborhood.

To implement the different neighborhoods, primitive `at-points` will be very useful. This primitive reports a subset of a given agentset that includes only the agents on the patches at the given coordinates (relative to the calling agent). As an example, the following code gives a patch's Von Neumann neighborhood of range 1 (including the patch itself):

```
patches at-points [[-1 0] [0 -1] [0 0] [0 1] [1 0]]
```

And the following code gives a patch's Moore neighborhood of range 1 (including the patch itself):

```
patches at-points [[-1 -1] [-1 0] [-1 1] [0 -1] [0 0] [0 1] [1 -1] [1 0] [1
1]]
```

Thus, the key is to implement procedures that report the appropriate lists of relative coordinates.[9] Let's do this!

9. Our implementation is heavily based on code example titled "Moore & Von Neumann Example", which you can find in NetLogo models library. Note, however, that this code example does not compute the correct neighborhoods if the center of the world lies at the edge or at a corner of the world (at least in version 6.1 and previous ones).

Implementation of relative coordinates for Moore neighborhoods

Our goal here is to implement a procedure that reports the appropriate list of relative coordinates for Moore neighborhoods, for any given range and letting the user choose whether the list should include the item [0 0] or not. Let us call this reporter to-report moore-offsets. Note that this reporter takes two inputs, which we can call r (for range) and include-center?.

```
to-report moore-offsets [r include-center?]
    ;; code to be written
end
```

Below we provide some examples of what reporter to-report moore-offsets should produce:

- If r = 1 and include-center? is true:

  ```
  [[-1 -1] [-1 0] [-1 1] [0 -1] [0 0] [0 1] [1 -1] [1 0] [1 1]]
  ```

- If r = 1 and include-center? is false:

  ```
  [[-1 -1] [-1 0] [-1 1] [0 -1] [0 1] [1 -1] [1 0] [1 1]]
  ```

- If r = 2 and include-center? is true:

  ```
  [[-2 -2] [-2 -1] [-2 0] [-2 1] [-2 2] [-1 -2] [-1 -1] [-1 0] [-1 1] [-1
  2] [0 -2] [0 -1] [0 0] [0 1] [0 2] [1 -2] [1 -1] [1 0] [1 1] [1 2] [2
  -2] [2 -1] [2 0] [2 1] [2 2]]
  ```

Note that the effect of input include-center? is just to include or exclude [0 0] from the output list, so we can worry about that at the end of the implementation. To produce the list of Moore offsets for range r, we can start building the list l = [–r, –r+1, …, r-1, r] and then build 2-item lists which each element of the list l together with each element of the same list l. Thus, let us build the list l = [–r, –r+1, …, r-1, r]:

```
let l (range (- r) (r + 1))
```

To build 2-items lists with first element *el1* and second element each of the elements of list l, we can use primitive map as follows:

```
map [el2 -> list el1 el2] l
```

And now we should make *el1* be each of the elements of list l. For this we can use primitive map again:

```
map [ el1 -> map [el2 -> list el1 el2] l] l
```

The only problem now is that we have several nested lists. For example, the code above for l = [-1, 0, 1] produces:

```
[[[-1 -1] [-1 0] [-1 1]] [[0 -1] [0 0] [0 1]] [[1 -1] [1 0] [1 1]]]
```

Note that the outmost list contains three sublists, each of which contains three 2-item lists. We can get rid of the extra lists using primitives reduce and sentence:

```
let result reduce sentence map [ el1 -> map [el2 -> list el1 el2] l] l
```

The code above creates the list of required offsets, including [0 0]. Now we just have to remove [0 0] if and only if input include-center? is false. Thus, the final code for reporter to-report moore-offsets is as follows:

```
to-report moore-offsets [r include-center?]
  let l (range (- r) (r + 1))
  let result reduce sentence map [ el1 -> map [el2 -> list el1 el2] l] l
  report ifelse-value include-center?
    [ result ]
    [ remove [0 0] result ]
end
```

Implementation of relative coordinates for Von Neumann neighborhoods

Our goal here is to implement a procedure that reports the appropriate list of relative coordinates for Von Neumann neighborhoods. Let us call this reporter to-report von-neumann-offsets and let us call its inputs r (for range) and include-center?, just like before.

```
to-report von-neumann-offsets [r include-center?]
   ;; code to be written
end
```

Note that, for any given r and include-center?, the list of offsets for a Von Neumann neighborhood is a subset of the list of offsets for the corresponding Moore neighborhood. In particular, the list of Von Neumann offsets is composed of the elements [*el1 el2*] in the list of Moore offsets that satisfy the condition $|el1| + |el2| \leq r$. Thus, we can create the corresponding list of Moore offsets and filter those coordinates that satisfy the condition using primitive filter. Do you want to give it a try?

Implementation of procedure to-report von-neumann-offsets

Yes, well done!

```
to-report von-neumann-offsets [r include-center?]
  let moore-list (moore-offsets r include-center?)
```

```
  report filter [l -> abs first l + abs last l <= r] moore-list
end
```

Putting everything together

Now that we have implemented to-report moore-offsets and to-report von-neumann-offsets, we can use them in procedure to setup-players to create the right neighborhood for each patch. The only lines we have to modify are the ones highlighted in bold below:

```
to setup-players
  let initial-distribution read-from-string n-of-players-for-each-strategy
  if length initial-distribution != length payoff-matrix [
    user-message (word "The number of items in\n"
      "n-of-players-for-each-strategy (i.e. "
      length initial-distribution "):\n" n-of-players-for-each-strategy
      "\nshould be equal to the number of rows\n"
      "in the payoff matrix (i.e. "
      length payoff-matrix "):\n"
      payoffs
    )
  ]

  if sum initial-distribution != count patches [
    user-message (word "The total number of agents in\n"
      "n-of-agents-for-each-strategy (i.e. "
      sum initial-distribution "):\n" n-of-players-for-each-strategy
      "\nshould be equal to the number of patches (i.e. "
      count patches ")"
    )
  ]

  ask patches [set strategy false]
  let i 0
  let offsets ifelse-value (neighborhood-type = "Von Neumann")
        [ von-neumann-offsets neighborhood-range self-matching? ]
        [ moore-offsets neighborhood-range self-matching? ]

  foreach initial-distribution [ j ->
    ask n-of j (patches with [strategy = false]) [
      set payoff 0
      set strategy i
      set my-coplayers patches at-points offsets
      set n-of-my-coplayers (count my-coplayers)
      set my-nbrs-and-me (patch-set my-coplayers self)
    ]
```

```
    set i (i + 1)
  ]

  set n-of-players count patches
end
```

Note that variable my-coplayers may or may not contain the patch itself (depending on the value of parameter *self-matching?*), but variable my-nbrs-and-me will always contain it, since we are setting its value to (patch-set my-coplayers self). This is perfectly fine even if my-coplayers already contains the patch itself, since agentsets do not contain duplicates. Adding an agent *a* to an agentset that already contains that agent *a* has no effect whatsoever.[10]

A nice final touch

Finally, we are going to write some code to let the user see the neighborhood of any patch in the 2D view by clicking on it. This is just for displaying purposes, so feel free to skip this if you're not really interested. Let us start by implementing a new procedure called to show-neighborhood as follows:

```
to show-neighborhood
  if mouse-down? [
    ask patch mouse-xcor mouse-ycor [
      ask my-coplayers [set pcolor white]
    ]
  ]
  display
end
```

You may want to read the documentation for primitives `mouse-down?`, `mouse-xcor` and `mouse-ycor`. Basically, this procedure paints in white the patches contained in the variable my-coplayers of the patch you click with your mouse. However, for this to work, the procedure must be running all the time. To do this, we can run this procedure within the button labeled show player's neighborhood in the interface, and make this button be a "forever" button.

Insert the following code within the button labeled show player's neighborhood:

```
with-local-randomness [show-neighborhood]
```

10. For instance, the following code reports true.

```
show (patch-set patch 0 0 patch 0 0) = (patch-set patch 0 0)
```

The use of primitive `with-local-randomness` guarantees that this piece of code does not interfere with the generation of pseudorandom numbers for the rest of the model.

> To clear the white paint, insert the following code within the button labeled clear (which should not be a "forever" button):
>
> ```
> with-local-randomness [ ask patches [update-color] ]
> ```

Figure 4 shows a patch's Von Neumann neighborhood of range 5 (excluding the patch itself) painted in white.

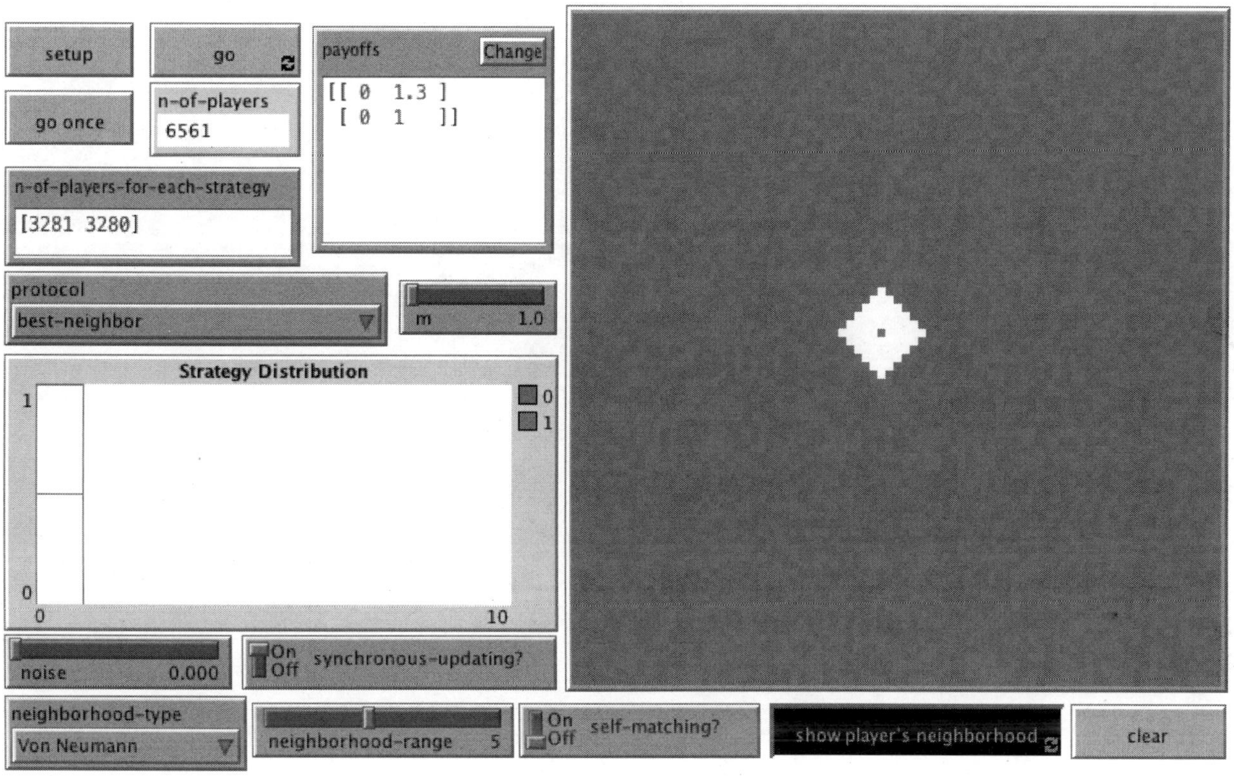

Figure 4. The 2D view shows in white a patch's set my-coplayers. Relevant parameters: neighborhood-type = "Von Neumann", neighborhood-range = 5, and self-matching? = false.

5.3. Extension II. Implementation of different revision protocols

The implementation of the revision protocol takes place in procedure to update-strategy-after-revision. Note that the effect of noise is the same regardless of the revision protocol, so we can deal with noise in a unified way, regardless of which revision protocol will be executed. One possible way of doing this is as follows:

```
to update-strategy-after-revision
  ifelse (random-float 1 < noise)
```

```
    [ set strategy-after-revision random n-of-strategies ]
    [
      ;; code to set strategy-after-revision
      ;; using the revision protocol indicated by the user
      ;; through parameter protocol
    ]
end
```

To make the implementation of revision protocols elegant and modular, we should implement a different procedure for each revision protocol. Let us call these procedures: best-neighbor-protocol, imitative-pairwise-difference-protocol, imitative-positive-proportional-m-protocol and imitative-logit-m-protocol. With these procedures in place, the code for procedure to update-strategy-after-revision would just look as follows:

```
to update-strategy-after-revision
  ifelse (random-float 1 < noise)
    [ set strategy-after-revision random n-of-strategies ]
    [ (ifelse
        protocol = "best-neighbor"
                    [ best-neighbor-protocol ]
        protocol = "imitative-pairwise-difference"
                    [ imitative-pairwise-difference-protocol ]
        protocol = "imitative-positive-proportional-m"
                    [ imitative-positive-proportional-m-protocol ]
        protocol = "imitative-logit-m"
                    [ imitative-logit-m-protocol ]
      )
    ]
end
```

Note that primitive `ifelse` can work with multiple conditions, just like switch statements in other programming languages.[11]

Now we just have to implement the procedures for each of the four revision protocols. Do you want to give it a try? The first one is not very difficult.

Implementation of procedure to best-neighbor-protocol

11. This functionality was added in NetLogo 6.1.

```
to best-neighbor-protocol
  set strategy-after-revision
      [strategy] of one-of my-nbrs-and-me with-max [payoff]
end
```

The implementation of procedure to imitative-pairwise-difference-protocol is significantly more difficult than the previous one, but if you have managed to read this book until here, you certainly have what it takes to do it!

Implementation of procedure to imitative-pairwise-difference-protocol

A possible implementation of this procedure is as follows:

```
to imitative-pairwise-difference-protocol
  let observed-player one-of other my-coplayers

  ;; compute difference in average payoffs
  let payoff-diff ([payoff / n-of-my-coplayers] of observed-player
                  - (payoff / n-of-my-coplayers))

  set strategy-after-revision
      ifelse-value (random-float 1 < (payoff-diff / max-payoff-difference))
        [ [strategy] of observed-player ]
        [ strategy ]
      ;; If your strategy is the better, payoff-diff is negative,
      ;; so you are going to stick with it.
      ;; If it's not, you switch with probability
      ;; (payoff-diff / max-payoff-difference)
end
```

Note that we are using a new variable, i.e. max-payoff-difference, to make sure that the agent changes strategy with *probability* proportional to the average payoff difference. Thus, we should define it as global (since this max-payoff difference will not change over the course of a run), as follows:

```
globals [
  payoff-matrix
  n-of-strategies
```

```
  n-of-players
  max-payoff-difference     ;; <== New line
]
```

We also have to set the value of this new variable. We can do that at the end of the setup-payoffs method, as follows:

```
to setup-payoffs
  set payoff-matrix read-from-string payoffs
  set n-of-strategies length payoff-matrix

  ;;New lines below
  set max-payoff-difference
      (max-of-matrix payoff-matrix) - (min-of-matrix payoff-matrix)
end
```

Finally, note that we have implemented two new procedures to compute the minimum and the maximum value of a matrix:

```
;;;;;;;;;;;;;;;;;;;;;;;;;;;;
;;; SUPPORTING PROCEDURES ;;;
;;;;;;;;;;;;;;;;;;;;;;;;;;;;

;;;;;;;;;;;;;;;;
;;; Matrices ;;;
;;;;;;;;;;;;;;;;

to-report max-of-matrix [m]
  report max reduce sentence m
end

to-report min-of-matrix [m]
  report min reduce sentence m
end
```

To implement procedure to imitative-positive-proportional-m-protocol, there is an extension that comes bundled with NetLogo which will make our life much easier: `extension rnd`. To use it, you just have to add the following line at the beginning of your code

```
extensions [rnd]
```

Having loaded the `rnd` extension, you can use primitive `rnd:weighted-one-of`, which will be very handy. With this information, you may want to try to implement this short procedure yourself.

Implementation of procedure to imitative-positive-proportional-m-protocol

```
to imitative-positive-proportional-m-protocol
  let chosen-nbr rnd:weighted-one-of my-nbrs-and-me [ payoff ^ m ]
  set strategy-after-revision [strategy] of chosen-nbr
end
```

If you wanted to use *average* rather than *total* payoffs, you would only have to divide the payoff by n-of-my-coplayers.

To avoid errors when payoffs are negative and this protocol is used, it would be nice to check that payoffs are non-negative, and if they are, let the user know. We can do this implementing the following procedure:

```
to check-payoffs-are-non-negative
  if min reduce sentence payoff-matrix < 0 [
    user-message (word
      "Since you are using protocol = imitative-positive-proportional-m,
all elements in the payoff matrix\n"
      payoffs
      "\nshould be non-negative numbers.")
  ]
end
```

An appropriate place to call this procedure would be at the end of procedure to setup-payoffs, which would then be as follows:

```
to setup-payoffs
  set payoff-matrix read-from-string payoffs
  set n-of-strategies length payoff-matrix

  ;; New lines below
  set max-payoff-difference
    (max-of-matrix payoff-matrix) - (min-of-matrix payoff-matrix)
  if protocol = "imitative-positive-proportional-m"
    [ check-payoffs-are-non-negative ]
end
```

The implementation of procedure to imitative-logit-m-protocol is not extremely hard after having seen the implementation of to imitative-pairwise-difference-protocol, and realizing that $\frac{e^{m\pi_j}}{e^{m\pi_j}+e^{m\pi_i}} = \frac{1}{1+e^{-m(\pi_j-\pi_i)}}$.

Implementation of procedure to imitative-logit-m-protocol

A possible implementation of this procedure is as follows:

```
to imitative-logit-m-protocol
  let observed-player one-of other my-coplayers

  ;; compute difference in average payoffs
  let payoff-diff ([payoff / n-of-my-coplayers] of observed-player
                - (payoff / n-of-my-coplayers))

  set strategy-after-revision
    ifelse-value (random-float 1 < (1 / (1 + exp (- m * payoff-diff))))
      [ [strategy] of observed-player ]
      [ strategy ]
end
```

5.5. Complete code in the Code tab

The Code tab is ready! Congratulations! With this model you can rigorously explore the effect of space in 2-player games.

```
extensions [rnd]        ;; <== New line

globals [
  payoff-matrix
  n-of-strategies
  n-of-players
  max-payoff-difference  ;; <== New line
]

patches-own [
  strategy
  strategy-after-revision
  payoff
  my-nbrs-and-me
  my-coplayers
  n-of-my-coplayers
]

to setup
  clear-all
  setup-payoffs
```

```
  setup-players
  setup-graph
  reset-ticks
  update-graph
  ask patches [update-color]
end

to setup-payoffs
  set payoff-matrix read-from-string payoffs
  set n-of-strategies length payoff-matrix

  ;; New lines below
  set max-payoff-difference
     (max-of-matrix payoff-matrix) - (min-of-matrix payoff-matrix)
  if protocol = "imitative-positive-proportional-m"
     [ check-payoffs-are-non-negative ]
end

to setup-players
  let initial-distribution read-from-string n-of-players-for-each-strategy
  if length initial-distribution != length payoff-matrix [
    user-message (word "The number of items in\n"
      "n-of-players-for-each-strategy (i.e. "
      length initial-distribution "):\n" n-of-players-for-each-strategy
      "\nshould be equal to the number of rows\n"
      "in the payoff matrix (i.e. "
      length payoff-matrix "):\n"
      payoffs
    )
  ]

  if sum initial-distribution != count patches [
    user-message (word "The total number of agents in\n"
      "n-of-agents-for-each-strategy (i.e. "
      sum initial-distribution "):\n" n-of-players-for-each-strategy
      "\nshould be equal to the number of patches (i.e. "
      count patches ")"
    )
  ]

  ask patches [set strategy false]
  let i 0
  let offsets ifelse-value (neighborhood-type = "Von Neumann")
       [ von-neumann-offsets neighborhood-range self-matching? ]
       [ moore-offsets neighborhood-range self-matching? ]

  foreach initial-distribution [ j ->
    ask n-of j (patches with [strategy = false]) [
      set payoff 0
      set strategy i
      set my-coplayers patches at-points offsets
      set n-of-my-coplayers (count my-coplayers)
```

```
      set my-nbrs-and-me (patch-set my-coplayers self)
    ]
    set i (i + 1)
  ]

  set n-of-players count patches
end

to setup-graph
  set-current-plot "Strategy Distribution"
  foreach (range n-of-strategies) [ i ->
    create-temporary-plot-pen (word i)
    set-plot-pen-mode 1
    set-plot-pen-color 25 + 40 * i
  ]
end

to go
  ifelse synchronous-updating?
    [
      ask patches [ play ]
      ask patches [ update-strategy-after-revision ]
        ;; here we are not updating the agent's strategy yet
      ask patches [ update-strategy ]
        ;; now we update every agent's strategy at the same time
    ]
    [
      ask patches [
        play
        ask my-coplayers [ play ]
          ;; since your coplayers' strategies or
          ;; your coplayers' coplayers' strategies
          ;; could have changed since the last time
          ;; your coplayers played
        update-strategy-after-revision
        update-strategy
      ]
    ]
  tick
  update-graph
  ask patches [update-color]
end

to play
  let n-of-coplayers-with-strategy-? n-values n-of-strategies [ i ->
    count my-coplayers with [strategy = i] ]
  let my-payoffs (item strategy payoff-matrix)
  set payoff sum (map * my-payoffs n-of-coplayers-with-strategy-?)
end

to update-strategy-after-revision
```

```
  ifelse (random-float 1 < noise)
    [ set strategy-after-revision random n-of-strategies ]
    [ (ifelse
        protocol = "best-neighbor"
                  [ best-neighbor-protocol ]
        protocol = "imitative-pairwise-difference"
                  [ imitative-pairwise-difference-protocol ]
        protocol = "imitative-positive-proportional-m"
                  [ imitative-positive-proportional-m-protocol ]
        protocol = "imitative-logit-m"
                  [ imitative-logit-m-protocol ]
      )
    ]
end

to best-neighbor-protocol
  set strategy-after-revision
      [strategy] of one-of my-nbrs-and-me with-max [payoff]
end

to imitative-pairwise-difference-protocol
  let observed-player one-of other my-coplayers

  ;; compute difference in average payoffs
  let payoff-diff ([payoff / n-of-my-coplayers] of observed-player
                  - (payoff / n-of-my-coplayers))

  set strategy-after-revision
      ifelse-value (random-float 1 < (payoff-diff / max-payoff-difference))
        [ [strategy] of observed-player ]
        [ strategy ]
      ;; If your strategy is the better, payoff-diff is negative,
      ;; so you are going to stick with it.
      ;; If it's not, you switch with probability
      ;; (payoff-diff / max-payoff-difference)
end

to imitative-positive-proportional-m-protocol
  let chosen-nbr rnd:weighted-one-of my-nbrs-and-me [ payoff ^ m ]
      ;; https://ccl.northwestern.edu/netlogo/docs/rnd.html#rnd:weighted-one-of
  set strategy-after-revision [strategy] of chosen-nbr
end

to imitative-logit-m-protocol
  let observed-player one-of other my-coplayers

  ;; compute difference in average payoffs
  let payoff-diff ([payoff / n-of-my-coplayers] of observed-player
                  - (payoff / n-of-my-coplayers))

  set strategy-after-revision
    ifelse-value (random-float 1 < (1 / (1 + exp (- m * payoff-diff))))
```

```
      [ [strategy] of observed-player ]
      [ strategy ]
end

to update-strategy
  set strategy strategy-after-revision
end

to update-graph
  let strategy-numbers (range n-of-strategies)
  let strategy-frequencies map [ n ->
    count patches with [strategy = n] / n-of-players ] strategy-numbers

  set-current-plot "Strategy Distribution"
  let bar 1
  foreach strategy-numbers [ n ->
    set-current-plot-pen (word n)
    plotxy ticks bar
    set bar (bar - (item n strategy-frequencies))
  ]
  set-plot-y-range 0 1
end

to update-color
  set pcolor 25 + 40 * strategy
end

;;;;;;;;;;;;;;;;;;;;;;;;;;;;;
;;; SUPPORTING PROCEDURES ;;;
;;;;;;;;;;;;;;;;;;;;;;;;;;;;;

to-report moore-offsets [r include-center?]
  let l (range (- r) (r + 1))
  let result reduce sentence map [ el1 -> map [el2 -> list el1 el2] l] l
  report ifelse-value include-center?
    [ result ]
    [ remove [0 0] result ]
end

to-report von-neumann-offsets [r include-center?]
  let moore-list (moore-offsets r include-center?)
  report filter [l -> abs first l + abs last l <= r] moore-list
end

to show-neighborhood
  if mouse-down? [
    ask patch mouse-xcor mouse-ycor [
      ask my-coplayers [set pcolor white]
    ]
  ]
  display
```

```
end

to check-payoffs-are-non-negative
  if min reduce sentence payoff-matrix < 0 [
    user-message (word
      "Since you are using protocol = imitative-positive-proportional-m, all
elements in the payoff matrix\n"
      payoffs
      "\nshould be non-negative numbers.")
  ]
end

;;;;;;;;;;;;;;;;
;;; Matrices ;;;
;;;;;;;;;;;;;;;;

to-report max-of-matrix [matrix]
  report max reduce sentence matrix
end

to-report min-of-matrix [matrix]
  report min reduce sentence matrix
end
```

6. Sample runs

Revision protocols

Now that we have implemented the model, we can explore the impact of the revision protocol on the promotion of cooperation in the spatially embedded Prisoner's Dilemma. Let us explore this question using the parameter values shown in figure 1 above. We start with the "imitate the best neighbor" protocol. The simulation below shows a representative run.

A video element has been excluded from this version of the text. You can watch it online here: https://wisc.pb.unizin.org/agent-based-evolutionary-game-dynamics/?p=1292

As you can see in the video above, with the "imitate the best neighbor" protocol, high levels of cooperation are achieved (i.e. about 90% of the patches cooperate in the long run). But, how robust is this result to changes in the revision protocol? To explore this question, let us run the same simulation with the other three revision protocols we have implemented. The simulation below shows a representative run with the "imitative-pairwise-difference" protocol.

A video element has been excluded from this version of the text. You can watch it online here: https://wisc.pb.unizin.org/agent-based-evolutionary-game-dynamics/?p=1292

With the "imitative-pairwise-difference" protocol, there is no cooperation at all in the long run. Let us now try the "imitative-positive-proportional-m" protocol with m = 1:[12]

A video element has been excluded from this version of the text. You can watch it online here: https://wisc.pb.unizin.org/agent-based-evolutionary-game-dynamics/?p=1292

We do not observe any cooperation at all with the "imitative-positive-proportional-m" (with m = 1) either. Finally, let us try the "imitative-logit-m" protocol with m = 1 (or any other positive value, for that matter):[13]

A video element has been excluded from this version of the text. You can watch it online here: https://wisc.pb.unizin.org/agent-based-evolutionary-game-dynamics/?p=1292

And we observe universal defection again! Clearly, as Roca et al. (2009a, 2009b) point out, the "imitate the best neighbor" protocol seems to favor cooperation in the Prisoner's Dilemma more than other revision protocols.

Neighborhoods

What about if we change the type of neighborhood? You can check that the simulations shown in the videos above do not change qualitatively if we use Von Neumann neighborhoods rather than Moore neighborhoods. However, what does make a difference is the size of the neighborhood. Note that if the size is so large that agents' neighborhoods encompass the whole population, we have a global interaction model (i.e. a model without population structure). Thus, the size of the neighborhood allows us to study the effect of population structure in a gradual manner. Having seen this, we can predict that, for the "imitate the best neighbor" protocol, if we increase the size of the neighborhood enough, at some point cooperation will disappear. As an exercise, try to find the minimum *neighborhood-range* (for both types of neighborhood) at which cooperation cannot be sustained anymore, with the other parameter values as shown in figure 1.

12. As long as $m \leq 5$, results are very similar, but for greater values of m (i.e. greater intensity of selection) cooperation starts to emerge.
13. In contrast with what happens under the "imitative-positive-proportional-m" protocol, parameter m does not seem to have a great influence in this case. This changes if *self-matching?* is turned on. In that case, for high values of m, cooperation can emerge.

Critical neighborhood size at which cooperation does not emerge in the simulation parameterized as in figure 1.

- *neighborhood-type* = "*Moore*". With *neighborhood-range* = 1, we observe significant levels of cooperation (about 90%) cooperation, but with *neighborhood-range* ≥ 2, we observe no cooperation at all.
- *neighborhood-type* = "*Von Neumann*". With *neighborhood-range* = 1, we observe significant levels of cooperation (about 75%) cooperation. Interestingly, with *neighborhood-range* = 2, we observe even more cooperation (usually more than 90%), but with *neighborhood-range* ≥ 3, we observe no cooperation at all.

Discussion

We would like to conclude this section emphasizing that the influence of population structure on evolutionary dynamics generally depends on many factors that may seem insignificant at first sight, and whose effects interact in complex ways. This may sound discouraging, since it suggests that a simple general theory of the influence of population structure on evolutionary dynamics cannot be derived. On a more positive note, it also highlights the importance of the skills you are learning with this book. Without the aid of computer simulation, it seems impossible to explore this type of questions. But using computer simulation we can gain some understanding of the complexity and the beauty of these apparently simple –yet surprisingly intricate– systems. The following quote from Roca et al. (2009b) nicely summarizes this view.

> To conclude, we must recognize the strong dependence on details of evolutionary games on spatial networks. As a consequence, it does not seem plausible to expect general laws that could be applied in a wide range of practical settings. On the contrary, a close modeling including the kind of game, the evolutionary dynamics and the population structure of the concrete problem seems mandatory to reach sound and compelling conclusions. With no doubt this is an enormous challenge, but we believe that this is one of the most promising paths that the community working in the field can explore. Roca et al. (2009b, pp. 14-15)

7. Exercises

You can use the following link to download the complete NetLogo model: nxn-imitate-best-nbr-extended.

Exercise 1. How can we parameterize our model to replicate the results shown in figures 1b and 1d of Hauert and Doebeli (2004)?

Exercise 2. How can we parameterize our model to replicate the results shown in figures 1, 2, 6 and 7 of Nowak et al. (1994a)?[14]

Exercise 3. How can we parameterize our model to replicate the results shown in figure 1 of Szabó and Tőke (1998)? Note that Szabó and Tőke (1998) use *total* payoffs and we use *average* payoffs in our "imitative-logit-m" protocol, but a clever parameterization can save you any programming efforts.

Exercise 4. How can we parameterize our model to replicate the results shown in figure 11 of Nowak and May (1993)?

A frame of the simulation shown in figure 11 of Nowak and May (1993).

Exercise 5. To appreciate the impact that *neighborhood-type* may have, run a simulation parameterized as in figure 1 above, but with *protocol* = "imitative-logit-m", *m* = 10, and *self-matching?* = true. Compare the results obtained using *neighborhood-type* = "Moore" and *neighborhood-type* = "Von Neumann". What do you observe?

CODE Exercise 6. The following block of code (in procedure to update-strategy-after-revision) can be replaced by one simple line using `run` (a primitive that can take a string containing the name of a command as an input, and it runs the command).

```
[ (ifelse
    protocol = "best-neighbor"
              [ best-neighbor-protocol ]
    protocol = "imitative-pairwise-difference"
              [ imitative-pairwise-difference-protocol ]
    protocol = "imitative-positive-proportional-m"
              [ imitative-positive-proportional-m-protocol ]
    protocol = "imitative-logit-m"
              [ imitative-logit-m-protocol ]
  )
]
```

Can you come up with the simple line?

14. Figures 1 and 2 in Nowak et al. (1994a) are the same as figures 1 and 2 in Nowak et al. (1994b).

Models implemented in this book

0. Introduction

0.2. Introduction to agent-based modeling

schelling-sakoda.nlogo

0.4. The fundamentals of NetLogo

schelling-sakoda-simple.nlogo

1. Our first agent-based evolutionary model

1.0. Our very first model

2×2-imitate-if-better.nlogo

1.1. Extension to any number of strategies

nxn-imitate-if-better.nlogo

1.2. Noise and initial conditions

nxn-imitate-if-better-noise.nlogo

1.3. Interactivity and efficiency

nxn-imitate-if-better-noise-efficient.nlogo

2. Spatial interactions on a grid

2.0. Spatial chaos in the Prisoner's Dilemma

2×2-imitate-best-nbr.nlogo

2.1. Robustness and fragility

2×2-imitate-best-nbr-extended.nlogo

2.2. Extension to any number of strategies

nxn-imitate-best-nbr.nlogo

2.3. Other types of neighborhoods and other revision protocols

nxn-imitate-best-nbr-extended.nlogo

References

Abar, S., Theodoropoulos, G. K., Lemarinier, P., and O'Hare, G. M. (2017). Agent based modelling and simulation tools: A review of the state-of-art software. *Computer Science Review*, 24 (Supplement C):13–33. https://doi.org/10.1016/j.cosrev.2017.03.001

Adami, C., Schossau, J., and Hintze, A. (2016). Evolutionary game theory using agent-based methods. *Physics of Life Reviews*, 19:1–26. https://doi.org/10.1016/j.plrev.2016.08.015

Aydinonat, N. E. (2007). Models, conjectures and exploration: an analysis of Schelling's checkerboard model of residential segregation. *Journal of Economic Methodology*, 14(4):429–454. https://doi.org/10.1080/13501780701718680

Bakshy, E. and Wilensky, U. (2007). NetLogo-Mathematica link. *Software*. Center for Connected Learning and Computer-Based Modeling, Northwestern University, Evanston, IL. http://ccl.northwestern.edu/netlogo/mathematica.html

Benaïm, M. and Weibull, J.W. (2003). Deterministic approximation of stochastic evolution in games. *Econometrica*, 71:873–903. https://doi.org/10.1111/1468-0262.00429

Biggs, M. B. and Papin, J. A. (2013). Novel multiscale modeling tool applied to pseudomonas aeruginosa biofilm formation. *PLOS ONE*, 8(10). https://doi.org/10.1371/journal.pone.0078011

Binmore, K. (2007). *Playing for Real: A Text on Game Theory*. Oxford University Press.

Binmore, K. (2011). *Rational Decisions*. Princeton University Press.

Binmore, K. (2013). Sexual drift. Biological Theory, 8(2):201–208. https://doi.org/10.1007/s13752-013-0103-5

Binmore, K. and Samuelson, L. (1994). An economist's perspective on the evolution of norms. *Journal of Institutional and Theoretical Economics*, 150(1):45–63. http://www.jstor.org/stable/40753015

Binmore, K., Samuelson, L., and Vaughan, R. (1995). Musical chairs: Modeling noisy evolution. *Games and Economic Behavior*, 11:1–35. Erratum, 21 (1997), 325. https://doi.org/10.1006/game.1995.1039

Binmore, K. and Shaked, A. (2010). Experimental economics: Where next?. *Journal of Economic Behavior and Organization*, 73(1):87–100. https://doi.org/10.1016/j.jebo.2008.10.019

Blume, L. E. (1997). Population games. In Arthur, W. B., Durlauf, S. N., and Lane, D. A., editors, *The Economy as an Evolving Complex System II*, pages 425–460. Addison-Wesley, Reading, MA. https://doi.org/10.1201/9780429496639

Boyd, R. and Richerson, P. J. (1985). *Culture and the Evolutionary Process*. University of Chicago Press.

Chung, K. L. (1960). *Markov Chains with Stationary Transition Probabilities*. Springer Berlin Heidelberg. http://dx.doi.org/10.1007/978-3-642-49686-8

Cohen, M. D., Riolo, R. L., and Axelrod, R. (1999). The emergence of social organization in the prisoner's dilemma: How context-preservation and other factors promote cooperation. Working Paper 99-01-002, Santa Fe Institute. https://www.santafe.edu/research/results/working-papers/the-emergence-of-social-organization-in-the-prison

Cohen, M. D., Riolo, R. L., and Axelrod, R. (2001). The role of social structure in the maintenance of cooperative regimes. *Rationality and Society*, 13(1):5–32. https://doi.org/10.1177/104346301013001001

Colman, A. M. (1995). *Game Theory and its Applications in the Social and Biological Sciences*. Routledge, 2nd edition.

Cornforth, D., Green, D. G., and Newth, D. (2005). Ordered asynchronous processes in multi-agent systems. *Physica D: Nonlinear Phenomena*, 204(1):70–82. https://doi.org/10.1016/j.physd.2005.04.005

Darwin, C. R. (1859). *On the origin of species by means of natural selection, or the preservation of favoured races in the struggle for life*. John Murray, London.

Dawes, R. M. (1980). Social dilemmas. *Annual Review of Psychology*, 31(1):169–193. https://doi.org/10.1146/annurev.ps.31.020180.001125

Dixit, A. K. and Nalebuff, B. J. (2008). *The Art of Strategy: A Game Theorist's Guide to Success in Business and Life*. W. W. Norton & Company.

Edmonds, B. (2001). The use of models – making MABS more informative. In Moss, S. and Davidsson, P., editors, *Multi-Agent-Based Simulation: Second International Workshop, MABS 2000 Boston, MA, USA*, 15–32. Springer Berlin Heidelberg. https://doi.org/10.1007/3-540-44561-7_2

Edmonds, B. and Hales, D. (2005). Computational simulation as theoretical experiment. *The Journal of Mathematical Sociology*, 29(3):209–232. https://doi.org/10.1080/00222500590921283

Ellison, G. (2000). Basins of attraction, long run equilibria, and the speed of step-by-step evolution. *Review of Economic Studies*, 67:17–45. https://doi.org/10.1111/1467-937X.00119

Epstein, J. M. and Axtell, R. (1996). *Growing Artificial Societies*. Brookings Institution Press/MIT Press, Washington/Cambridge.

Foster, D. P. and Young, H. P. (1990). Stochastic evolutionary game dynamics. *Theoretical Population Biology*, 38:219–232. Corrigendum, 51 (1997), 77-78. https://doi.org/10.1016/0040-5809(90)90011-J

Fudenberg, D. and Imhof, L. A. (2008). Monotone imitation dynamics in large populations. *Journal of Economic Theory*, 140:229–245. https://doi.org/10.1016/j.jet.2007.08.002

Fudenberg, D. and Levine, D. K. (1998). *The Theory of Learning in Games*. MIT Press, Cambridge.

Fudenberg, D. and Tirole, J. (1991). *Game Theory*. MIT Press, Cambridge.

García, J. and van Veelen, M. (2016). In and out of equilibrium I: Evolution of strategies in repeated games with discounting. *Journal of Economic Theory*, 161:161–189. http://dx.doi.org/10.1016/j.jet.2015.11.007

García, J. and van Veelen, M. (2018). No strategy can win in the repeated prisoner's dilemma: Linking game theory and computer simulations. *Frontiers in Robotics and AI*, 5:102. https://doi.org/10.3389/frobt.2018.00102

Gilbert, N. (2007). *Agent-Based Models*, volume 153 of *Quantitative Applications in the Social Sciences*. Sage Publications, London.

Gintis, H. (2009). *Game Theory Evolving Game Theory Evolving: A Problem-Centered Introduction to Modeling Strategic Interaction*. Princeton University Press, 2nd edition.

Gintis, H. (2013). Markov models of social dynamics: Theory and applications. *ACM Trans. Intell. Syst. Technol.*, 4(3), Article 53. http://dx.doi.org/10.1145/2483669.2483686

Gintis, H. (2014). *The Bounds of Reason: Game Theory and the Unification of the Behavioral Sciences*. Princeton University Press, revised edition.

Gotts, N., Polhill, J., and Law, A. (2003). Agent-based simulation in the study of social dilemmas. *Artificial Intelligence Review*, 19(1):3–92. https://doi.org/10.1023/A:1022120928602

Hamill, L. and Gilbert, N. (2016). *Agent-based Modelling in Economics*. John Wiley & Sons, Ltd. http://dx.doi.org/10.1002/9781118945520

Hamilton, W. D. (1967). Extraordinary sex ratios. *Science*, 156:477–488. http://dx.doi.org/10.1126/science.156.3774.477

Harsanyi, J. C. (1967). Games with Incomplete Information Played by "Bayesian" Players. Part I. The Basic Model. *Management Science*, 14(3):159–182. https://doi.org/10.1287/mnsc.14.3.159

Harsanyi, J. C. (1968a). Games with Incomplete Information Played by "Bayesian" Players. Part II. Bayesian Equilibrium Points. *Management Science*, 14(5):320-334. https://doi.org/10.1287/mnsc.14.5.320

Harsanyi, J. C. (1968b). Games with Incomplete Information Played by "Bayesian" Players. Part III. The Basic Probability Distribution of the Game. *Management Science*, 14(7):486-502. https://doi.org/10.1287/mnsc.14.7.486

Hauert, C. (2002). Effects of space in 2×2 games. *International Journal of Bifurcation and Chaos*, 12(07):1531–1548. https://doi.org/10.1142/S0218127402005273

Hauert, C. (2006). Spatial effects in social dilemmas. *Journal of Theoretical Biology*, 240(4):627–636. https://doi.org/10.1016/j.jtbi.2005.10.024

Hauert, C. (2018). *EvoLudo: Interactive tutorials in evolutionary games*. https://wiki.evoludo.org/

Hauert, C. and Doebeli, M. (2004). Spatial structure often inhibits the evolution of cooperation in the snowdrift game. *Nature*, 428:643–646. http://dx.doi.org/10.1038/nature02360

Head, B. (2018). NetLogo Python extension. *Software*. https://github.com/NetLogo/Python-Extension.

Hegselmann, R. (2017). Thomas c. schelling and james m. sakoda: The intellectual, technical, and social history of a model. *Journal of Artificial Societies and Social Simulation*, 20(3):15. https://doi.org/10.18564/jasss.3511

Helbing, D. (1992). A mathematical model for behavioral changes by pair interactions. In Haag, G., Mueller, U., and Troitzsch, K. G., editors, *Economic Evolution and Demographic Change: Formal Models in Social Sciences*, pages 330–348. Springer, Berlin. https://doi.org/10.1007/978-3-642-48808-5_18

Hindersin, L., Wu, B., Traulsen, A., and García, J. (2019). Computation and simulation of evolutionary game dynamics in finite populations. *Scientific Reports*, 9(1):6946. https://doi.org/10.1038/s41598-019-43102-z

Hofbauer, J. (1995). Imitation dynamics for games. Unpublished manuscript, University of Vienna.

Hofbauer, J. and Sigmund, K. (1988). *Theory of Evolution and Dynamical Systems*. Cambridge University Press, Cambridge.

Holt, C. A. and Roth, A. E. (2004). The Nash equilibrium: A perspective. *Proceedings of the National Academy of Sciences*, 101(12):3999–4002. http://dx.doi.org/10.1073/pnas.0308738101

Huberman, B. A. and Glance, N. S. (1993). Evolutionary games and computer simulations. *Proceedings of the National Academy of Sciences*, 90:7716–7718. https://doi.org/10.1073/pnas.90.16.7716

Isaac, A. G. (2008). Simulating evolutionary games: a python-based introduction. *Journal of Artificial Societies and Social Simulation*, 11(3):8. http://jasss.soc.surrey.ac.uk/11/3/8.html

Izquierdo, L. R., Izquierdo, S. S., Galán, J. M., and Santos, J. I. (2009). Techniques to understand computer simulations: Markov chain analysis. *Journal of Artificial Societies and Social Simulation*, 12(1):6. http://jasss.soc.surrey.ac.uk/12/1/6.html

Izquierdo, L. R., Izquierdo, S. S., Galán, J. M., and Santos, J. I. (2013). Combining mathematical and simulation approaches to understand the dynamics of computer models. In Edmonds, B. and Meyer, R., editors, *Simulating Social Complexity: A Handbook*, chapter 11, pages 235–271. Springer Berlin Heidelberg. http://doi.org/10.1007/978-3-540-93813-2_11. Second edition (2017) available at: https://doi.org/10.1007/978-3-319-66948-9_13

Izquierdo, L. R., Izquierdo, S. S., and Sandholm, W. H. (2019). An introduction to ABED: Agent-based simulation of evolutionary game dynamics. *Games and Economic Behavior*, 118:434–462. https://doi.org/10.1016/j.geb.2019.09.014

Izquierdo, L. R., Izquierdo, S. S., and Vega-Redondo, F. (2012). Learning and evolutionary game theory. In Seel, N. M., editor, *Encyclopedia of the Sciences of Learning*, pages 1782–1788. Springer US, Boston, MA. https://doi.org/10.1007/978-1-4419-1428-6_576

Izquierdo, L. R. and Polhill, J. G. (2006). Is your model susceptible to floating-point errors? *Journal of Artificial Societies and Social Simulation*, 9(4):4. http://jasss.soc.surrey.ac.uk/9/4/4.html

Izquierdo, S. S. and Izquierdo, L. R. (2013). Stochastic approximation to understand simple simulation models. *Journal of Statistical Physics*, 151(1):254–276. http://dx.doi.org/10.1007/s10955-012-0654-z

Janssen, M.A. (2020). *Introduction to Agent-Based Modeling: With applications to social, ecological and social-ecological systems*. https://intro2abm.com

Janssen, J. and Manca, R. (2006). *Applied semi-markov processes*. Springer-Verlag, New York. http://dx.doi.org/10.1007/0-387-29548-8

Jaxa-Rozen, M. and Kwakkel, J. H. (2018). PyNetlogo: Linking NetLogo with Python. *Journal of Artificial Societies and Social Simulation*, 21(2):4. https://dx.doi.org/10.18564/jasss.3668

Karr, A. F. (1990). Markov processes. In Heyman, D. P. and Sobel, M. J. (eds.), *Stochastic Models*, volume 2 of *Handbooks in Operations Research and Management Science*, chapter 2, pages 95–123. Elsevier. https://doi.org/10.1016/S0927-0507(05)80166-5

Killingback, T. and Doebeli, M. (1996). Spatial evolutionary game theory: Hawks and doves revisited. *Proceedings of the Royal Society of London. Series B: Biological Sciences*, 263(1374):1135–1144. https://doi.org/10.1098/rspb.1996.0166

Kosfeld, M., Droste, E., and Voorneveld, M. (2002). A myopic adjustment process leading to best reply matching. *Journal of Economic Theory*, 40:270–298. https://doi.org/10.1016/S0899-8256(02)00007-6

Kravari, K. and Bassiliades, N. (2015). A survey of agent platforms. *Journal of Artificial Societies and Social Simulation*, 18(1):11. https://doi.org/10.18564/jasss.2661

Kulkarni, V. G. (1995). *Modeling and Analysis of Stochastic Systems*. Chapman & Hall, Ltd., London, UK.

Kulkarni, V. G. (1999). *Modeling, Analysis, Design, and Control of Stochastic Systems*. Springer New York, NY. https://doi.org/10.1007/978-1-4757-3098-2

Loginov, G. (2019). Ordinal Imitative Dynamics. Unpublished manuscript. https://arxiv.org/abs/1907.04272

Lytinen, S. L. and Railsback, S. F. (2012). The evolution of agent-based simulation platforms: A review of NetLogo 5.0 and ReLogo. In *Proceedings of the fourth international symposium on agent-based modeling and simulation (21st European Meeting on Cybernetics and Systems Research)*.

Marden, J. R. and Shamma, J. S. (2015). Game theory and distributed control. In Young, H.P. and Zamir, S., editors, *Handbook of Game Theory with Economic Applications*, volume 4, chapter 16, pages 861–899. Elsevier, Amsterdam. https://doi.org/10.1016/B978-0-444-53766-9.00016-1

Maynard Smith, J. (1982). *Evolution and the Theory of Games*. Cambridge University Press, Cambridge.

Maynard Smith, J. and Price, G. R. (1973). The logic of animal conflict. *Nature*, 246:15–18. https://doi.org/10.1038/246015a0

Mukherji, A., Rajan, V., and Slagle, J. R. (1996). Robustness of cooperation. *Nature*, 379(6561):125–126. http://dx.doi.org/10.1038/379125b0

Myerson, R. B. (1997). *Game theory: Analysis of Conflict*. Harvard University Press.

Nash, J. F. (1950). Equilibrium points in n-person games. *Proceedings of the National Academy of Sciences*, 36:48–49. https://doi.org/10.1073/pnas.36.1.48

Nelson, R. R. and Winter, S. G. (1982). *An Evolutionary Theory of Economic Change*. Harvard University Press.

Newth, D. and Cornforth, D. (2009). Asynchronous spatial evolutionary games. *Biosystems*, 95(2):120–129. https://doi.org/10.1016/j.biosystems.2008.09.003

Newton, J. (2018). Evolutionary game theory: A renaissance. *Games*, 9(2), 31. https://doi.org/10.3390/g9020031

Nikolai, C. and Madey, G. (2009). Tools of the trade: A survey of various agent based modeling platforms. *Journal of Artificial Societies and Social Simulation*, 12(2):2. http://jasss.soc.surrey.ac.uk/12/2/2.html

Norris, J. R. (1997). *Markov Chains*. Cambridge University Press, Cambridge. https://doi.org/10.1017/CBO9780511810633

Nowak, M. A., Bonhoeffer, S., and May, R. M. (1994a). More spatial games. *International Journal of Bifurcation and Chaos*, 4:33–56. https://doi.org/10.1142/S0218127494000046

Nowak, M. A., Bonhoeffer, S., and May, R. M. (1994b). Spatial games and the maintenance of cooperation. *Proceedings of the National Academy of Sciences*, 91:4877–4881. https://doi.org/10.1073/pnas.91.11.4877

Nowak, M. A., Bonhoeffer, S., and May, R. M. (1996). Robustness of cooperation. Nature, 379(6561):126–126. https://doi.org/10.1038/379126a0

Nowak, M. A. and May, R. M. (1992). Evolutionary games and spatial chaos. *Nature*, 359:826–829. http://dx.doi.org/10.1038/359826a0

Nowak, M. A. and May, R. M. (1993). The spatial dilemmas of evolution. *International Journal of Bifurcation and Chaos*, 3:35–78. https://doi.org/10.1142/S0218127493000040

Ohtsuki, H., Nowak, M. A., and Pacheco, J. M. (2007a). Breaking the symmetry between interaction and replacement in evolutionary dynamics on graphs. *Phys. Rev. Lett.*, 98:108106. https://doi.org/10.1103/PhysRevLett.98.108106

Ohtsuki, H., Pacheco, J. M., and Nowak, M. A. (2007b). Evolutionary graph theory: Breaking the symmetry between interaction and replacement. *Journal of Theoretical Biology*, 246(4):681–694. https://doi.org/10.1016/j.jtbi.2007.01.024

Osborne, M. (2004). *An Introduction to Game Theory*. Oxford University Press, Oxford.

Osborne, M. J. and Rubinstein, A. (1998). Games with procedurally rational players. *American Economic Review*, 88:834–847. https://www.jstor.org/stable/117008

Oyama, D., Sandholm, W. H., and Tercieux, O. (2015). Sampling best response dynamics and deterministic equilibrium selection. *Theoretical Economics*, 10:243–281. https://doi.org/10.3982/TE1405

Perc, M. and Szolnoki, A. (2010). Coevolutionary games—a mini review. *Biosystems*, 99(2):109–125. https://doi.org/10.1016/j.biosystems.2009.10.003

Polhill, J. G., Izquierdo, L. R., and Gotts, N. M. (2006). What every agent-based modeller should know about floating point arithmetic. *Environmental Modelling & Software*, 21(3):283–309. https://doi.org/10.1016/j.envsoft.2004.10.011

Probst, D. (1999). Book review of "Evolutionary Game Theory" by Jörgen W. Weibull. *Journal of Artificial Societies and Social Simulation*, 2(1). http://jasss.soc.surrey.ac.uk/2/1/review3.html

Python Software Foundation (2019). Python. *Software*. http://www.python.org.

Quijano, N., Ocampo-Martinez, C., Barreiro-Gomez, J., Obando, G., Pantoja, A., and Mojica-Nava, E. (2017). The role of population games and evolutionary dynamics in distributed control systems: The advantages of evolutionary game theory. *IEEE Control Systems Magazine*, 37(1):70–97. https://doi.org/10.1109/MCS.2016.2621479

R Core Team (2019). R: A Language and Environment for Statistical Computing. *Software*. R Foundation for Statistical Computing, Vienna, Austria. https://www.R-project.org.

Railsback, S., Ayllón, D., Berger, U., Grimm, V., Lytinen, S., Sheppard, C., and Thiele, J. (2017). Improving execution speed of models implemented in netlogo. *Journal of Artificial Societies and Social Simulation*, 20(1):3. https://doi.org/10.18564/jasss.3282

Railsback, S. F. and Grimm, V. (2019). *Agent-Based and Individual-Based Modeling: A Practical Introduction*, Second edition. Princeton University Press, Princeton, NJ. http://www.railsback-grimm-abm-book.com. First edition (2011) at http://www.jstor.org/stable/j.ctt7sns7

Railsback, S. F., Lytinen, S. L., and Jackson, S. K. (2006). Agent-based simulation platforms: Review and development recommendations. *Simulation*, 82(9):609–623. https://doi.org/10.1177/0037549706073695

Roca, C. P., Cuesta, J. A., and Sánchez, A. (2009a). Evolutionary game theory: Temporal and spatial effects beyond replicator dynamics. *Physics of Life Reviews*, 6(4):208 – 249. https://doi.org/10.1016/j.plrev.2009.08.001

Roca, C. P., Cuesta, J. A., and Sánchez, A. (2009b). Effect of spatial structure on the evolution of cooperation. *Phys. Rev. E*, 80:046106. https://doi.org/10.1103/PhysRevE.80.046106

Roth, G. and Sandholm, W. H. (2013). Stochastic approximations with constant step size and differential inclusions. *SIAM Journal on Control and Optimization*, 51:525–555. https://doi.org/10.1137/110844192

Sakoda, J. M. (1949). *Minidoka: An Analysis of Changing Patterns of Social Behavior*. PhD thesis, University of California.

Sakoda, J. M. (1971). The checkerboard model of social interaction. *The Journal of Mathematical Sociology*, 1(1):119–132. https://doi.org/10.1080/0022250X.1971.9989791

Samuelson, L. (1997). *Evolutionary Games and Equilibrium Selection*. MIT Press, Cambridge.

Sandholm, W. H. (2001). Almost global convergence to p-dominant equilibrium. *International Journal of Game Theory*, 30:107–116. https://doi.org/10.1007/s001820100067

Sandholm, W. H. (2003). Evolution and equilibrium under inexact information. *Games and Economic Behavior*, 44:343–378. https://doi.org/10.1016/S0899-8256(03)00026-5

Sandholm, W. H. (2007). Simple formulas for stationary distributions and stochastically stable states. *Games and Economic Behavior*, 59:154–162. https://doi.org/10.1016/j.geb.2006.07.001

Sandholm, W. H. (2009). Evolutionary game theory. In Meyers, R. A., editor, *Encyclopedia of Complexity and Systems Science*, pages 3176–3205. Springer, Heidelberg. https://doi.org/10.1007/978-3-642-27737-5_188-3

Sandholm, W. H. (2010). *Population Games and Evolutionary Dynamics*. MIT Press, Cambridge.

Sandholm, W. H., Izquierdo, S. S., and Izquierdo, L. R. (2019). Best experienced payoff dynamics and cooperation in the Centipede game. *Theoretical Economics*, 14: 1347–1385. https://doi.org/10.3982/TE3565

Sandholm, W. H., Izquierdo, S. S., and Izquierdo, L. R. (2020). Stability for best experienced payoff dynamics. *Journal of Economic Theory*, 185:104957. https://doi.org/10.1016/j.jet.2019.104957

Sandholm, W. H. and Staudigl, M. (2018). Sample path large deviations for stochastic evolutionary game dynamics. *Mathematics of Operations Research*, 43(4):1348–1377. https://doi.org/10.1287/moor.2017.0908

Schelling, T. C. (1969). Models of segregation. *The American Economic Review*, 59(2):488–493. http://www.jstor.org/stable/1823701

Schelling, T. C. (1971). Dynamic models of segregation. *The Journal of Mathematical Sociology*, 1(2):143–186. https://doi.org/10.1080/0022250X.1971.9989794

Schelling, T. C. (1978). *Micromotives and Macrobehavior*. Norton, New York.

Schlag, K. H. (1998). Why imitate, and if so, how? A boundedly rational approach to multi-armed bandits. *Journal of Economic Theory*, 78:130–156. https://doi.org/10.1006/jeth.1997.2347

Selten, R. (1965). Spieltheoretische Behandlung eines Oligopolmodells mit Nachfrageträgheit. *Zeitschrift für die gesamte Staatswissenschaft / Journal of Institutional and Theoretical Economics*, 121(2):301–324. http://www.jstor.org/stable/40748884

Selten, R. (1975). Reexamination of the perfectness concept for equilibrium points in extensive games. *International Journal of Game Theory*, 4(1):25–55. https://doi.org/10.1007/BF01766400

Seri, R. (2016). Analytical approaches to agent-based models. In Secci, D. and Neumann, M., editors, *Agent-Based Simulation of Organizational Behavior*, chapter 13, pages 265–286. Springer International Publishing. https://doi.org/10.1007/978-3-319-18153-0_13

Sethi, R. (2000). Stability of equilibria in games with procedurally rational players. *Games and Economic Behavior*, 32:85–104. https://doi.org/10.1006/game.1999.0753

Sethi, R. (2019). Procedural Rationality in Repeated Games. http://dx.doi.org/10.2139/ssrn.3468993

Sklar, E. (2007). NetLogo, a multi-agent simulation environment. *Artificial Life*, 13(3):303–311. https://doi.org/10.1162/artl.2007.13.3.303

Szabó, G. and Tőke, C. (1998). Evolutionary prisoner's dilemma game on a square lattice. *Phys. Rev. E*, 58:69–73. https://doi.org/10.1103/PhysRevE.58.69

Taylor, P. D. and Jonker, L. (1978). Evolutionarily stable strategies and game dynamics. *Mathematical Biosciences*, 40:145–156. https://doi.org/10.1016/0025-5564(78)90077-9

The MathWorks, Inc. (2019). Matlab. *Software*. Natick, Massachusetts. https://mathworks.com

Thiele, J. C. (2014). R marries NetLogo: Introduction to the RNetLogo package. *Journal of Statistical Software*, 58(2):1–41. http://dx.doi.org/10.18637/jss.v058.i02

Thiele, J. C. and Grimm, V. (2010). NetLogo meets R: Linking agent-based models with a toolbox for their analysis. *Environmental Modelling & Software*, 25(8):972–974. https://doi.org/10.1016/j.envsoft.2010.02.008

Thiele, J. C., Kurth, W., and Grimm, V. (2012a). Agent-based modelling: Tools for linking netlogo and R. *Journal of Artificial Societies and Social Simulation*, 15(3):8. http://dx.doi.org/10.18564/jasss.2018

Thiele, J. C., Kurth,W., and Grimm, V. (2012b). RNetLogo: An R package for running and exploring individual-based models implemented in NetLogo. *Methods in Ecology and Evolution*, 3(3):480–483. http://dx.doi.org/10.1111/j.2041-210X.2011.00180.x

Thiele, J. C., Kurth, W., and Grimm, V. (2014). Facilitating parameter estimation and sensitivity analysis of agent-based models: A cookbook using netlogo and R. *Journal of Artificial Societies and Social Simulation*, 17(3):11. http://dx.doi.org/10.18564/jasss.2503

Thomas, B. (1984). Evolutionary stability: States and strategies. *Theoretical Population Biology*, 26:49–67. https://doi.org/10.1016/0040-5809(84)90023-6

Traulsen, A. and Hauert, C. (2009). Stochastic evolutionary game dynamics. In Schuster, H. G., editor, *Reviews of Nonlinear Dynamics and Complexity*, volume 2, pages 25–61. Wiley, New York. https://doi.org/10.1002/9783527628001.ch2

Vega-Redondo, F. (2003). *Economics and the Theory of Games*. Cambridge University Press, Cambridge, UK.

von Neumann, J. and Morgenstern, O. (1944). *Theory of Games and Economic Behavior*. Prentice-Hall, Princeton.

Wallace, C. and Young, H. P. (2015). Stochastic evolutionary game dynamics. In Young, H.P. and Zamir, S., editors, *Handbook of Game Theory with Economic Applications*, volume 4, chapter 6, pages 327–380. Elsevier, Amsterdam. https://doi.org/10.1016/B978-0-444-53766-9.00006-9

Weibull, J. W. (1995). *Evolutionary Game Theory*. MIT Press, Cambridge.

Wilensky, U. (1999). *NetLogo*. Software. Center for Connected Learning and Computer-Based Modeling, Northwestern University, Evanston, IL. http://ccl.northwestern.edu/netlogo/

Wilensky, U. (2019). *The NetLogo User Manual*. Version 6.1.1. https://ccl.northwestern.edu/netlogo/6.1.1/docs/

Wilensky, U. and Rand, W. (2015). *An Introduction to Agent-Based Modeling: Modeling Natural, Social, and Engineered Complex Systems with NetLogo*. The MIT Press. https://www.jstor.org/stable/j.ctt17kk851

Wilensky, U. and Shargel, B. (2002). Behaviorspace. *Software*. Center for Connected Learning and Computer-

Based Modeling, Northwestern University, Evanston, IL. http://ccl.northwestern.edu/netlogo/behaviorspace.html

Wilensky, U. and Stroup, W. (1999). Hubnet. *Software*. Center for Connected Learning and Computer-Based Modeling, Northwestern University, Evanston, IL. http://ccl.northwestern.edu/netlogo/hubnet.html

Wolfram Research, Inc. (2019). Mathematica. *Software*. Champaign, Illinois. https://www.wolfram.com

Young, H. P. (1998). *Individual Strategy and Social Structure*. Princeton University Press, Princeton.

Young, H. P. (2004). *Strategic Learning and Its Limits*. Oxford University Press, Oxford.

Index

$$p^N(x) = (1-x)\frac{xN}{N-1}\frac{xN-1}{N-1}$$

$$q^N(x) = x\frac{(1-x)N}{N-1}\frac{(1-x)N}{N-1}\frac{(1-x)N-1}{N-1}$$

